Psychology and Social Work

Psychology and Social Work

Applied Perspectives

GABRIELA MISCA AND PETER UNWIN

polity

First published in 2017 by Polity Press

Polity Press
65 Bridge Street
Cambridge CB2 1UR, UK

Polity Press
350 Main Street
Malden, MA 02148, USA

ISBN-13: 978-0-7456-9630-0
ISBN-13: 978-0-7456-9631-7 (pb)

A catalogue record for this book is available from the British Library.

Library of Congress Cataloging-in-Publication Data

Names: Misca, Gabriela, author. | Unwin, Peter (Peter Frederick) author.
Title: Psychology and social work : applied perspectives / Gabriela Misca, Peter Unwin.
Description: Malden, MA : Polity Press, 2016. | Includes bibliographical references and index.
Identifiers: LCCN 2016028150| ISBN 9780745696300 (hardback) | ISBN 9780745696317 (pbk.)
Subjects: LCSH: Social psychology. | Social service.
Classification: LCC HM1033 .M57 2016 | DDC 302--dc23 LC record available at https://lccn.loc.gov/2016028150

Typeset in 10.5 on 13 pt Utopia by
Servis Filmsetting Ltd, Stockport, Cheshire
Printed in Great Britain by CPI Group (UK) Ltd, Croydon

For further information on Polity, visit our website: www.politybooks.com

Contents

Acknowledgements   vi

1   The Place of Psychological Knowledge and Research in Social Work Training and Practice   1

2   Signposts from Developmental Psychology on Human Development over the Life Course   23

3   Perspectives from Clinical and Counselling Psychology on Mental Health and Illness   48

4   Perspectives from Social and Community Psychology: Understanding Values, Attitudes, Diversity and Community Change   71

5   Health Psychology: Understanding Health, Illness, Stress and Addiction   94

6   Organizational Psychology: Understanding the Individual and the Organization in the Social Work Structure   119

7   Forensic Psychology: Understanding Criminal Behaviour and Working with Victims of Crime   143

8   Conclusions   166

References   173

Index   199

Acknowledgements

Both authors would like to thank their families for their support and forbearance during the wiriting of this book.

Gabriela would like to acknowledge the support she received from the US-UK Fulbright Commission, the book being completed during her Fulbright Scholar award in the USA. Particular thanks are due for the generous hosting she received from colleagues at the Williams James College Boston, MA; from friends in Newburyport, MA; and from many other academic colleagues and friend across the USA.

1 The Place of Psychological Knowledge and Research in Social Work Training and Practice

Introduction

The social work profession has changed dramatically in its comparatively short life. Social work in the UK was founded on humanistic and counselling principles that were greatly influenced by key psychological theories. In recent decades, however, the influence of psychological theories and approaches has declined as social work has become increasingly concerned with the targeted and aggregated world of performance management (Harris and Unwin, 2009). This book is intended to help reclaim social work by placing renewed energy and importance on understanding the psychological theories that lie at the heart of every contemporary social worker's caseload (Ferguson, 2008). The recent plethora of social work standards and frameworks place continuing importance on the need for a core understanding of psychological theories and research within contemporary social work, partly driven by lessons learned from tragedies wherein a lack of relational work and a lack of understanding between professionals and clients have contributed to failures.

The increasing professionalization and raising of standards in social work means that the Professional Capabilities Framework (PCF) of the British Association of Social Workers (BASW, 2015) and the Standards of Proficiency from the regulatory body the Health Care Professions Council (HCPC, 2012) must be adhered to at all times. Accordingly, each chapter in this book is prefaced with both the relevant PCF domain (pitched at the end of last placement level) and the relevant HCPC standard of proficiency which applies to all registered social workers in England.

The social work subject benchmark for higher education in the UK clearly highlights 'the relevance of psychological perspectives to understanding individual and social development and functioning' (QAA, 2008, 5.1.4). The Social Work Reform Board (SWRB, 2010) states the importance of psychological knowledge to all social workers:

> Social workers understand psychological, social, cultural, spiritual and physical influences on people; human development throughout

1

the life span and the legal framework for practice. They apply this knowledge in their work with individuals, families and communities. They know and use theories and methods of social work practice. (Professional Capabilities Framework: Domain 5, Knowledge)

The above statements recognize that a fundamental part of social work's theoretical base is drawn or 'borrowed' from other disciplines, among which psychology makes a substantive contribution (along with sociology, political sciences, anthropology, medicine and health sciences). Psychology is defined as the scientific study of human behaviour and has an established tradition of empirical inquiry linked with theoretical developments. Historically, many empirical approaches in psychology have led to important applications which have significantly influenced professional practice in clinical, educational, business and social care settings. The current climate of research-mindedness in social work education and practice (SWRB, 2010) is clearly an example of such influence. The role of psychological knowledge is seen as providing relevant scientific and evidenced-informed frameworks for those who train to be or are social workers within the context of the most up-to-date research. Successful and expert social work practice needs to be underpinned by theories and research findings from the variety of disciplines that contribute to its knowledge base, and this book explains and applies a range of psychological perspectives towards that end.

Public engagement with psychology

Modern society is fascinated by psychology, and this fascination comes in a variety of guises – for example, reality TV shows, soap operas, *Woman's Hour*, documentaries, child sexual exploitation, internet dating, celebrity, corrupt politicians, jihadists, nationalist politics, health and social care scandals, and the obesity epidemic. We all ask ourselves questions about why certain behaviours occur and often come up with our own theories. These, and the debates you have about such issues with family and friends, could probably be located among the theories debated in this book around such issues as identity, self-esteem, intelligence and peer pressure.

Psychologists are increasingly called upon to advise and intervene in a variety of social issues, with an emphasis on the impact of psychological knowledge and research on professional practice (British Psychological Society, 2015a). In the current climate of public engagement with psychology and psychologists' engagement with public issues, this book will also provide a unique resource for students to enhance their understanding of the applications of psychology in social work practice and aid their further study and career choices. According to the Quality Assurance Agency for Higher Education (QAA, 2010), psychology is the largest scientific discipline and the second largest discipline overall taught at higher education level in the UK and so can be seen to enjoy great popularity. The key issue, however, is not popularity but what we, as human beings and social workers, can truly learn from the wealth of psychological knowledge out there and how we can adapt this knowledge for the betterment of our own well-being and also that of our clients and communities.

This book is not intended as an exhaustive monograph of all psychological knowledge applied in social work but aims to provide signposts from various psychological theories to understanding human development, behaviour and interactions in social work practice. It is beyond our scope to provide this here and, indeed, most likely impossible to achieve, given the breadth and depth of both psychology and social work knowledge. The book aims to challenge the dominant ideologies in contemporary social work and calls for a re-emphasis on relational ways of working with individuals, families and communities as a way to bring about change and also as a way of helping social work professionals achieve greater job satisfaction (Ferguson, 2008). This in turn will hopefully lead to a workforce that is more consistent and committed than that of today, with its constant 'daily churn' of staff and high levels of sickness and stress (SWRB, 2010; Munro, 2011).

There are many textbooks that present the traditional theories and approaches of psychology and, while this volume will respect such received and established wisdom, some of these traditional theories will be challenged, interpreted and applied in new contexts to help social workers make better sense out of the day-to-day psychological complexities they encounter. Recent research findings will be used to illuminate links between the discipline of psychology and its application to social work, thus helping bridge that gap between theory and practice that many student social workers find hard to grasp.

There is hardly a case open in social work practice today that is not inherently complex: as thresholds for intervention have risen, social work students on their first placement are given 'straightforward cases' that routinely include sexual abuse or drug addiction, neglect, and serious family dysfunction. The more advanced practitioner might work with families that are more difficult to engage and that, additionally, have issues of mental illness, self-harm, sexual exploitation, intra-familial collusion and criminality. These cases are all supposed to fit within organizational systems, thresholds, budgets and outcomes measurements. Such families will, however, never fit neatly into bureaucratic boxes, and it is a false premise to pretend that the social work 'business' will be able to achieve the same types of outcomes and 'win–win' scenarios strived for in the world of business (Harris and Unwin, 2009). Everyone cannot possibly be a 'winner' in a family torn apart by sexual abuse, and there is no 'win–win' outcome in a family where a member is compulsorily detained in a psychiatric hospital. There will, however, be lots of individuals with serious psychological problems, the pain and extent of which can be greatly ameliorated by the effective involvement of social workers and others who are skilled in developing insights, relationships and effective interventions.

The aim of this book is to empower social workers to better understand and empathize with their clients and fellow professionals in their daily encounters, using relational forms of working to explore the cause of problems rather than being competent only as social administrators. It is not expected that, as a result of reading it, social workers will become expert in one or more fields of psychology. Rather, it is expected that the deeper levels of knowledge they will be able to reflect on and critically examine will lead to better, more considered interventions in the lives of individuals, families and communities. Both psychology and social work are in reality eclectic disciplines that take the most relevant knowledge and interventions and adapt them to particular situations. It must be appreciated that interventions based on a single theoretical stance are only ever likely to have limited efficacy unless other factors in the whole of that person's life are in balance. For example, introducing a cognitive-behavioural therapy (CBT) programme for a person who abuses drugs may be excellent, but if the person involved completes the programme and then returns to their social circle of substance-abusing friends they are unlikely to show sustained recovery. However, a more eclectic approach that looked perhaps at different lifestyle or relocation options or facilitated an introduction to a supportive network is likely to have a greater chance of success.

The realities of contemporary social work

Real-life scenarios, personal testimonies, and the findings of serious case reviews and inquiries will be used throughout the book as rich and contemporary sources of information about psychology and social work. It is unfortunate that much learning in the field of social work (as opposed to, say, the fields of medicine and education) comes from scenarios that enter the public domain because things have gone wrong (e.g., Laming, 2003: Haringey LSCB, 2009). The everyday successes of social work, which far outweigh the failures, are usually private affairs – the young person protected from internet abuse; the personalization package for a severely disabled adult; the older person with dementia whose move to residential care is sensitively handled – with no place in the public domain. These successes take place against a most difficult background of public-sector cuts and reorganizations which make it all the more remarkable that social work does as well as it does.

The emotional demands of being a social worker are great, and it is difficult to keep a healthy balance between one's own psychological health when working with stressful family situations while also having to meet an increasing number of targets and deadlines brought about by the business culture. Getting to the heart of the individual psychologies that lie behind those numbers is, however, altogether a different reality. There is an argument that social workers and their professional organizations – for example, the British Association of Social Workers (BASW) – should be less self-effacing about their successes and broadcast them in an appropriate manner in ways that counter the prevalent negative media image of the profession (Munro, 2011).

Recent government-commissioned reports such as that by the SWRB (2010) have been vociferous in their condemnation of the current culture of compliance and performance management within social work and have called for a return to a learning culture which respects social workers as professionals dealing with the most complex individuals and families (Munro, 2011). However, since the publication of these reports, the performance management ethic has become increasingly dominant, and there is little sign of learning cultures truly having been re-established within social work, despite some improvements in support for newly qualified social workers in the form of an assessed and supported first year of practice characterized by reduced caseloads in order to allow for personal growth and development.

The individualistic basis of social work

As mentioned above, social work was initially based on individualized humanistic principles, and social workers prided themselves on this non-judgemental approach towards the complexities and dysfunctions of many of their clients (the term 'clients' is preferred to the term 'service users' in this book on account of its more personalized connotations). While social services were originally known as 'the personal social services', many social work organizations might now more accurately be described as 'the impersonal social services' as a result of the rapid turnover of staff, the closure of local offices, and the generic call centre model that now acts as gateway to services. Partly because of 'brand failure' following a series of scandals and the deaths of children known to social workers (e.g., Laming, 2009), social services departments became reorganized into separate children's social care and adult services departments designed to be more specialist and focused. An interesting organizational psychology has emerged from this specialization structure in that children's social care, especially the safeguarding arena, is often perceived as where the really challenging social work takes place, whereas other fields, such as mental health and work with older people, are somehow less demanding. It takes a special type of resilience in any professional to work day in, day out, with cases of child abuse and the adults who may be its perpetrators, but this culture is not psychologically healthy for the workforce, and too much time spent with a narrow focus can lead to unsound practice as well as stress and burnout (Ferguson, 2008). In the following chapters of this book the psychological complexities of work in learning disabilities, mental health and older persons' services will be presented as being equally as complex as work with children, even if they do not attract the same political and media attention. We call here for a return to a family and 'family as part of a community' approach to social work, wherein the psychologies of different individuals will be recognized as having key impacts upon the health, the well-being and often the safety of vulnerable adults and children. Sadly, comments such as 'I am there to work with the drug issue – I am not a child-care worker' and 'That's Health's responsibility, not ours' can still be heard in daily practice. Such comments are understandable to an extent because everybody is busy being expert in their own field of legislation, policy and practice, but it is argued in this book that a more holistic recognition and respect for each other's perspectives would lead to a healthier working environment for all concerned. The increasingly culturally diverse workforce in the profession (Zanca and Misca, 2016) brings its own challenges to practice, and such challenges can be overcome by social workers possessing a sound knowledge base (Misca and Neamţu, 2016).

Reflective point

In recent years, across England and Wales, there has been an increase in recruitment of social workers trained and qualified abroad, from countries such as Australia, Canada and Romania, among others. Partly because of the shortage of social workers in England and Wales, such social workers are 'headhunted' by recruitment agencies, immigrate to the UK as skilled professionals, and practise social work in local authorities, where the turnover and shortage of social workers tend to be problematic. What are the potential challenges that social workers who trained and qualified outside the UK may face when practising social work here? Consider the challenges that may arise from the potentially different knowledge base as well as the different culture.

The complex psychological demands of social work

Contemporary social work takes place in a complex and psychologically demanding environment. How might the seminal theories and approaches of the various disciplines of psychology be able to help the hard-pressed social worker, struggling with a high caseload, being pressured for a court report, and having a flashing computer screen tell them that they are behind on any number of performance deadlines? We hope that a better understanding of psychological knowledge will bring greater insight into day-to-day realities, greater empathy for others, a better sense of self, and some cognitive learning that can be put to good use in supporting and advocating for vulnerable clients. For example, reflecting on organizational psychology might empower social workers to operate in more flexible and creative ways described by Lipsky (1980) as street-level bureaucracy. An informed and aware social worker might develop the street wisdom to know just how little needs to go on a computer screen to stop the flashing light and then be freed up to do the home visits. Some social workers might prefer to sit all day in the office (less volatile than some home visits can be) and others might be perfectionists who spend days having to get a court report just right. Perfectionists are unlikely to experience good health and well-being in a social work role because the work is never-ending and there is never a perfect solution. The core challenge is how social workers might find that line between performing at a level that meets their own standards of professional self-esteem and ascertaining what work might be completed with a lighter touch. 'Meetings – the practical alternative to work' is one of those jokey phrases you might see on office walls, but how much time do social workers needlessly spend in meetings or on systems compliance and how much time with vulnerable people? Also, how much quality time do social workers spend with their own families, and do they achieve that much talked about work–life balance? Contemporary social work organizations claim to value and support employees, but such managerial claims often ring hollow in the face of staff shortages, public-sector cutbacks and increasing performance measurement demands. The challenge is that, if you want to be a social worker who makes a difference, you somehow have to find a way of making sense of a range of competing demands and keep yourself, your family and your clients as psychologically healthy as you can. An understanding of key psychological theories and their application will help social workers be resilient in practice and better placed to advocate for their clients.

The research base underpinning psychological sciences and social work practice

Psychology is an eclectic discipline, as can be seen in the many strands outlined above, and accordingly its research base is also eclectic. Behaviourist and cognitive disciplines will favour scientific empirical approaches in their search for psychological truths, using methods that range from randomized controlled trials, simulated laboratory experiments and quantitative surveys. Hypotheses and potential for the replication of studies and experiments will guide the importance they ascribe to research findings. In contrast, humanistic psychologists will not be looking for universal truths but will use qualitative methodologies to interpret individual experiences and narratives in ways that seek to explain the phenomena of phobias, anxieties, aggression and depression.

Evidence-based practice, where scientific evidence is used to deliver the most effective care on a systematic basis, became a core feature of health services across the UK in the 1980s. Most medical and psychological research is increasingly concerned with evidence-based outcomes in a world that strives to measure and provide examples of effectiveness and value for money. The research resources of the NHS are huge, whereas social work has no public body whose responsibility it is to ensure appropriate funding and prioritizing of research. The Social Care Institute for Excellence (SCIE) was introduced in 2002, but this body largely disseminates best practice and research and is not a statutory funder of research. Some social work organizations are wary of adopting evidence-based research as a model from health and argue that the complexity of social work – its reflective and relationship-based core; its championing of social justice; its commitment to treating clients and carers as partners in knowledge; and its claim to be the profession of individualization – means that the term 'evidence-informed' is perhaps a more appropriate one (Holloway et al., 2009). This term means that social workers will both welcome and critically evaluate research and use its findings to inform the unique and complex variables involved in supporting individuals, families and communities. What works across the whole population in terms of medical best practice (e.g., diabetes or asthma medication regimes) is not the same as taking a successful intervention, say, with perpetrators of domestic violence in one community and transferring it to another community. The psychological and sociological differences across communities of social work practice may involve psychological and sociological variables that are not usually present in health scenarios. For example, all social workers can think of people they have met whose life pattern has gone against the predicted course suggested by research – the child in care who makes it to university, the severely disabled person who enjoys excellent mental health, or the survivor of domestic abuse who broke free and brought her children up in a safe and nurturing environment.

In order to develop and gain political and public confidence, however, social work needs to have its distinct research base to inform best practice and also to share research bases with other professions such as psychology (Marsh and Fisher, 2005). All research methods have their strengths and weaknesses, and a social worker should possess the skills of critical analysis to be able to ask the following questions of any research claims:

- When and where was the research carried out?
- How big was the sample?
- Is the method used appropriate to address the research question?
- Does it under-claim or over-claim validity?
- Is the research widely applicable or very limited in scope?
- What was the influence of the researcher or the research design?
- Was consent truly 'informed consent'?

- Who paid for the research?
- What criticisms can be made about the research?
- What are the interpretations of the findings?
- In what ways could the findings benefit your practice and your clients?

Different criteria to evaluate a piece of research will be applied, depending on whether the methodology is qualitative or quantitative. In the further reading section at the end of the chapter there is a selection of articles offering an accessible guide to evaluation of quantitative and qualitative research studies.

The many strands of psychology

Psychology has many different academic and applied strands, all eloquently detailed in a range of standard textbooks, and it is not the purpose of this book to replicate such knowledge in detail; rather, it is our purpose to help hard-pressed social work students and practitioners to make sense of what can be a most complex discipline. Psychology is a longer established discipline than social work and has championed various theories and practices over the past century, social and political mores often shaping its messages. For example, Bowlby's (1958) views about the critical role of the mother in respect of healthy attachment in babies and children were modified when economic demands meant that women were needed in the workforce. His modified theory suggested that consistency in caregivers rather than a unique attachment with the mother was the key to positive child developmental outcomes (Bowlby, 1982).

Essentially, psychology might be seen as being concerned with all matters of mind and behaviour, whether with core issues of intelligence, perception, relationships or counselling. A social worker is going to need to understand how their clients think and behave in order best to support, assess and plan for interventions that are increasingly geared towards the safeguarding of young people and adults from various forms of exploitation and abuse. A social worker needs to understand and interpret the importance of developmental milestones, to recognize how families can both support and collude, to appreciate the psychologies of other professionals, to be aware of the organizational psychologies of their places of work, and to have some insight into the psychologies of the communities within which they operate. These communities may be geographic communities – e.g., a housing estate – or they may be communities of interest – e.g., drug-using communities or communities of survivors of domestic abuse.

Therefore in this book we will be looking in detail at developmental psychology, health psychology, social psychology, organizational psychology, counselling psychology and forensic psychology, particularly as the last relates to perpetrators and victims of crime. We will also explore the nature of the research behind received knowledge across the various fields of psychology and help readers to critique and challenge the credibility of various claims made regarding psychological findings. Much received wisdom across the fields of psychology has been derived from white ethnocentric studies, many of which are limited by nature of being specific to their time or by their small scale, meaning that they may not be wholly relevant today, particularly given our fast-changing and increasingly diverse society. We want social workers to be critical thinkers and to be able to interpret research findings appropriately in ways that inform their practice by providing the insights and knowledge that will better equip them to act as advocates for their clients.

We will now briefly examine the seminal psychological schools of thought and theory in order that the reader can place the following chapters into context. A grounding of knowledge in these core theories will also provide the necessary platform from which to challenge some established wisdom and to reflect on how psychological theory and practice might fit or need to be adapted in order to understand better the new and diverse communities of social work practice. Later chapters will explore these areas in more depth and provide opportunities for critical thinking, reflection and the application of theory to practice via case studies and practical exercises. Each one will be prefaced with the relevant domain of BASW's Professional Capabilities Framework (PCF), which pertains to the qualifying level for social work, and the relevant Standard of Practice set by the Health Care Professions Council (HCPC), both of which are essential requirements of the social work profession in England. The PCF is concerned with capabilities in ongoing learning and the application of that learning, whereas the HCPC standards are concerned primarily with how professional social work is delivered in the field.

Psychodynamic psychology

The psychodynamic approach is a grand set of theories that view human interaction as being based upon the ways in which inner drivers, particularly unconscious ones, interact with personalities. Freud's original psychoanalytical theory and its therapeutic applications are now seen as part of a range of psychodynamic theories, as are those of Jung and Klein. The principles of psychodynamic theories will be developed further in chapter 2.

Many people will be familiar with the name of Freud and will have a vague notion that he was concerned with the unconscious mind and with presenting impulses as key to behaviour. His seminal model consisted of the id, the ego and the superego: the id was made up of the primal, largely sexual, drivers that determine behaviour; the ego was the sense of self responsible for mediating some of the impulses of the id; and the superego was the social sense of the self which was able to contextualize both the id and the ego from a higher control point. A century's worth of therapy around the world flowed from Freud's most interesting theory, but increasing recognition that this was a theory based on very small numbers of middle-class patients in Vienna at the turn of the twentieth century and critique from various psychologists of the behaviourist persuasion have challenged his work ever since (e.g., Sulloway, 1991; Webster, 1995).

Increasingly, parts of the scientific community after the Second World War viewed Freudian psychology as not being rooted in scientific evidence, and by the end of the twentieth century psychoanalytical theory and the psycho-therapeutic interventions such as free association and dream interpretation that accompanied it largely fell from favour (Sulloway, 1991). Although they still exist in psychotherapeutic practice, they have been modified.

Behaviourism

The essence of behaviourism is a belief that individual behaviours are largely determined and modified by the immediate environment, and behaviour-ist theories rose in popularity as psychoanalytic theories lost ground. Much experimental research involving rewards and sanctions led to a very wide body of knowledge, champions of behaviourism being Watson (1913) and Skinner (1971). Skinner believed that the human mind as such could not be explained or predicted – only its subsequent behaviours could. Skinner developed the concept of 'operant conditioning', which stated that people behave in ways that are consequential – i.e., behaviour that brings reward will be reinforced, whereas behaviour that meets with disapproval or sanc-tion will be curtailed. As might be expected in a field as contentious as psychology, critics of behaviourism emerged with the work of psychologists such as Seligman (1972). Seligman's theory of 'learned helplessness' contra-dicted Skinner's theory of operant conditioning and was based on laboratory experiments in which animals would give up and accept that they were not going to get rewards, only sanctions – a state which apparently persisted even when the animals were subsequently given the option of positive reward. The concept of learned helplessness provides a clinical model for helping under-stand depression.

Therapeutic responses to learned helplessness in the human world include those such as cognitive behavioural therapy (CBT), in which strategies of breaking the cycle are brought about by way of encouraging new and differ-ent ways of thinking about how to change situations. CBT is popular today in social work arenas and is used particularly for people with depression or addictions and for those caught up in seemingly hopeless situations of domes-tic abuse and violence. It has also become popular in recent decades because it is relatively cost-effective and claims to bring about change over compara-tively short periods of time. Drug and alcohol services are now commissioned by the current government only if they show tangible results, particularly in terms of reduction in offending behaviours (Department of Health and Home Office, 2015). Short-term and relatively inexpensive interventions such as CBT are hence very popular within these services, but the question must be asked about the real purpose of such a singular commitment to a specific therapy which largely ignores an individual's wider social and economic context.

Social workers and psychologists who practise from an eclectic theory base do not believe that all substance users are the same but recognize the complexities of issues such as cognition, early childhood experiences, family context and community environment interplaying in ways that impact on the problem. How easy it would all be if there were really a simple, single and inexpensive solution to the complex, multiple and expensive issues facing social workers!

Humanistic psychology

The humanistic school of psychology, which embraces core social work values, developed partly as a rejection of rational scientific theories such as behaviourism and took a whole-person or holistic approach to the various problems of mind and relationships. An awareness of self and an appreciation that people need to be viewed as more than their presenting problems lie at the heart of humanistic psychology. These models were also rather radical in that the key to changing behaviours and mood was seen as being located in the inherent strength of the person seeking help and not with the 'expert' insight of the psychoanalyst or professional behaviour therapist. Most humanistic therapies are characterized by a relationship of equals rather than a differentiated status between therapist and the person seeking help. For example, Rogers et al.'s (1967) core conditions of congruence, empathy and unconditional positive regard are seen as setting the atmosphere in which any change might take place – change which is not imposed but which is self-initiated. Saleebey (1996) is a social work academic who exhorts professionals to adopt a strengths-based approach which starts by looking for the strengths that are to be found in everyone, regardless of how dire their circumstances and histories may seem on the outside. Many local authorities now promote strengths-based approaches such as Signs of Safety (Edwards and Turnell, 1999) in respect of their safeguarding responsibilities for children. Such positive psychology must have benefit for practitioners as well as clients and is a useful antidote when organizational cultures can be so weighed down with negativity and poor morale.

Maslow's seminal work regarding the existence of a hierarchy of needs in humans is one that has largely stood the test of time and one of the few theories, along with attachment theory, that seems to have pervaded the social work profession (Maslow, 1968). According to Maslow, whose hierarchy represents a holistic model of human needs, 'higher order' needs such as self-esteem are addressed only once the more basic needs of food and shelter have been met. Certainly social workers often support individuals and families whose basic needs for food and shelter are not met and where surviving, rather than thriving, is the task in hand. Maslow's seminal 'Triangle of Need' has been criticized for its failure to give enough attention to the importance of social networks in helping people find positive ways of functioning, even if their higher level needs are not all met. Despite its hierarchical nature, Maslow's model remains influential within social work, largely because it embraces the concept that people can change and can aspire to more fulfilling lives. All social workers can recall someone who has broken a personal or family pattern of behaviour or low aspirations and gone on to achieve higher order success and satisfactions in life. Examples such as these can make social work a great job capable of bringing with it feelings of achievement and satisfaction not found in many other career paths.

Cognitive psychology

Cognitive psychology is concerned with the ways in which the conscious mind processes information in order to make sense of the environment via perception, learning, memory, emotion, judgement and problem-solving. The scientific interest in the mechanisms and factors that lead to individuals making choices in their daily functioning has largely been built on laboratory and quantitative studies. Chomsky (1965) threw out a particular challenge to the behaviourist school by stating that all behaviour is not learned and is not subject to stimulus-response. Rather, he argued that much human behaviour, such as the ability to acquire language, is innate. Cognitive theorists have been encouraged by recent technological advances – e.g., the ability to scan brain activity – to further their positions. Neuroscience and its application to social work scenarios such as the development of neglected children is particularly contentious, and the extensive political and professional take-up of 'truths' about some of these neurological claims, for example the irreparability of damage done to children's brains by neglect in the first two years of life, has been challenged (e.g., Munro and Musholt, 2014; Williams, 2014). The developmental advances observed in Romanian children who were adopted overseas from deprived institutional settings (Misca, 2014b) are both a powerful lesson in human resilience and a renewed warning of the impact that negative early experiences have on subsequent development – a situation that calls for a balanced consideration.

Developmental psychology

Sometimes referred to as 'lifespan psychology' or 'life-course psychology', this discipline is concerned with how the conscious mind adapts and develops across the ageing process. Such an approach places importance on the link with sociological as well as psychological perspectives in understanding the life course.

Knowledge of normative development is critical for social workers, who need to be able to determine and debate what constitutes development that is 'good enough' and what amounts to real concern for individuals. Most studies around developmental stages are Western in orientation and do not necessarily embrace the cultural changes, cultural norms and expectations that present challenges to social workers. Developmental psychological knowledge is constantly changing as society changes, and it sets the norms against which social workers need to base their contemporary assessments, plans and expectations. Many social work clients, both young and old, will not have experienced relationships, families and communities in which the core building blocks and stimuli for optimum development are received. Sometimes a child will move into a foster home, or an isolated older person into residential care, and their development, or levels of personal and social competence and well-being, will change dramatically.

Social norms such as those regarding sexuality and relationships are constantly changing, particularly in a technological age when advances in communications and medical technology are altering our views about what is 'normal'. Many people now begin their personal relationships online in ways that would have been unimaginable twenty years ago, and advances in medical technology mean that the medical knowledge base regarding developmental heath and psychology is constantly expanding. For example, 'old age' in Western societies in the 1950s might have been considered to have begun at age sixty, whereas advances in health and overall living standards mean that many older people now have good health and choose to work and be active through their seventies and eighties. Such social changes challenge previous development theories of old age, such as that of disengagement theory (Cummings and Henry, 1961), which saw it as natural that many old people would simply want to fade away from the mainstream of life once they were no longer economically active.

Attachment theory (Bowlby 1958, 1982) grew out of the psychodynamic school and has seen a renaissance in social work in the fields of both adults and children, where concerns regarding human growth and development are core. There are attachment theorists and practitioners focused on applying attachment theory in the social work area of foster care and adoption (Cairns, 2002; Golding, 2008) in particular. Attachment theory has been embraced wholeheartedly by the social work profession, who see it as offering valuable insight into behaviours by considering the models of insecure ambivalent attachment, insecure avoidant attachment, and disorganized attachment (Bowlby, 1982) that otherwise would make no sense. It is used to inform best intervention strategies by carers and social workers – strategies that are usually based on consistencies and commitment in order to enable the child or adult to develop a secure emotional base from which to experience and explore their world.

Organizational psychology

Organizational psychology, also known as work psychology, emerged from industrial contexts in the early 1900s and can be defined as the science and study of behaviour in the workplace. Taylor's (2006) book on scientific management depicted workers as essentially needing to be managed and directed in order for productivity and profit to be maximized. Organizational psychology still has a focus on the maximization of efficiency and quality – the 1980s, for example, having seen a rise in competitive global initiatives such as 'total quality management' (Hoyle, 2007), which purported to mix the best of business efficiency with a concern for worker satisfaction. Public services in the UK also increasingly adopted practices from business from the 1980s (Harris, 1998). Many of the contemporary pressures within social work stem from clashes between a business-oriented managerialist culture (Unwin, 2009), which asserts a manager's right to manage, and a social work culture based on humanism, rights, relationships and the exercise of professional judgement. The increasing importation of business models by a succession of neo-liberal governments since the 1980s is partly responsible for the issues of low morale, staff turnover and vacancy levels in contemporary social work organizations (Harris, 1998; Munro, 2011). Organizational psychology is also now concerned with issues of equity and well-being in the workplace, and since the 1990s employment law has reflected the influence of the discipline around issues of rights, harassment and equality of opportunity. Despite many advances in workers' rights and protections in these areas, however, there remain huge problems in social work organizations, and high-profile cases such as the government's intervention in the firing of Sharon Shoesmith, director of children's services in Haringey, following the death of baby Peter Connelly (Jones, 2014) have demonstrated how easily these rights can be overridden.

Social and community psychology

Among the academic branches of psychology, social psychology is most closely related to social work and is concerned with social settings and how interaction with the behaviour of others affects individual behaviour.

Social psychology is the empirical study of how people's thoughts, feelings and behaviours are influenced by the actual, imagined or implied presence of others (Allport, 1985). It is concerned primarily to explain how feelings, beliefs and prejudices influence the way we interact with others and hence has particular relevance to social work situations where issues of discrimination or bullying and exploitation might be present – e.g., the standards of domiciliary care being offered to people with disabilities or the attitudes of groups of professionals towards young people in care who go missing and become involved in sexual exploitation. Importantly, the 'social' in social psychology brings in the sociological and political aspects missing, say, from behaviourist or psychoanalytical approaches, which embrace neither an individual's wider social settings nor the influence of others.

Research in social psychology might take the form of experiments that measure how people react across a range of artificially constructed social settings or be undertaken using naturalistic observations of people in social settings – e.g. to determine how people react to the physical closeness of others. Goffman (1961) was a seminal social psychologist whose participant observations in psychiatric institutions in the USA led both to a greater understanding about how staff and patient worlds are separately constructed and to the theory of institutionalization. Such realities still hold true, as can unfortunately be seen in scandals such as that at Mid Staffordshire General Hospital (Francis, 2013) and Winterbourne View (Department of Health, 2012b), where vulnerable adults were systematically abused by the very people who were supposed to be providing care and protection. Social work remains an advocate of anti-oppressive practice and can be more effective in its challenges to racism, ageism, sexism and disablism once a clear understanding is developed regarding the causes of discriminatory behaviour. The effective championing of such principles can only be enhanced by social workers learning from the discipline of social psychology regarding the causes of discrimination, group and peer dynamics.

Community psychology is a relatively recent branch of psychology that concerns the relationships of the individual to communities and the wider society. The values at the heart of community psychology include those of inclusivity, social justice and the improvement of health and well-being, all of which are social work values (BASW, 2012). Despite their valuable insights, community-based approaches have been neglected in social work education and practice. However, there has recently been a renewed interest in community, influenced largely by the government's promotion of 'the Big Society' (Scott, 2011), which led to most local authorities investing in some type of community-based approaches to well-being alongside traditional, statutory-based approaches to the problems of social work. An understanding of the complex psychology of diversity within communities will help social workers understand the perspectives taken by others and hopefully lead to better practice in the pooling of ideas and resources, all communities having their hidden strengths that just need to be tapped.

These key psychological schools of theory will be explored more fully later in this book. Meanwhile, the following case study provides the opportunity to reflect on how a range of theories and interventions might help alleviate a situation involving psychological and social distress.

Case study: Exploring the relevance of psychological knowledge for social work

Karen, aged twenty-six, is the only woman in a five-place community home which has been carrying a vacancy for two months. This facility is one of many such homes owned and managed by CommoCare, a private provider organization. The reason for this is that Karen enjoys being the only woman in the house and having the attention of three (possibly, four) men and refuses to have another woman. Karen has mild learning disabilities and holds down a shelf-stacking job at a local supermarket four days per week. Her progress in terms of confidence and social ability has been excellent over the two years she has lived at the community home. She was initially housed at the facility because she was assessed as being too vulnerable to predatory sex offenders when living in a partially supported flat in the local community. All the applicants on the waiting list are women.

Task
Imagine that you are a social worker employed by CommoCare called in to try to sort out this scenario. You believe that clients should have the right to choose their fellow residents, but you are under pressure from the organization's accountant and also from Karen's parents, who are threatening to complain to the press if their daughter is forced to accept another woman housemate, as they know her behaviour will deteriorate and that she will become very depressed and possibly at risk. What can psychological theories (e.g., psychodynamic/behaviourist/humanistic/cognitive/development theories) offer to a social worker's understanding of the dynamics and issues at play in the case scenario in terms of Karen, her parents, and the other residents.

Discussion
A humanistic approach might consider the well-being of all the people involved and focus on the feelings and fears about the intended life-course change. A behaviourist approach might reflect on any previous behaviour on Karen's part that had brought her rewards and might try to deal with the issue of change from a perspective that concentrated on positive behavioural change. A psychodynamic approach might be limited in the light

of Karen's cognitive impairment, but considering psychodynamics might be a constructive way of exploring her parents' fears about separation, loss and risk. A cognitive approach would have to take into account levels of understanding, but exploring skills and capabilities in new settings could be a way forward, particularly if done on an incremental basis.

Task
Can you expand on any ways in which the above theoretical approaches could help shape your approach to Karen's situation? How might an organizational or social/community psychology intervention be structured to help address the impasse in this community home?

Discussion
The previous discussion did not consider the strengths that an organizational or social/community-based approach might hold for Karen and those affected by her situation. The nature of her friendships could be explored, her key worker at the home could be involved and her parents also involved as appropriate, notwithstanding that she is an adult. If this 'community' can be seen as a resource supporting Karen during and after any transition, that may provide her and her parents with the confidence to effect the move and enable her to continue to develop as an adult. Issues such as the risks and opportunities presented by a wider community that may be discriminatory towards people with learning disabilities is also a reality that needs to be taken into consideration, particularly given Karen's earlier experiences regarding her vulnerability.

Outline of book: next chapters

A keen working knowledge of psychology is core to effective social work practice. There is no one right way for psychological knowledge to be interpreted and used, but a good social worker will find out about any area of concern being addressed with a client and read around a range of perspectives on that subject. Humanistic and qualitative research and theory are most likely to resonate with social work concerns, but quantitative and cognitive, even psychoanalytical, insights may equally illuminate cases and systems in ways that provide a way forward. Throughout the following chapters, social workers will be encouraged to critically analyse key research in their chosen areas and to adopt practices that are informed by best research findings.

Chapter 2 will explore the relevance of developmental psychology for social work practice. Of all the branches of psychology, developmental psychology is perhaps most familiar to social workers, students and professionals, as it contributes prominently to social work training under topics such as 'human growth and development' and/or 'life-course development'. There are entire books dedicated to these topics that are typically studied over the course of a semester or an entire academic year during social work training. It is beyond the scope of this chapter to provide an exhaustive account of the many and various ways in which developmental psychology is relevant or applied in social work. Instead, it aims to offer signposts to the reader towards further exploration of the contributions to social work of developmental psychology around two main topics. One strand will explore some of the main concepts and theories of development and their application to social work. The second strand will focus on exploring a topical issue in contemporary developmental psychology and social work – that of resilience, or positive development 'against the odds'. Current debates on resilience as concept and process will be explored, with evidence drawn from up-to-date research and its relevance for social work practice.

Chapter 3 will bring together perspectives from clinical and counselling psychology on understanding mental health and illness. Much contemporary social work is concerned with risk assessment, rationing resources and managing performance to budget. At the core of social work, however, lies relationship-based practice, even if modern-day social work relationships may be brief in nature. Counselling skills are at the heart of this, and an understanding of core counselling skills, types of counselling and likely successes is key to effective social work. Clinical and counselling psychologies share similar goals to social work and are concerned with the integration of psychological theory and research with therapeutic practice. This chapter will explore, from a psychological perspective, the concepts of mental health, psychological distress and well-being. Theoretical models explaining mental health problems and approaches to their treatment will be central.

Chapter 4 will look in detail at the branches of social and community psychology and the understanding of group and social influence, prejudice and discrimination. The interaction of individuals in social contexts and issues such as attitudes and social cognitions, including cognitive dissonance, will be examined. Social influences and group processes, among them cultural differences apparent in roles, self and social identity, will be related to social work situations. This chapter will explore the contribution of community psychology to the understanding of communities, their contexts, and attitudes and relationships within them. The challenges of community psychology and how best to understand and work with political structures in ways that are effective for clients and their families will also be discussed.

Chapter 5 focuses on health psychology and its contribution to helping our understanding of health and illness, stress and addiction. This chapter is particularly important to social workers because health, both mental and physical, is a crucial determinant of many client and carer worlds. An understanding of the psychological models and phenomena of health conditions will stand social workers in good stead when working with other professionals and enable them to demonstrate empathy with the presenting conditions of their clients. Social workers with such knowledge should be better able to advocate for services and to be more focused in their views about the appropriateness of a range of services. This chapter will explore the application of psychological theories and research to understanding biological, psychological, environmental and cultural factors involved in health and the prevention of illness. It will also look in some depth at the particular issues of dementia, obesity in children and substance abuse as key concerns of social work that might helpfully be conceptualized and addressed through the lens of health psychology.

Chapter 6 addresses organizational psychology and the understanding of organizational behaviour and the work environment. This is a hot topic in social work at present, with its high levels of stress and vacancies and its modernized methods of working, such as hot-desking and the use of IT. An understanding of the ways in which organizations behave and of ways to 'look after yourself' in social work's ever changing systems is of vital importance to the profession and to the health and well-being of individual social workers. Healthy social workers are also far more likely to carry out their work in ways that lead to more successful outcomes for clients and their carers.

Chapter 7 brings insights from forensic psychology, since many social workers encounter situations where knowledge of forensic psychology could prove invaluable. Again, such knowledge not only enables social workers to understand better what might be going on in the lives of the families with whom they work; it also gives them a shared platform of knowledge from which to share and debate issues with colleagues from different backgrounds. Forensic psychology is placed at the intersection between psychology and the criminal justice system and aims to apply psychological theory to the understanding of criminal behaviour in working with perpetrators and victims of crime.

Chapter 8 reviews the main themes explored in our book and their relevance for social work practice. A conclusion will be that the appropriate use of a range of psychological knowledge can both empower social workers to experience a more fulfilling job and enable them to work with and challenge other professionals more constructively. Such knowledge should always lead to better outcomes for clients of all ages.

Meet the Brightwells

This case study will be referred to throughout the rest of the book to help illuminate and contextualize reflective and critical thinking. The Brightwell family's problems are of a nature and extent that would be likely to bring them to the attention of a range of professionals, notably social workers and psychologists in specialist areas. We will introduce more detail and context about the family in the relevant chapters through the book concerned with topics such as development psychology, health psychology and forensic psychology. The Brightwells live in Mossford, a large ex-council estate in the English Midlands. They rent their house from a housing association. Mossford is characterized by high levels of unemployment, racial tension, poor health outcomes and low aspirations.

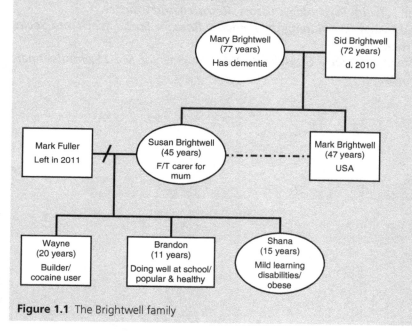

Figure 1.1 The Brightwell family

Further reading and resources

(For full bibliographic details, see the References.)

On overarching debates around psychology and social work:

BASW, Professional Capabilities Framework, www.basw.co.uk/pcf/ [the BASW site also contains free articles and position statements on a range of contemporary social work issues].

British Psychological Society *Psychology and the Public*, www.bps.org.uk/psychology-public/psychology-and-public [the BPS site contains very useful free information on contemporary issues within different fields of psychology].

Ferguson, *Reclaiming Social Work.*

Gross, *Psychology: The Science of Mind and Behaviour.*

Harris and White, *Modernising Social Work: Critical Considerations.*

On critical evaluation of research:

Different evaluation criteria are applied to qualitative and quantitative research. The articles below offer an accessible guide to evaluation.

Hoare and Hoe, Understanding quantitative research: part 2.

Hoe and Hoare, Understanding quantitative research: part 1.

Lietz and Zayas (2010) Evaluating qualitative research for social work practitioners.

Marks et al., *Health Psychology: Theory, Research and Practice*.

Marsh and Fisher, *Developing the Evidence Base for Social Work and Social Care Practice*.

Rutter, *Practice Enquiry Guidelines: A Framework for SCIE Commissioners and Providers*.

2 Signposts from Developmental Psychology on Human Development over the Life Course

The following are the key relevant capabilities and standards in this chapter for social workers.

Professional Capabilities Framework (BASW, 2015)	Standards of Proficiency (HCPC, 2012)
5 Knowledge 5.4 Recognise the short and long term impact of psychological, socio-economic, environmental and physiological factors on people's lives, taking into account age and development, and how this informs practice 5.6 Acknowledge the centrality of relationships for people and the key concepts of attachment, separation, loss, change and resilience	**13 Understand the key concepts of the knowledge base which are relevant to their profession** 13.4 Human growth and development across the lifespan and the impact of key developmental stages and transitions

Introduction

Social work addresses issues with individuals at all stages in life, from infancy, through to childhood, adolescence, adulthood and old age. Developmental psychology is a branch of psychology which studies the systematic changes (psychological, cognitive, emotional) occurring over the life course. It is not in itself an applied field, but it is prolifically applied in many other fields, such as educational, forensic and health psychology. Of all the branches of psychology, developmental psychology is perhaps most familiar to social workers, students and professionals, as it contributes prominently to social work training under topics such as 'human growth and development' and/or 'life-course development'.

Social work takes place with individuals and families in challenging and often extreme situations, but judgements and risk assessments need to be made against an understanding of 'normative' development. Children who have been neglected or abused will develop in different ways to children with a positive experience of nurture. Adults who have been sexually abused will need particular understanding with regard to their mental health and their parenting. Adults and children involved in domestic violence will need to be understood by social workers in reference to how past experiences might or might not affect future experiences, mental health relationships and ability for child care. Social work takes place in multicultural settings, and this chapter will also consider the influence of culture on development across the life course, taking note of the findings of recent inquiries regarding the importance of cultural understanding to child-centred decisions.

Psychology as a scientific and practical field became established much earlier than social work and, as such, provided many fundamental concepts and theories for developing tools and techniques for social work, some of which will be explored throughout his chapter. Having a basic knowledge and understanding of developmental theories and concepts is important for social workers, who need to assess and intervene in the lives of a range of different individuals and environments in their everyday practice. Many of the fundamental assumptions, concepts, principles, theories, methods and techniques used within social work are derived from developmental psychology.

What is developmental psychology and how is it relevant to social work?

According to the British Psychological Society (2015b), developmental psychology is the scientific study of cognitive, emotional, social, perceptual and biological age-related changes in both mind and behaviour. Original ideas about human development proposed that the formation of all our skills and abilities was completed in childhood; indeed many of the initial developmental psychology theories – such as Piaget's theory of cognitive development and Bowlby's attachment theory – were essentially concerned with childhood development. Nowadays, however, development is seen as a *lifelong process*, and, as lifespans increase and technology impacts on development and communication, it is accepted that the life course of any individual involves constant development and readjustment. Moreover, human development is *multidimensional* and incorporates psychological, biological, cognitive, social and cultural influences which overlap and interact interchangeably and shape individual development across the life course. Developmental psychology is informed by *scientific* methods of studying human behaviour and theories which aim to further our understanding of how development evolves, offering a growing body of knowledge of the general principles and models and of the differences and similarities in development across individuals. However, the study of human development is an endeavour that has been influenced by a multiplicity of disciplines, including psychology, biology, anthropology, sociology and history.

Reflective point

As you read this chapter, consider how knowledge of developmental psychology might help inform social work practice with the Brightwell family. The Brightwells certainly have a lot of issues, but their case is fairly typical of those open to statutory social workers and, if we are honest, there are elements of the Brightwell family in all of our families. Social workers should always be aware of this shared humanity and strike that difficult balance between empathy and authoritative practice – a balance that is more achievable from a sound and inquisitive knowledge base about developmental psychology.

Discussion: Exploring issues around the Brightwell family
Consider the situation of Susan Brightwell as an abused partner, single parent and carer for her mother. It is likely that her experiences impacted on her own life chances and potential for development. For example, caring responsibilities have made it unlikely that she would have been able to develop any educational or career aspirations and, given the pressing demands of close family, it is also likely that she neglects her own physical and mental health. Her self-esteem, after an unhappy relationship, is likely to be low, and Wayne's abusive behaviour towards her will only serve to reinforce those feelings. There are several junctures in the Brightwell family's life course when social workers might be involved, and the reflective social worker, equipped with an understanding of developmental psychology, will look further than the specific presenting problem and hopefully be able to make a difference to the family's overall level of functioning.

Debates within developmental psychology

There are a number of long-standing debates within developmental psychology that are still being explored by continued research and theoretical developments. Some of the key elements of these debates are presented below, although it should be borne in mind that the families and individuals known to social workers have often experienced distorted, rather than normative, patterns of development likely to include issues such as the mental health of carers, the neglect of children, domestic violence and poor living conditions. Hence it should be expected that certain developmental milestones will be met within differing timescales.

Nature vs. nurture

The nature vs. nurture debate (Rutter, 2006) is one of the oldest debates in psychology and in essence refers to the relative contribution of nature and environment to human development. For example, the argument that development is rooted in *nature* can be traced back to philosophers such as Plato and Descartes, who supported the notion that babies are born with *innate* skills that are somehow programmed in the human mind. Nowadays, the nature argument encompasses advances in genetics and refers to the position that our genetic make-up and inheritance are the primary influence on development, while nurture refers to those primary influences being provided by our environment. This latter view evolved from early ideas in the seventeenth and eighteenth centuries of the child being a 'blank slate' at birth (John Locke, 1632–1704) and that environmental experiences are key in shaping the individual through their life course.

The contemporary view of the debate captures the complex interplay between nature *and* nurture. For example, the concept of temperament (Chess and Thomas, 1977) refers to individuals' ways of responding to the emotional events and problems they may face; the child's temperament appears to be affected in part by their genetic make-up but may be altered as a result of the environment in which they live (Rothbart et al., 2000).

Case studies: The nature vs. nurture debate

1) Consider the situation of Laura, a child brought up from birth in a home environment characterized by neglect and the drug abuse of both her parents. At age sixteen Laura decided that she was going to make something of her life and rejected what she saw as the 'inherited self' (low aspirations, low self-esteem, the beginnings of depression). She began attending school regularly, moved out of her parents' home to live with an aunt and went on to complete a degree at university.

Discussion
Laura's early life path has clearly been one shaped by nature. Consider how the nature vs. nurture perspectives might help explain her life path.

2) Consider the situations of Stella and Paul, both adopted at a few months of age from different birth families of mixed-race heritage. Adopted by a middle-class white couple in the 1970s, Stella developed as a happy child at primary school but, once at secondary school, began truanting and getting involved in shoplifting. Despite the loving and non-judgemental care given by her adoptive parents, Stella escalated her criminality to include an assault on her peers. She left home at sixteen to live in a series of bedsits, where she became dependent on heroin, and she died alone at the age of thirty-two, not having seen her adoptive family for five years. Paul, in contrast, flourished throughout his childhood, married a local girl and now holds down a teaching job and has two young sons of his own.

Discussion
Consider how the nature vs. nurture perspectives might help explain the differing life-paths of Stella and Paul.

Continuity vs. discontinuity in development

This debate is concerned with whether development follows a smooth and continuous path or whether it is a discontinuous stage-based process. If development is seen as continuous, then later development can be predicted from early life. Historically this corresponds to the view of children being mini-adults – as observed by historians of childhood in records and the arts as early as the seventeenth century (James and Prout, 1997). Contemporary research confirms the importance of early experiences – for example, quality of child care – in predicting such outcomes as a good level of language development in later youth (e.g., National Institute of Child Health and Human Development, 2006). These large cohort studies found that higher quality early child care also predicted less externalizing, acting-out behaviour in youth and that more hours of non-relative care (such as nursery care) predicted greater risk-taking and impulsivity at the age of fifteen.

Other longitudinal studies (Weinfeld et al., 2000, 2004) have explored the stability of attachment security representations from infancy to early adulthood in a sample consisting of individuals living in poverty and at high risk of poor developmental outcomes. The researchers found that, in this sample, some participants who, as infants, had formed a secure attachment with their main caregiver (usually the mother), as a result of intervening life events, by the age of nineteen had undergone a change in their attachment pattern to insecure. This is an important finding as, although attachment has been found to be stable over time in other samples, it shows that attachment is vulnerable to difficult and chaotic life experiences. In other words, a secure infant attachment does not provide immunity from adverse outcomes such as deprivation and poverty. This contradicts the original view of secure attachment in infancy as the 'vaccine' against later poor developmental outcomes. By the same token, poor early attachments do not result directly in adverse later outcomes, as intervening experiences may change the attachment patterns (Misca, 2009). This has positive implications for successful adoption practice, whereby poor infant attachment effects can be moderated by positive parenting experiences. Thus attachment is better seen as an adaptation to the individual environment. This is confirmed by emerging longitudinal research on attachment in adopted children. For example, a study of 125 adopted children showed that sensitive maternal support in early childhood and adolescence predicted continuity of secure attachment from one to fourteen years (Beijersbergen et al., 2012), thus highlighting the importance of such support both early and later in adopted children's lives to ensure secure attachments.

Discussion

Children who are taken into care are at a high risk of poor developmental outcomes as a result of their early experiences, including unsatisfactory early attachments to their caregivers. However, despite statistics indicating that young people leaving care are far more likely to experience poor mental health and relationship problems than their peers, there are many examples of such youngsters who have developed into successful adults.

Consider the situations of Mick and Michelle, two unrelated children who came into care aged three and four, respectively, after serious neglect and abuse by their respective birth parents. After a succession of foster and residential placements, Mick found security and stability with Mary and Phil, an older fostering couple who stuck by him, despite his teenage years of aggressive and rejecting behaviours. This period of security was identified by Mick as being the factor that led him to turn his life around.

Michelle, however, who suffered a similarly abusive childhood, never achieved any kind of continuity in her fractured life and went from foster placement to foster placement and then on to a series of supported lodgings, breaking down all placements through her violent outbursts and heavy drinking. In her adult life Michelle continued to drink heavily and to associate with a series of abusive men, which led to her three children being taken into care in their early years.

The above two cameos suggest that the role played by attachment is a critical one for children in care.

Critical vs. sensitive periods of development

In developmental psychology, a *critical period* usually implies that certain environmental stimuli are needed if healthy development is to occur. An example is the assumption that, if an infant does not form a secure attachment with a mother figure in the first months of life, he or she may not develop the ability to form secure attachments with other adults. Early research during the 1930s and 1940s with children brought up in institutions or orphanages where, because of high levels of staff turnover, they did not have the opportunity to form stable and secure attachment to a specific adult showed that they subsequently displayed a range of behavioural and relationship difficulties. These studies (comprehensively reviewed by Clarke and Clarke, 2000) supported the idea of a critical period in attachment formation.

However, ideas regarding the critical period were revised later on. Research on children adopted from Eastern European orphanages by foreign families in the 1990s indicated that their development showed impressive catch-up, and they were able to form relationships with their adoptive parents (Misca, 2014a, 2014b). However these children appear to be more likely to develop attachments characterized by insecurity and *indiscriminate friendliness*

(Chisholm et al., 1995; Chisholm, 1998), which can in turn place children in danger – for example, indiscriminately trusting stranger adults who could pose significant risks for a child's safety.

Most developmental psychologists now agree that, rather than suffering permanent damage from a lack of stimuli during early or critical periods of development, it is more likely that people can use later experiences to help overcome deficits to some extent (Misca, 2014b). Therefore the concept of a critical period has been replaced with that of *sensitive* periods.

Theories of development

In applied professions such as social work, it is often difficult to understand theory. Students, as well as experienced practitioners, often ask why we actually need theories. A theory provides a systemic way of observing and interpreting behaviours, thus offering a conceptual framework upon which practice is based. In psychology, a theory is based on testable hypotheses and supported by (research) evidence. Developmental theories inform the way in which social workers assess and shape interventions for individuals across the life course. For social workers, the function of a theory is to inform practice, which then enables them to interpret and make sense of different behaviours and circumstances and guide the intervention. Substantive parts of social work theory are borrowed from other disciplines as well as being developed from qualitative and phenomenological studies that explore the uniqueness and richness of the lived experience. Thus the disciplines contribute to each other's theoretical bases and should not be seen as mutually exclusive.

The theory of cognitive development

The cognitive theory, initially developed by Piaget (1896–1980), views human development as driven by a person's thought processes and explores how these influence an individual's understanding and interaction with the world around them. Piaget studied the intellectual development of children, and his theory transformed the way that children were viewed. Based upon his observations, Piaget rejected previous ideas of children as 'blank slates' and passive in their development and proposed a theoretical framework that has at heart the idea that children are active in constructing their knowledge and understanding of the world. Thus they are not less intelligent than adults; they simply think differently. Piaget's theory (1964) suggests that children are born with fundamental and genetically inherited mental structures or *schemas* – starting with very basic motor activities such as reflexes, which evolve into sophisticated mental activities through a process of *assimilation and accommodation* in interaction

Table 2.1 Piaget's stages of cognitive development

Stage	Age range	Development
Sensorimotor	Birth to age 2	Infants progress from understanding the world in terms of their simple reflexes and physical actions by making perceptual and motor reactions to objects and events; the emergence of internal mental representations occurs towards the end of the stage.
Pre-operational	2–7 years	Supported by the growth in language, children use symbols to represent objects and events; however, there remain difficulties in grasping *transformations* – i.e., recognizing that a quantity (e.g., of liquid) remains the same despite changes in the shape of a container, known as 'conservation' – and seeing the world from another's perspective (*egocentrism*).
Concrete operational	7–12 years	Children acquire certain logical structures – *cognitive schemas* – that allow them to perform various mental operations such as transformations and overcome egocentrism; difficulties with abstract reasoning remain.
Formal operational	12+	Mental operations are no longer limited to concrete objects and are applied to abstract concepts engaged in logical reasoning and problem-solving.

Source: Adapted from Duckworth (1964).

with the environment. Thus cognitive development is a progressive reorganization of mental processes resulting from both *maturation and experience*.

Piaget developed a four-stage model of how the mind processes new information in a staged manner (see table 2.1) and how development progresses though these qualitatively different stages (Flavell, 1971). The age stages are seen as developmental milestones triggered by maturation that allow children to move from one stage to the next. Piaget's ideas have been very influential, particularly in educational practice, and are at the root of child-centred approaches to education which acknowledges that progress in early learning can be attained only when the child is ready by having the necessary structures in place.

Discussion

Children coming into the care system are unlikely to have progressed steadily through the above stages, particularly if they have not been stimulated or have been abused by their birth parent(s) and environment. Consider the child whose cognitive stimulation during their first two years of life consists predominantly of being left for long periods of time in front of a TV set. Their sensorimotor period of development will necessarily be restricted, and their ability to negotiate through Piaget's stages will be at a different pace to that of their peers. Foster carers and adoptive parents need an understanding of the stages of development and of the need to view each child as an individual whose progress will be different to that of children brought up in stimulating and nurturing environments.

Many of the children who come to the attention of social workers will not follow Piaget's milestones. Developmental delays will necessarily occur when parents or carers are neglectful or abusive, and children brought up to experience the world as a fearful rather than a loving place will see little logic or hope in their existence. Some may withdraw or display their upset in particularly aggressive ways. Social workers, social care workers and foster carers need to show empathy and insight when assessing and designing plans of support and intervention. Similarly, children with learning disabilities will meet some milestones at different stages and in different ways and may not achieve others at all. What is important is that such children are viewed holistically and their strengths emphasized.

Unwin and Hogg (2012) proposed the 'dry stone wall model of development' to demonstrate how children may not always follow a linear or predictable path of development but, in general terms, somehow 'get there', just like the random stones of a dry stone wall, made up of irregularly shaped building blocks, hold together as a whole.

The socio-cultural theory of development

At about the same time as Piaget was developing his cognitive theory, Vygotsky (1978) put forward his idea of a theory focusing on the connection between individuals and the socio-cultural context in which they act and share experiences, thus bringing to the fore the importance of relationships and interactions between children and adults or their peers. Humans use cultural tools, such as language, speech and writing, to mediate their social environments. Unlike Piaget, who saw the child as a 'lone scientist' discovering the world through stages, Vygotsky saw the child as learning within social interactions that involve communications.

The main concept of Vygotsky's theory is the *zone of proximal development* (ZPD), which is the 'distance' (the gap) between an individual's ability to perform a task independently and what they can do with help. Vygotsky argued that, if a task is within an child's zone of proximal development, the appropriate assistance – or *scaffolding* – will give them enough of a 'boost' to achieve it. Once the individual, with the benefit of scaffolding, masters the task, the scaffolding can then be removed and the child will then be able to complete the undertaking again on their own. However, if the task is currently outside

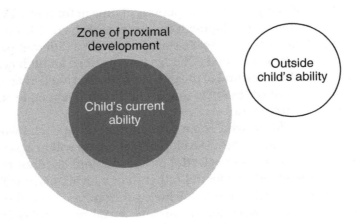

Figure 2.1 The zone of proximal development

their zone of proximal development, the scaffolding will not be efficient in helping the child achieve the task, as illustrated in figure 2.1.

The socio-cultural theory brings into focus the active role of parents, teachers and more experienced peers in a child's development. Its main contribution, in contrast to Piaget's theory, is that the influence of culture is seen as important.

Reflective point

Consider the development opportunities for a young child being brought up primarily by a single mother prone to bipolar depressive episodes who often spends her days in bed isolated from the rest of the world.

Discussion

The likelihood of the mother engaging in close forms of communication and hence helping scaffold the child's development is severely circumscribed. It may be that, if the child's wider social network – such as extended family or attendance at school or play groups – is sufficiently supportive, this might compensate for the shortcomings of the mother, but there may be cause for concern if such compensatory networks do not exist. The threshold for child protection intervention under the Children Act 1989 is that of 'significant harm' – this threshold to be measured by comparing the child's health and development with what could reasonably be expected from a child of similar age.

Reflective point

When might a lack of opportunities to develop be considered to constitute a risk of significant harm to a child or young person? You might take into account issues such as the child's social and cultural environment, any special needs the child may have, the parents' ability to provide effective care and stimulation, and how any impact on the child's development might be measured. Are there any other areas you might consider in weighing up the contested nature of significant harm with reference to Vygotsky's theory of zones of proximal development?

Attachment theory

Attachment theory, in its initial formulation by John Bowlby (1907–1990), is about a child forming a secure relationship with one primary caregiver in order for typical or normal social and emotional development to occur. Such an attachment allows the child to feel secure enough to explore the world. Bowlby postulated that behaviours such as crying and searching for parents or caregivers were adaptive responses to separation from a primary attachment figure. He put forward the idea that there was a link between *maternal deprivation* (Bowlby, 1951) and subsequent problematic behaviours in adolescence and adulthood, including poor mental health and criminal activity. Such ideas were highly influential at the time, leading to the gradual closure of children's homes and the expansion of foster care arrangements.

Attachment theory is highly influential in contemporary social work, specifically in the area of practice with children and families. The original formulation of the theory spoke of *maternal deprivation* and proposed explanations of behaviour based on early experiences (under the influence of the psychodynamic perspective predominant at the time) and, importantly, the quality of relationship and/or separation from primary carers, who were then almost exclusively the mothers (Bowlby, 1958). Bowlby's initial views were also highly influenced by ethology – the study of animal behaviour – in particular by the seminal study by Konrad Lorenz on animal imprinting in the 1930s (i.e., young geese followed the mother goose substitute instinctively), which suggested that attachment may be innate and thus an important survival mechanism (Bretherton, 1992). At the centre of social work practice is the endeavour to support children being cared for within their (birth) families, although many of the children with whom social workers come into contact may be unable to live with their birth parents. What these children have in common is that they have had their primary attachment bonds interrupted in ways that affect their later adjustment (Bowlby, 1982).

Social workers and psychologists need to know the essential types of attachment patterns that affect children if they are to play a part in helping them develop secure bases. There are four main types of attachment – secure attachment; insecure ambivalent attachment; insecure avoidant attachment; and disorganized attachment (Research in Practice, 2014). Secure attachment occurs when a child is sensitively nurtured by parents/carers, leading to that child demonstrating a range of regulated emotions; insecure avoidant attachment occurs when the child closes off emotions as a result of feeling unloved due to rejecting or hostile care from parents/carers. Insecure ambivalent attachment may be present when nurturing by parents/carers is inconsistent, often leading to needy and angry behaviours from children. Disorganized attachment patterns occur in children who are brought up in fear of their parents/carers, meaning that they are often unable to understand or regulate their own emotions. Many children who come to the attention of social workers fall into this latter category, and it is vital that the ways in which social workers and psychologists might approach their interactions with children and young people should take account of the underlying effect that such patterns of attachment may have had over several years. Moreover, recent research findings call for the critical evaluation and use of attachment concepts in practice; they also favour more holistic, child-centred approaches to understanding child development in a variety of family settings (Misca and Smith, 2014).

Case study: Applying developmental psychology knowledge in social work with children

You are a student social worker in placement with a local authority foster care team. One of the foster children, Maria, aged fifteen, has been living with foster carers Fred and Josie Heath since she was thirteen. Maria is subject to a care order, having been removed from her parents due to issues of physical and emotional neglect. Over recent months, she has become more unsettled at the Heaths, who found that her constant boundary pushing and answering back led to their asking for a two-week respite period, to coincide with the holiday break that they had booked. Maria herself wanted to go back to her parents' home for these two weeks, but this has not been allowed as conditions there are still very poor, the electricity currently being cut off for non-payment. Maria was eventually placed with a respite care foster family, the O'Reillys. She refuses to go back to the Heaths after the respite period, saying that the O'Reillys treat her with more respect and are a 'fun' family, whereas the Heaths are 'boring'. The O'Reillys also have a thirteen-year-old son, Josh, who Maria says is 'cool' as he plays in a local rock band.

Discussion
Developmental psychology can help explain Maria's attitude and explore her behaviours in respect of insecure attachment, which may have led her to attach so quickly to the O'Reillys. She may have become close to other carers

who then let her down by ending a placement, hence making her wary of becoming too close to adults for fear of being hurt again.

Developmental psychology theories and models that are helpful in this case might include the discontinuity vs. continuity perspective, particularly if Maria has had a history of repeatedly changing placements. Her cognitive development may also have taught her that 'honeymoon' periods with foster carers can bring material rewards and treats, whereas the realities of longer term commitments might lead to a lessening of such rewards, hence encouraging her to move on again. Vygotsky's theory regarding the importance of culture might help explain why being part of a 'fun' family, with the added attraction of having a young male who is in a rock band, appears to be Maria's preference. Among the strategies that a social worker might use with Maria are exploring some of the above perspectives with her and trying to facilitate her gaining insight into her situation. Depending on her cognitive abilities, she may be empowered to make decisions based on a more holistic appreciation of how her behaviour is affecting her current and future development.

Recent government policy (Department for Education, 2016) has promoted adoption as the preferred choice for children at risk, as compared to previous practices and policies which afforded parents several attempts at rehabilitation with birth children. The belief in the critical need for stable early attachment is a key theory underpinning this policy change. Some social workers object to the new policies intended to speed up adoption and use the rather derogatory term 'forced adoption', which is criticized for denying parents' rights to prove they can change (Unwin and Misca, 2013).

Reflective point

Do you think it is legitimate for the government to use a theory to promote a political policy which might really be led by other considerations (e.g., adoption is a lot cheaper for the state than long-term foster care)? If so, why?

Attachment in adults

Consequent developments in attachment theory focused on providing an explanation for adult relationships in terms of their emotional, romantic and caregiving patterns. We all know people who are very close or not very close to friends and family, and we also know people in long-term relationships and others who 'flit' in and out of relationships. Initial formulations provided a model of adult attachment mirroring infant attachment styles based on the continuity assumption that early patterns last throughout an individual's lifetime. For example, Hazan and Shaver (1987, 1994) argue that there are similar concerns in adult relationships around intimacy, insecurity and feelings of safety, suggesting that an attachment style adopted in infancy can have resonance in adult life. However, a meta-analysis of longitudinal studies (studies that followed up and compared the attachment style of an individual from infancy through to adulthood) failed to evidence the continuity (Fraley, 2002).

Bifulco and Thomas (2013) looked at adult attachment with a particular focus on an individual's ability to access social networks of support, which are a key factor in social work interventions with older people. They identified a range of styles of adult attachment:

- *clearly secure* – able to make and maintain relationships with others while also being appropriately autonomous;
- *enmeshed* – a dependent style of relationship-making with low autonomy;
- *fearful* – anxious about rejection or being let down; sensitive and avoidant of commitment in relationships;
- *angry-dismissive* – high levels of mistrust and anger; a need to have strong controls;
- *withdrawn* – private and highly self-reliant; avoidant of close relationships.

Such typologies of attachment are useful ways for social workers to think broadly about what needs a person might have in terms of relating to others, what kind of approach to take, and what types of interventions might have the greatest likelihood of success. This developing area of research is interesting in its critique of Bowlby's (1958) early concepts and in developing other theories to capture the complexity of adult relationships. Although it is insufficiently researched in the later life stages, attachment theory may be a useful framework to understand the changes in relationship for adults requiring social work intervention.

Discussion

Returning to the Brightwells, let us consider the patterns of attachment that might characterize relationships between the adults in the family and their relevance for any planned social work interventions. Brandon (aged eleven) might be seen as securely attached, whereas fifteen-year-old Shana's attachment pattern might be seen as insecure/avoidant. Adult son Wayne's aggressive behaviour and ongoing drug usage perhaps indicate an angry-dismissive style of adult attachment, or perhaps this presenting behaviour masks an underlying 'fearful' style in which he is sensitive and afraid of commitment in relationships. Susan's attachment to her mother, Mary, would seem to fall within the enmeshed, dependent style of adult attachment which is characterized by low autonomy.

A social worker or psychologist with such a holistic vision of a family has opportunities to effect change that would not be open to a professional who considered only individual attachment styles or thought that attachment concerns were limited to issues of development and relationship-building within childhood.

Reflective point

Reflect on whether you think the adult attachment styles of Susan and Wayne Brightwell discussed above mirror the childhood attachment styles they were likely to have experienced.

You can assess and reflect on your own adult attachment style by using the questionnaire on the following link. Discuss the findings in a small group where you feel comfortable sharing some level of personal issues: www.web-research-design.net/cgi-bin/crq/crq.pl.

Behaviourist theories

Behaviourist theories are concerned with observable behaviour, as opposed to internal processes such as thinking and emotions, and explain *development as a learning process* through stimulation and rewards. They deal only with observable behaviours and consider development a reaction to *rewards, punishments, stimuli and reinforcement.* Ivan Pavlov (1849–1936) proposed the seminal concept of *classical conditioning* in an experiment involving the study of conditioned response in dogs given food immediately after a bell sounded. After a short while the dogs salivated at the sound of the bell, anticipating that they would be fed, even though no food was actually forthcoming (Pavlov, 2010).

The principle of classical conditioning was later applied to children, notably in Watson and Rayner's (1920) famous 'Little Albert' experiment. Watson and Rayner prompted a fear response in eleven-month-old Albert by associating loud noises with the appearance of certain stimuli, such as a white rabbit. They found that fear was induced in Albert even when that stimulus – e.g., seeing a white rabbit – had not previously done so. It would not be permitted under today's standards to submit an infant to distress in such a highly unethical way for research purposes. Despite this and some later concern about the lack of rigour in the 'Little Albert' experiment, Watson's early work around classical conditioning has been very influential ever since. B. F. Skinner (1904–1990) expanded the behaviourist methods to include the phenomenon of operant conditioning by investigating ways that certain behaviours can be encouraged and others discouraged – coined as positive or negative reinforcement (Skinner, 1948).

The behaviourist tradition has contributed to several methods of therapeutic interventions as social work has developed, with basic reward systems such as star charts being regularly used, particularly in residential settings, to reward good behaviour. Such systems may be welcomed in addressing some issues – e.g., a star when a young child has a dry bed in the morning – but they only ever deal with symptoms of underlying issues and can be used in patronizing ways, especially with adults who have various forms of cognitive impairment. Reward charts and sanctions regimes are commonplace in educational settings (where the need to control behaviours is often a prerequisite of the class being able to learn), and star charts and naming a pupil of the week, month or year are part of established educational culture. Behavioural approaches have been used effectively by social workers with individuals who have various anxiety-related conditions, and behaviour modification is an important approach where there is concern about problems in the context of family and community environments.

Case study

The Brightwell family exhibit some behaviours that could possibly escalate in ways that may require social work assessment or intervention. Let us consider the issues surrounding Shana's problems with her weight and her mother Susan's behaviour in attending to all of her own mother's needs.

Discussion
Shana had been obese and a victim of bullying, but she had begun to lose a lot of weight, threw away her packed lunches, and would not eat tea or supper. Her behaviours put her health at risk. Shana has mild learning disabilities, and her limited cognitive abilities suggest that responses which directly linked reward with behaviour might be effective. For example, if Shana was rewarded with praise and maybe some particular attention by her mother every time when even the smallest amounts of food were eaten, this could build up, and 'treats' such as going shopping one-to-one with Susan could be introduced. A star chart could possibly be kept in Shana's bedroom with a star reflecting every successful mealtime, reinforcing such behaviours until a point when she ate well without thinking about other rewards.

Susan's response of attending to all her mother's care needs, as well as those of her children, are likely to lead to high levels of stress and associated health problems. A behaviourist approach to Susan's habit of responding to all of her mother's demands might involve her setting very strict boundaries on the duration of visits to Mary. The need to control the length of these visits could possibly be reinforced by a technique such as setting the alarm on her mobile phone to go off at diminishing intervals as a prompt for her to leave. Mary might set a particular alarm in order to remind her to have some quality time for herself.

Psychodynamic theories

Historically, the 'original' theory of human development, the psychoanalytic theory, emerged in the clinical work of Sigmund Freud (1856–1939),
who proposed a collection of ideas forming the basis of the psychodynamic
approach to psychology. Freud's psychoanalytic theory evolved into a broad
framework which is still used today as a therapeutic technique within applied
practice. The main tenet of psychodynamic theory is that early childhood
experiences and unconscious desires influence behaviour.

Freud believed that the human mind is divided into three different areas:

- the conscious – the part of the mind where ideas and perceptions originate;
- the preconscious – the part of the mind representing aspects and ideas
  that require substantial effort to be brought into the conscious mind;
- the unconscious – the part of the mind representing content and thoughts
  which are kept 'hidden' from the conscious part of the mind.

Freud ([1923] 2001) proposed three concepts illustrating human personality:
the id, the ego and the superego. Each of these different areas serves a specific function and is a key component of psychoanalysis personality theory.
The *id* is the subconscious and instinctive component and consists of inherited aspects of personality, the *ego* mediates between the instincts of the *id*
and the external real world, and the *superego* incorporates values and morals
of society, which are learned from various other individuals.

Based on clinical observations and a range of case studies, Freud developed a theory that described development in terms of a series of fixed
psychosexual stages (see table 2.2). As an individual grows physically, certain
areas of the body become important as sources of frustration or pleasure.

Although widely influential in practice over time, Freud's theory of staged
psychosexual development has been subject to vigorous critical evaluation. Like other stage theories, it postulates that development can result in
either successful completion or a healthy personality or alternatively in failure, leading to an unhealthy personality. This prediction is too simplistic to
explain the complexity of the human mind and personality. A further criticism is in relation to the methodology used throughout Freud's work, which
was limited to clinical case studies (drawn from predominantly middle-class
female patients displaying clinical symptoms) which are highly susceptible to researcher bias. More recent re-examination of Freud's clinical work

Table 2.2 Stages of psychosexual development

Stage	Age	Development
Oral stage	Birth to 18 months	Focus on oral stimulations (breastfeeding and feeding); too much or too little oral gratification can result in oral fixation. A fixation at this stage may result in the individual having a tendency to smoke, overeat and drink alcohol.
Anal stage	18 months to three years	Focus on toilet training. A fixation at this stage may result in an obsession with cleanliness, perfection and control or the individual being messy and disorganized.
Phallic stage	Three years to six years	Focus on unconscious sexual desires; this stage is often referred to as the Oedipus/Electra complex. A fixation at this stage could result in sexual deviancies and weak or confused sexual identity.
Latency stage	Six years to puberty	Sexual urges remain repressed and children interact and play mostly with same-sex peers. Conscious energy is focused primarily on academic and practical skills.
Genital stage	Puberty onwards	Coinciding with the start of puberty, the focus of pleasure is the genitals and sexual urges. Through the lessons learned during the previous stages, adolescents direct their sexual desires towards opposite-sex peers.

Source: Adapted from Rutter (1970).

suggests that he sometimes distorted his patients' case histories to 'fit' with his theory (Sulloway, 1991).

Psychoanalysis has fallen from popularity in social work as professionals have looked to use interventions that are informed by evidence. Much emphasis today is on working with individuals within their families and social environments, which psychoanalytical interventions, focusing only on the individual, do not consider. Social work's preoccupation with targets and systems (Harris and White, 2009) has been at the expense of therapeutic work and relational work in general, and a great strength of psychoanalysis is in its challenge to professionals to think deeply, beyond the surface and appearances, about what drives a person.

Reflective point

Harry, an outwardly successful businessman, is fifty years old and has always been a heavy drinker, both socially and at home. As a child he always felt unloved and rather a nuisance to his parents, who were in their forties when he was born. Harry has seen two marriages break down, partly through his excessive drinking and partly because he did not want children, having initially told his wives that he did. He has recently been suffering from anxiety and has been advised by his GP to seek help. He has decided to pay for psychodynamic therapy.

Discussion

What is encouraging in the above scenario is that Harry clearly has some motivation to change his drinking habit and has already displayed a level of emotional awareness by recognizing that he felt unloved as a child. Psychoanalysis will be used to seek out the reasons that underlie his compulsion to drink. Psychoanalysis, whereby the therapist lets the client lead by exploring any areas with which they are comfortable, may be supportive in nature, whereas the more traditional form of psychotherapy is therapist-led and explores early experiences, considering Freud's stages of development and their possible links to present behaviours. Discussions about dreams and fantasies may form part of this exploratory unlocking process, which is often reported by clients as being very therapeutic, especially once trust is established with the therapist.

Harry might well have subconsciously become stuck at the oral stage, and his dependence on alcohol may well bring him feelings of comfort or escape. If psychotherapy can be used to help him bring his underlying emotions to the surface, there is potential for understanding and insight that may lead to change.

Reflective point: Professionals' attitudes towards children being sexually exploited

Recent high-profile cases of child sexual exploitation (CSE) in England (Berelowitz et al., 2012; Firmin, 2013) raised concerns not only about the widespread nature of the phenomenon but also about the (limited) ability of professionals to identify, understand and support the victims. For example, research for the Office of the Children's Commissioner identified that a disproportionate number of victims of CSE were in the care system, particularly in residential care. Moreover, children and young people who were being sexually exploited were frequently described by professionals in many localities as being 'promiscuous', 'liking the glamour', engaging in 'risky behaviour' and being generally 'badly behaved'. Some of the most common phrases used to describe the behaviour in question were 'prostituting herself', 'sexually available' and 'asking for it'. The Office of the Children's Commissioner's Inquiry Panel into Child Sexual Exploitation in Gangs and Groups (Berelowitz et al., 2012: 12) found that 'this labelling reflects a worrying perspective held by some professionals, namely that children are complicit in, and responsible for, their own abuse.' For the various reports produced by the panel, see www.childrenscommissioner.gov.uk/info/csegg1.

Task
How could knowledge of developmental psychology help professionals to understand the phenomenon of child sexual exploitation and the behaviour of children who are sexually exploited in developmentally inappropriate ways?

The life-course perspective

Paul Baltes (1936–2006) and his colleagues (Baltes, 1987; Baltes and Smith, 2004; Baltes et al., 1999) identified a range of key principles of life-course or lifespan development. These principles act as a conceptual framework and blend biological knowledge with environmental and cultural determinants of healthy development:

- Development is a *lifelong process*; thus each period is affected by what has gone before and will influence what will follow. This perspective rejects the traditional assumption that childhood is the main period of development.
- Development is *multidimensional*; it occurs along numerous interacting biological, psychological and social dimensions.
- Development is *multidirectional*; as individuals gain in one area of their development they may lose in another; the process is influenced by both biology and culture, and the balance between these changes over time.
- Development involves flexible *resource* allocations; resources may be used for growth, or for maintenance, or for dealing with loss when maintenance is not possible.
- Development shows *plasticity*; this refers to the fact that individual development trajectories are not predetermined and can be modified.
- Development is influenced by the *historical and cultural context*; individuals develop within several different contexts.

As mentioned above, many of the children and adults who come into contact with social workers will not have followed a number of psychology's typical pathways of development, and thus taking a life-course approach to understanding their trajectories might be more practical. This will be illustrated in the following case study.

Case study: Applying developmental psychology to social work across the life course

Alicia is seventeen years old and lives with her maternal grandmother, Yvonne, aged seventy-five. Alicia's mother abandoned her to be cared for by Yvonne soon after she was born. Alicia does not have contact with her mother, and the last news she heard was that she was in prison for drug dealing.

'Alicia was an angelic child but such a troubled teenager', Yvonne says, and at the age of fourteen Alicia was placed in Section 20 (Children Act 1989) foster care as her grandmother could no longer cope with her behaviour: she was missing from home frequently, drinking and taking drugs, and Yvonne suspected her of being involved in promiscuous behaviour with older men, several of whom had bought her gifts such as jewellery and clothes. 'She got in with the wrong crowd', Yvonne said about her at the time.

Last year, Alicia returned from her foster home to live with Yvonne, who was glad to have her back as she seemed to have 'sorted out' her behaviour. Yvonne said that she could use her help now in her old age, as she felt physically frail and her health was visibly declining.

A week ago Alicia proudly announced to Yvonne that she was five months' pregnant. She told Yvonne: 'When I have my baby, then I'll have someone who'll really love me.' However, Yvonne is very worried about the news, as she does not think that Alicia is mature enough to care for a baby and she does not feel able herself to take on looking after another baby at her age, particularly given her poor health. When she told Alicia what she thought, they had a massive row. Alicia was very angry and accused Yvonne of never caring about her and shouting abuse at her. A neighbour, who overheard the argument, saw Yvonne the next day with bruising on her face and left arm.

Discussion

A social worker would clearly be concerned about an apparent injury to an older person and will need to assess risk in this situation. Rather than perhaps pathologizing an individual as being deviant, having an understanding of life-course development might be helpful in viewing individual actions as falling within a range of normative behaviours associated with a particular stage of development. As a teenager, Alicia is striving for independence and asserting her own autonomy, and she may well have got pregnant deliberately to show that she can do what she wants with her life. Peer pressure, a very significant force in adolescence, may have encouraged her to take sexual risks at a stage in life when sexual exploration is normative, the extra concern in Alicia's situation being her alleged association with older men.

Holistic assessment of this situation should also involve a consideration of risks to the unborn baby, whose physical and emotional development will be affected by Alicia's lifestyle and by any stress in the environment. There is intergenerational conflict within the home environment, and Alicia's grandmother, Yvonne, is at a stage when she may well not want to bring up a new grandchild in her home, especially given Alicia's rather volatile situation and disposition. In other families, a willing and healthy grandmother could be a great source of help and support, able perhaps to model some of the parenting behaviours that young people such as Alicia missed out on in their own childhoods. As regards the injury to Yvonne, Alicia may well have been physically chastised by Yvonne when she was younger, and a skilful social worker will explore, advise and set down boundaries about acceptable behaviour in a situation where an older person and an unborn baby may be at risk.

The theory of psychosocial development

Erik Erikson (1902–1994) proposed a stage theory of development which encompassed human growth throughout the entire life course, representing a shift away from the initial work done by Freud and Piaget. Erikson's basic premise, emphasizing the dynamic relationship between the individual and his or her social environment (Erikson, 1956, 1959), brought about a psychosocial view of lifelong development.

Erikson's theory proposes that the individual's personality is the result of the successful resolution of the stages through which they progress (see table 2.3). Originally, he focused on child development, but his later research encompassed adult development and later stages, right up to death. Moreover, Erikson introduced a multicultural perspective to the formulation of the life cycle and postulated that individuals experience a conflict through each stage, which results in a turning point in growth and development.

Reflective point: Applying theory in practice

Revisit the case study of Alicia above. Consider how psychosocial theory might help your understanding of the situation of both Alicia and Yvonne. In light of psychosocial theory, how might the different life stages of Alicia and

Table 2.3 Psychosocial stages of development

Stage/Age	Psychosocial conflict
Birth to 1 year	Trust vs. mistrust
18 months to 3 years	Autonomy vs. shame
3 years to 5 years	Initiative vs. guilt
5 years to 12 years	Industry vs. inferiority
13 years to 20 years	Identity vs. role confusion
20 years to 25 years	Intimacy vs. isolation
25 years to 60 years	Generativity vs. stagnation
Over 65 years	Integrity vs. despair

Source: Adapted from Rosenthal et al. (1981).

Yvonne explain their interactions? Evaluate the effectiveness of a theoretical framework that could encompass both early and later stages of life and its application to family situations.

Early life experiences and resilience in development

The assumption that early experiences are important for subsequent development has generated continual debate. Recent research reinforces the message that early experiences have a great influence on brain development and structure. For example, across studies involving previously institutionalized children who have been adopted, findings suggest that early severe deprivation leads to a dramatic reduction in overall brain volume (Nelson, 1999). However, the interplay between genes and environment underlies such influences, as outlined earlier in the nature vs. nurture section of this chapter, as well as in recent research (Misca, 2014a).

It is thus important to understand that the impact of early experience is not a singular causal relationship but one which depends on various environmental and genetic factors interacting in a complex manner (Schaffer, 2000). Moreover, such impact is not constant throughout life, and early experiences appear to have a strong influence on the immature brain. Such time-frames of high susceptibility to change are often referred to as *sensitive or critical periods*. For example, adverse childhood experiences are important contributing factors to psychiatric disorders, and these can potentially manifest across the life course (Zubin and Spring, 1977).

Munro (2011) and Munro and Musholt (2014) call for caution in the extrapolation of the limited neuroscientific base regarding areas such as brain imaging and have challenged the basis on which established medical research about early brain development has been used inappropriately to support government policies regarding child protection and adoption strategies.

To add to the complexities of such debates, individuals have demonstrated the capacity to adapt well to adversity and to thrive against the odds – a concept known as *resilience*. Resilience describes the 'relative resistance to psychosocial risk experiences' (Rutter, 1999: 119). Initial understanding of the concept tended to focus on the personal qualities of strong individuals, such as high self-esteem or high intelligence in children, which have been shown to act as protective factors against poor early experiences. Researchers increasingly acknowledge that resilience might derive from factors external to the child and that it is best thought of as a process rather than as an individual trait. Cross-cultural research on resilience (Ungar, 2008) among children, adolescents and young adults has found a positive relationship between both external variables (such as spirituality, social support, social capital and income) and personal traits (such as self-efficacy, normal attachment, healthy attributions and coping) alongside 'resistance' to a variety of risk factors, including psychiatric disorders and school failure.

The influence of culture on development

How social workers think about culture can help them to move towards greater sensitivity or can create additional barriers in their ability to engage and work with different families. The concept of culture has evolved dramatically over the last few years and can aid social workers to understand the individual's lived experience, which can help bridge the distance between the individual and community. Recent definitions of culture focus on the beliefs and values that underlie observable behaviours and customs. For example, Western cultures centre on individualism, whereas Eastern cultures are known for having a more collectivist focus. Such cultural differences can lead to different variations in how children are raised, further impacting on their psychological development (Quintana et al., 2006). The increasingly culturally diverse workforce itself (Misca and Neamţu, 2016; Zanca and Misca, 2016) brings its own challenges to social work practice.

Case study: Understanding the socio-cultural contexts of development

A fourteen-year-old Irish traveller girl is regularly going missing from home, and her mother has been told by her daughter's friends that she is meeting groups of older men for sex, using local hotels.

Task
How would you explain such behaviour culturally and with reference to theories of adolescence, and how would you become knowledgeable about attitudes towards development within Irish travelling communities?

How might developmental theory help you form a view regarding whether the young person was at risk of 'significant harm' (Children Act 1989)? What is your core consideration – cultural sensitivities or the safeguarding of a young person?

Summary

It is easy for a social worker, or indeed a psychologist, to be overwhelmed by the volume of and differences between the various strands of psychology. Most psychologists are specialists in a particular field, whereas social workers specialize largely in either children or adults while maintaining a world view that embraces the ecosystem around a family – children, adults, friends, neighbours and community – often looking for the strengths rather than the pathologies that exist. There are no right or wrong answers regarding how an individual should develop, but the vast array of knowledge and agreement arrived at over the last century and more is to be both respected and critically interpreted. Some social workers, and their clients, will have a preference for certain ways of working, and no interventions need to be mutually exclusive. Hopefully, this chapter has made you reflect not just on the Brightwell family but on the families with whom you are actually working. You might now look at those families in a different light and be able to come up with a fresh perspective or new questions to ask them or fellow professionals from other disciplines.

Further reading and resources

(For full bibliographic details, see the References.)

On theoretical perspectives on development:

Baltes and Smith, Lifespan psychology: from developmental contextualism to developmental biocultural co-constructivism.
Bretherton, The origins of attachment theory: John Bowlby and Mary Ainsworth.
Duckworth, Piaget rediscovered.
Erikson, *Identity and the Life Cycle: Selected Papers.*
Hazan and Shaver, Attachment as an organizational framework for research on close relationships.

On critical evaluations of theories of development:

Misca and Smith, Mothers, fathers, families and child development.
Quintana et al., Race, ethnicity, and culture in child development: contemporary research and future directions.
Schaffer, The early experience assumption: past, present, and future.
Sulloway, Reassessing Freud's case histories: the social construction of psychoanalysis.
Ungar, Resilience across cultures.
Weinfield et al., Continuity, discontinuity, and coherence in attachment from infancy to late adolescence: sequelae of organization and disorganization.

On attachment theory:

The short video *Theories of Attachment in Young Children* (www.youtube.com/watch?v=uyO0qY49bW8) is a useful overview of attachment and presents historical and contemporary perspectives.
The website Research in Practice (http://fosteringandadoption.rip.org.uk/) contains a wealth of useful information and learning tools regarding fostering and adoption.

3 Perspectives from Clinical and Counselling Psychology on Mental Health and Illness

The following are the key relevant capabilities and standards in this chapter for social workers.

Professional Capabilities Framework (BASW, 2015)	Standards of Proficiency (HCPC, 2012)
5 Knowledge 5.4 Recognise the short and long term impact of psychological, socio-economic, environmental and physiological factors on people's lives, taking into account age and development, and how this informs practice **7 Intervention and Skills** 7.1 Identify and apply a range of verbal, non-verbal and written methods of communication and adapt them in line with people's age, comprehension and culture 7.3 Demonstrate the ability to engage with people, and build, manage, sustain and conclude compassionate and effective relationships 7.4 Demonstrate a holistic approach to the identification of needs, circumstances, rights, strengths and risks.	**1 Be able to practise safely and effectively within their scope of practice** Know the limits of their practice and when to seek advice or refer to another professional **2 Be able to practise within the legal and ethical boundaries of their profession** 2.9 Recognise the power dynamics in relationships with service users and carers and be able to manage those dynamics appropriately **3 Be able to maintain fitness to practise** 3.4 Be able to establish and maintain personal and professional boundaries 3.5 Be able to manage the physical and emotional impact of their practice **7 Be able to maintain confidentiality** 7.2 Be able to recognise and respond appropriately to situations where it is necessary to share information to safeguard service users and carers or others **9 To be able to work appropriately with others** 9.10 Be able to understand the emotional dynamics of interactions with service users and carers

Introduction

This chapter will explore the concepts of mental health, psychological distress and well-being via examination of the issues of discrimination and stigma so often experienced by the clients of social workers – and, indeed, by social workers themselves – with the aim of providing a broad overview of professional clinical and counselling psychology theory and practice. It is intended that it will offer readers an introductory map to understand the complexities at the interface between social work and clinical and counselling psychology practice and thus will act as a signpost towards further in-depth exploration of these issues.

Much contemporary social work is concerned with risk assessment, rationing resources and managing performance to budget. Counselling skills remain central to the practice of effective social work, and an understanding of these, as well as types of counselling and their likely success, is key to effective social work. Clinical and counselling psychology is concerned with the integration of psychological theory and research with therapeutic practice. It is important that social workers understand and have insights into the types of therapies and treatments that their clients will be receiving. This knowledge will enable them to be more empathic in their interactions with clients and psychological professionals, empowering them to collaborate or challenge as necessary.

The differences between clinical and counselling psychology

Clinical and counselling psychology are applied fields of psychology concerned with the integration of psychological theory and research with clinical and therapeutic practice. Their aims are to understand, prevent and relieve psychological distress. Clinical psychology can be considered as the original branch of psychology given that it emerged from the medical field of psychiatry, which had been concerned with finding cures for mental illnesses. The early work of Freud at the end of the nineteenth century saw the advent of claims of mental illness being cured through a novel method, the 'talking cure'. However, it was only after the Second World War that the roots of clinical psychology as a discipline distinct from psychiatry started to emerge, leading to its professional recognition in the 1970s and 1980s.

By contrast, counselling psychology has its roots in the humanistic paradigm influenced by postmodernist thinking, and it aims to apply psychological principles to psychotherapeutic practices in order to enhance growth, well-being and mental health. Counselling psychology is informed by values grounded in the supremacy of the counselling relationship, and its practice guidelines include the need to engage with clients empathically, to respect their accounts as valid, not to assume superiority of any particular way of experiencing, feeling and knowing, and to 'recognise social contexts and discrimination and work in ways that empower rather than control and demonstrate high standards of anti-discriminatory practice appropriate to the pluralistic nature of society today' (British Psychological Society, Division of Counselling Psychology, 2005: 1–2).

Social workers will come into contact with a range of adults and children who are receiving different clinical inputs from the field of psychology – adults who are experiencing mental health problems, older people who have been bereaved, carers under stress, victims of sexual and other abuse. Much contemporary social work is concerned with risk assessment, the rationing of resources and managing performance to budget, but it is important that social workers are curious and have insight into the nature of the clinical interventions being experienced by their clients. All social workers need counselling skills, but they also need some additional understanding of the skills and interventions which colleagues may be employing in working towards common goals of rehabilitation or improvement in mental well-being.

Definitions

The applied field of clinical psychology is preoccupied with understanding, defining and identifying mental health disorders in people. Clinical psychologists use different theoretical frameworks to understand how mental illness is caused and how mental illnesses are classified and identified or diagnosed and treated. Their aim is to reduce long-term psychological distress and to alleviate its associated problems in individual ability to function, and they work mainly within health and social care settings with individuals presenting with, among a range of other conditions and issues:

- mental health problems (such as depression, anxiety and schizophrenia)
- physical health problems (chronic physical illness with a significant mental impact, such as cancer)
- personal and family relationship problems.

Clinical psychologists try to help people to understand their thoughts and behaviours, and in this respect it is important to distinguish them from psychiatrists, who are medical professionals whose main interventions for clients with mental illness involve the assessment and monitoring of medication regimes. In the UK, mental health provisions are delivered by multidisciplinary teams of professionals, who provide a range of skills. Clinical psychologists and social workers will often work together with doctors, nurses and occupational therapists across a range of settings; it is therefore important that social workers have a good understanding of the role of a clinical psychologist.

Counselling psychology is a discipline closely linked to clinical psychology and is concerned with the integration of psychological theory and research within therapeutic practice to empower clients and enhance their self-determination, rather than to 'treat' or 'cure' mental illness. The term 'counselling' can mean different things to different people, and counselling psychologists work with a variety of people – from those with severe and enduring mental health problems to those who are seeking support to adapt to life's changes. The focus is less on diagnosis and treatment and more on working with an individual to improve psychological functioning and well-being, as well as empowerment to reach their potential (see the website of the British Psychological Society, Division of Counselling Psychology, www.bps. org.uk/networks-and-communities/member-microsite/division-counsel-ling-psychology). One tension in counselling practice arises from this desire to 'empower', which at times challenges the oppression prevalent in our unequal society and in the hierarchical nature of health and social services.

There are two main models that inform the training and professional development of clinical and counselling psychologists – the scientist-practitioner and the reflective practitioner. These models will be explored, and parallels with social work practice models will be drawn.

The scientist-practitioner model

At the core of the identity of all applied psychologists is the scientist-practitioner model, indicating that the 'scientist' and the 'practitioner' should inform each other (Corrie and Callahan, 2000). For clinical and counselling psychologists, this implies an active commitment to integrate current research findings into their work, to promote evidence-based practice, and to 'think scientifically' in all areas in which they operate. They are also expected to be actively involved with the production of evidence-based research (Blair, 2010). Thus the model sees clinical and counselling psychologists as practitioners, consumers and producers of research.

The reflective practitioner

However, stemming from humanistic values of reflection and the recognition of the importance of the therapist's self-knowledge, the reflective-practitioner model also needs to be incorporated into practice. This involves the use of supervision, continuing professional development, a self-critical stance and openness to experience (Stoltenberg et al., 2000; Johns, 2013). Many of the reflective skills valued by clinical psychologists are the same as those valued in social work (Ruch, 2005, 2007).

Howe (2008) suggested that effective social work practitioners should critically reflect on both previous and current experiences as they occur in practice. Schön (1983) refers to such techniques as 'reflection on practice' and 'reflection in practice'. The essential belief is that reflection will lead to continuous improvement through deeper and better empathy and insights, both on self and on clients. Influenced by Rogers's (Baldwin, 1987) core conditions deemed essential for effective humanistic counselling – empathy, respect, positive regard for others, genuineness and congruence – social work has long promoted humanistic forms of working. Horner (2012) reminds us, however, that reflective practice is only beneficial if it produces outcomes. Certainly, practitioners will develop greater critical awareness of themselves by embracing reflective practice, but it is more difficult to argue empirically for client benefits that are attributable to humanistic counselling input. Ixer acknowledges this difficulty and argues that reflective practice helps social workers to 'develop transferable skills which are lifelong and not context-specific' (1999: 523). A move towards personalization in adult services, whereby clients organize their own care rather than have services arranged on their behalf, has been seen by many as an empowering move – one which puts clients more in charge of their own lives. However, other commentators (e.g., Harris, 2009) have put forward the view that personalization policies are part of a neo-liberal ideology designed to strip away state liability and enforce responsibilities on individuals, regardless of their vulnerabilities.

The PCF (BASW, 2015), which promotes the significance of a person-centred approach in practice, was developed partly to facilitate social workers' championing of the use of values and ethics, which in turn should better serve their clients. However, it can be argued that social workers in front-line services have little time to develop professional relationships with service users on account of the bureaucratic environment of modern social work (Unwin and Hogg, 2012).

In conclusion, reflective practice is seen as an essential part of social work which enables practitioners to become more effective by developing self-awareness and an understanding of the impact of self on others, skills closely aligned to the concept of 'emotional intelligence' (Howe, 2008; Morrison, 2007). However, as discussed previously, time constraints and a lack of opportunities for reflection within organizations are just two of the challenges that practitioners currently face in modern social work. It can be argued that, in order to promote reflection and to increase the efficiency of social workers, organizations need to allow space and time for reflection to occur. This could take the form of encouraging reflective conversations between colleagues, although formal, structured supervision is also crucial for effective continuing professional development.

Reflective point

In what ways might you be able to promote a working culture of reflection even if your workplace is a very busy one?

Defining mental health problems

According to the Health and Social Care Information Centre (2015) over 1.7 million adults accessed NHS services in 2013–14 for severe or enduring mental health problems. According to the UK charity Mind (2015b), one in four people in the UK will experience a mental health problem each year, and at any one time 17 per cent of adults and 10 per cent of children are affected. This statistical data reflects the reality that mental health problems are common and affect all population groups, across age, gender and social class. A Care Quality Commission (2015) review of crisis mental health services confirmed that black and minority ethnic (BME) people have traditionally been over-represented in the mental health services, partly as a result of racism and partly because services are not reaching out to minorities. For example, the review found that black people were less likely to be offered talking therapies, were more dependent on long-term medication, and were more likely to be detained under compulsory orders.

Social work has a role in challenging such injustice, a particularly difficult role given the predominance of the medical profession in the field of mental health. Historically, in the UK, the treatment of those suffering from a mental illness took place within large institutions, but a series of scandals regarding patient care, together with criticisms of institutional mistreatment by authors such as Goffman (1961) and Townsend (1962), led to moves towards smaller units and contemporary care in the community. Goffman viewed institutions as essentially self-serving organizations wherein the needs of the establishment and the key staff took precedence over the needs of patients.

The 'medical model' (Laing, 1971) of treating mentally ill people in ways that sought to 'cure' them was increasingly challenged, and the 1960s saw a continued move away from large hospitals and a new generation of psychiatry which questioned traditional treatments. The medical model basically views mental illness in terms of diagnostic categories that are usually best treated by expert diagnosis and clinical intervention, often involving pharmacological treatments. Psychological and social factors are not given prominence under this model, which measures success in terms of individuals' ability to accord with social norms and values as reflected in the categorizations of the main diagnostic framework, the International Classification of Diseases (ICD). By way of contrast, psychosocial models or systems theory (Payne, 2014) attach great significance to the wider factors that impact on individual well-being, such as the influences of family, culture, race and environment.

Distinguishing between the behaviour of a person who is mentally unwell and that of someone who is just different is not a straightforward task. There are multiple ways of defining mental illness. One definition is based on the deviation from the 'statistical norm' – i.e., comprising all behaviour that falls outside the 'normal range' of behaviours. This approach is problematic, as it ignores individual differences. Moreover, deviation from the norm is not necessarily bad – for example, individuals with exceptionally high intelligence levels (IQ) fall outside the norm, but this is not a negative behaviour. Another perspective in defining mental illness is based on the maladaptive behaviour of mentally ill people, such as the inability to face, or a degree of difficulty in coping with, everyday life. This approach is used in official classification of mental disorders such as in the *Diagnostic and Statistical Manual* (DSM); however, these carry negative and stigmatizing connotations. Moreover, for a condition to be defined as a mental illness, symptoms are commonly required to provoke significant impairment or distress in the sufferer. This allows people to judge the impact of their condition on their own quality of life and not have 'norms' imposed upon them by mental health professionals or society. This definition, however, fails to capture certain mental illnesses that do not feature symptoms of distress (e.g., personality disorders), and it raises further moral questions in practice if a person must be distressed by their condition in order to be treated.

Stigma and mental health problems

The view that mental illness is present when behaviours deviate significantly from social and cultural norms has historically led to the inappropriate labelling of many forms of behaviour. For example, homosexuality, although decriminalized in the UK in 1967, was categorized as a mental illness in the UK until 1987, and in many other societies it still is. Repressive societies may misuse the label of mental illness to oppress and control undesirable groups: during the late twentieth century, communist authorities in Eastern European countries classified political protesters as mentally ill in order to discredit and control them.

Individuals labelled as mentally ill are the targets of various forms of discriminatory actions, emotions and prejudices that create a range of barriers to life opportunities (Ociskova et al., 2013). Thus, individuals with mental disorders have to cope with the symptoms of the disease along with the misunderstandings of society about various mental disorders, resulting in stigma. For example, public opinion polls suggest that individuals with mental health problems are dangerous and hard to engage in conversation and that some mental illnesses (such as eating disorders) are self-inflicted (Crisp et al., 2000). Paradoxically, although the quality and effectiveness of mental health treatments and services have improved over recent decades, many of the individuals who may benefit from such services choose not to access them, partly due to reasons of stigma (Corrigan, 2004).

The stigma of mental illness is a heavy burden for sufferers, and thus it is important to define mental illness with consideration and sensitivity. Unfortunately the media is often unsympathetic and sensationalizes news stories involving mental health, as in the coverage of the Germanwings plane crash in 2015, when the co-pilot appeared to have committed suicide and taken a further 149 people with him to their deaths. In reality this incident was an exceptional and tragic one. The headline of *The Sun* newspaper in the UK on 27 March 2015 read 'Madman in Cockpit. Crazed Rookie Pilot Murdered 149'. MIND, the UK mental health charity, responded as follows:

> Clearly assessment of all pilots' physical and mental health is entirely appropriate – but assumptions about risk shouldn't be made across the board for people with depression, or any other illness. There will be pilots with experience of depression who have flown safely for decades, and assessments should be made on a case by case basis. (MIND, 2015a)

Other advocacy groups try to balance such media distortions of mental illness. Examples include Mad Pride (http://madpride.org.uk/index.php), which is a voice for individuals willing to speak openly and positively about their mental health issues, and Time to Change (2014), the biggest programme in England to challenge mental health stigma and discrimination.

Developments in mental health services

Generally, if someone develops a mental health problem, their first port of call will be their GP, who can provide medication or refer an individual to more specialist services such as therapy. In the UK, the National Institute for Health and Clinical Excellence (NICE) recommends treatment for specific mental health problems should be based on evidence.

A recent significant and important development in mental health services affecting both clinical and counselling psychologists has been the introduction of the Improving Access to Psychological Therapies (IAPT) programme (Williams, 2015), which is run by the Royal College of General Practitioners (RCGP) and offers psychological help online for adults with common mental health problems (MIND, 2013). This programme claims to equip practitioners 'with the knowledge and skills to conduct a patient-centred consultation for people with anxiety and depressive disorders. An enhanced understanding of effective psychological interventions and the IAPT programme will improve the availability of psychological therapies for patients' (RCGP, 2015). Hollinghurst et al. (2014) reviewed the effectiveness of IAPT at the end of its first three years and found that more than 1 million people had used the service. Recovery rates across a range of conditions had improved by 45 per cent, indicating some considerable success for this new mental health service.

Classification of mental health problems

The predominance of the medical model has been maintained by the acknowledgement that some mental illnesses have a biological component, usually linked to brain injuries or abnormalities (e.g., brain abnormalities in dementia), although this is not the case for all mental illnesses.

The two commonly used methods or standards for classifying mental health problems are the World Health Organization's *International Classification of Diseases* (ICD), which is currently in its tenth edition (ICD-10), and the American Psychological Association's *Diagnostic and Statistical Manual* (DSM), currently in its fifth edition (DSM-5). The DSM, which describes diagnostic criteria for a mental health problem and classifies individuals on five separate axes, is the one most commonly used in clinical practice, and it is important that social workers understand its significance and application.

Why do we need such a system?

Classification systems such as the ICD and DSM allow professionals to differentiate types of mental illness and their specific contributory factors in order to provide appropriate treatment. For example, anxiety-related disorders, depression and psychotic disorders have very different aetiologies, and those suffering from them have different needs. However, such classification systems are not free from controversy. These systems have been developed from the medical model and tend to focus on symptoms and define disorders as separate entities, despite the evidence suggesting mental health may be better understood as being a continuum (Larsson et al., 2012). Moreover, by giving diagnostic labels to disorders, there is a risk of inappropriate labelling of a client's difficulties, and many people are diagnosed with multiple problems, a phenomenon known as comorbidity. The medical model that underpins both the ICD and the DSM places the problem within the individual, a focus on disease and the desire to return the patient to a previous 'healthy' state. As mentioned above, the issue of homosexuality has been a subject of great controversy in terms of DSM categorization: it was listed as a disorder until DSM-II, then in DSM-III this 'diagnosis' was changed to 'ego dystonic homosexuality' (i.e., in conflict with the ego or one's self-image). It was only with the publication of the DSM-III-R in 1987 that this was dropped, following a long process of political debate about what constitutes 'normality'. A social model, as found in counselling psychology and practice, emphasizes health, choice and self-help and would view homosexuality as a matter of choice, not a 'problem' that needed solving.

Common mental health problems

There now follows a brief overview of the most common mental health problems and their characteristics to facilitate familiarization with the terminology, its abbreviations and the general area of mental health concerned.

MIND (2015b) provides clear evidence of the prevalence of mental health problems in the UK across age and social class.

Anxiety-based problems

Anxiety is an excessive negative state of mind characterized by bodily symptoms of physical tension and by feelings of apprehension, uncertainty and fear. Anxiety is a normal human emotion felt by most people at some point in their life; it is therefore important that social workers are able to recognize differing levels of anxiety in individuals. Some anxiety disorders, however, cause such distress that it interferes with a person's ability to function normally.

Anxiety-based problems are common, with around 4.7 in 100 people in England affected by such a problem yearly (estimates from MIND, 2015b, based on 2009 survey data). The five most common anxiety disorders are as follows.

1   Specific phobia is defined as an excessive and persistent fear triggered by a specific object or situation. Phobic individuals develop irrational beliefs that the phobic object or situation is certain to cause harm (phobic beliefs).
2   Panic disorder is characterized by repeated panic or anxiety attacks associated with a variety of physical symptoms, including heart palpitations, perspiration, dizziness, hyperventilation, nausea and tremor. In addition, the individual may experience real feelings of terror or severe apprehension and depersonalization.
3   Generalized anxiety disorder (GAD) is a condition in which the sufferer experiences continual anxiety about the future. While worry is a normal feature of life, GAD worrying can lead to catastrophizing, feeling out of control and experiencing distress to an extent that leaves an individual unable to function.
4   Obsessive-compulsive disorder (OCD) is less understood, despite being the fourth most common mental health disorder (Jast, 2011). It has two components – obsessions (intrusive and recurring thoughts that the individual finds disturbing and uncontrollable) and compulsions (repetitive or ritualized behaviour that the individual feels is necessary to prevent something negative occurring). OCD can cause anxiety and repetitive irrational urges to carry out certain acts, such as hand-washing.
5   Post-traumatic stress disorder (PTSD) consists of a set of persistent symptoms that occur after experiencing or witnessing an extremely traumatic event, including increased arousal, avoidance and numbing of emotions, and re-experiencing the event.

In the social work arena, severe anxieties are encountered across a range of client groups and situations – the partner who is terrified of violence and sexual abuse, the carer of a person with advanced dementia, or the homeless person not knowing whether they will be attacked and robbed in the night. Hence it is vital that social workers recognize the signs and types of anxiety in order best to advocate for their client or support the interventions of psychologist colleagues.

Depression and mood disorders

An individual suffering from depression is likely to experiences feelings of anxiety, hopelessness and negativity. When an individual suffers from depression it can be difficult for them to identify it, to know what they can do about it and where to seek help. Living with depression is difficult for the sufferer, but it can also make life difficult for family members and friends (MIND, 2015b).

There are different forms of depression. While mild depression has limited negative effects, major or unipolar depression interferes with an individual's daily life and stops them doing things they would usually be able to do. Bipolar disorder, also called manic depression, involves major mood swings, whereby periods of depression alternate with periods of mania. Seasonal affective disorder (SAD) is a disorder related to reduced exposure to sunlight and usually develops in the autumn and winter months; symptoms gradually decrease as days become longer (MIND, 2015b). The most common form of depression is unipolar depression and the second is bipolar disorder.

Depression manifests at emotional, behavioural, physical and cognitive levels. For example, clinically depressed individuals are limited to experiencing negative emotions and often feel sad and hopeless, struggling to enjoy things that previously brought them pleasure. They are also likely to have predominantly pessimistic and negative thoughts. Individuals with bipolar disorder fluctuate between mania – an emotion characterized by frenzied energy and feelings of euphoria – and depression. The biggest risk in such individuals is that of suicide, and there are many views regarding who is likely to be serious when they talk about taking their own life. One tragic example of a health professional keeping a 'secret' may have contributed to the suicide of a depressed girl in Birmingham (Barnett, 2006).

Case study: Suicide risk

A 27-year-old white British man, Jed, has recently been telling you that he wants to 'end it all', especially since the breakdown of his last relationship, after which his partner took their three-year-old child abroad and has refused to contact him. You were involved as a result of domestic violence having taken place in the partnership and knew also that the couple misused alcohol. Jed currently does not have any contact with his child and does not know where his ex-partner lives. He tells you that he is thinking of going to his ex-partner's mother's house and 'scaring' the address out of her. You also suspect that he is not taking his anti-depressant medication and is again drinking heavily. Jed has always spoken positively of the counselling he has been receiving until recently at his GP surgery.

Task

What theories, insights and possible interventions might be appropriate in this scenario? For example, would you take any notice of what Jed was saying, or would you dismiss it because he was drunk? Would you contact the police? Would you contact his ex-partner and her mother? Would you stay with him while he sobered up? Would you ring his GP or psychologist on his behalf if he made such a request?

Schizophrenia and psychotic illnesses

Psychotic illnesses are characterized by distortions in thought, language, sensory perception, emotion regulation and behaviour (Zubin and Spring, 1977). Sufferers may experience sensory hallucinations, false beliefs or delusions about themselves or their environment and also social withdrawal. Social workers in the field of mental health will have frequent contact with clients suffering from psychosis, and such individuals pose threats at times to their own well-being and that of others. An extreme example of psychosis or delusion would be that of 'fabricated or induced illness', previously known as Munchausen's syndrome by proxy, whereby a person subjects an individual under their care to various administrations of noxious substances to make them sick and may even take them to hospital for invasive surgery, all on false pretexts. This often involves a mother, who may be suffering from mental illness, either being deluded that something is seriously wrong with their child or having deliberate intention to cause significant harm to the child. The prognosis in all cases of fabricated or induced illness is very low for successful rehabilitation of both parties (Stirling, 2007).

Case study: Fabricated or induced illness

A mother has presented six times over the past three weeks at various A & E services at hospitals across the county. She is convinced that her eight-week-old baby has cancer of the bowel. Medical investigations have taken place, and there appears to be no problem with the child's digestive system. The baby is small but healthy for her age, and the mother is very co-operative with health staff. You have just received a call that the child has been admitted to hospital with an extreme case of diarrhoea, and the medical staff are suspicious about the mother's account of the onset of the symptoms and suspect 'fabricated or induced illness'.

Discussion

Firstly, a swift but in-depth social history needs to be compiled, working with the mother and any close contacts or family able to corroborate her claims relating to the baby's illness or previous patterns of behaviour in this sphere.

Clearly, if this is determined a case of 'fabricated or induced illness', then both mother and child are vulnerable. However, under the Children Act 1989, it is the welfare of the child that is of paramount concern. While the mother would doubtless be in need of appropriate therapeutic intervention and social support, the key consideration for the social worker is whether the child is judged to be at risk of significant harm. If, for example, it can be medically proved that the diarrhoea was brought about by the administration of a substance rather than as the result of an infection, the child would need to be removed from the mother's care by means of application to the court for an Emergency Protection Order. Seeking a Section 20 voluntary agreement to care is unlikely to be sufficient in this scenario, as the mother could demand her child back at any time.

Substance misuse and addiction

Substance misuse can be defined as a harmful pattern of substance use. The impact on the misuser's life is varied and can involve increased social and personal difficulties, failing to keep up with daily obligations or harm to health. Cleaver et al. (1999), in their 'toxic trio', clearly identify drug or alcohol abuse as one of the key dangers to children, alongside the presence of domestic violence and mental illness in families. Social workers should be very aware of the culture of drug taking, its risks and indicators (e.g., smells or identification of drug paraphernalia). In chapter 5, there is a section dedicated to exploring parental substance misuse and its impact on children.

Eating disorders

One common eating disorder is anorexia nervosa, characterized by an individual's distorted view of their body image and engagement in sustained excessive dieting. Severe weight loss is the most notable feature of anorexia, accompanied by an irrational fear of obesity and a desire to be thin (Fairburn et al., 1999). Individuals with anorexia employ various strategies to achieve weight loss, through either obsessive caloric restriction or purging or a combination of both.

Another common eating disorder is bulimia nervosa, which involves eating excessive amounts of food (Fairburn and Cooper, 1993). Individuals with bulimia identify with this description, even though the actual caloric intake for binges varies between different individuals (Fairburn et al., 1999). Individuals suffering from bulimia maintain roughly the same weight, making this disorder difficult to identify and so harder for individuals to get the appropriate support and help they require (MIND, 2015b). Depression also commonly occurs in individuals with bulimia (Agras, 2001).

Theoretical perspectives in understanding mental illness and treatment approaches

This section of the chapter will explore the key contemporary psychological approaches to the treatment of mental health problems and their supporting evidence. It is important that social workers have an understanding of different types of psychological therapy and their effectiveness if they are to work efficaciously with clients and colleagues. Psychological models have often emerged as alternatives to the medical model, and many such approaches view mental health problems as having an underlying social or psychological cause.

From medical model to talking therapies

Psychological therapies – or 'talking therapies' (Mental Health Foundation, 2009) – involve a range of interventions aimed at helping people to understand and make changes to their behaviour in order to relieve distress (Callan and Fry, 2012). Talking therapies generally fall into three different categories based on their major theoretical underpinning: psychodynamic therapies, behavioural therapies and humanistic therapies. Stiles et al. (2008) explored a range of different talking therapies within a UK primary care setting and found evidence of their effectiveness, illustrated by 58 per cent of clients having achieved an improvement. Importantly, talking therapies appear to have been steadily increasing in popularity compared to treatment with medication. For example, in a cross-sectional survey of GP surgeries, when patients were asked to rate their preferences regarding treatment for depression, counselling emerged as more popular than drug therapy. This was particularly the case among women, those who believed that antidepressant drugs were addictive and those who had received talking therapies in the past (Churchill et al., 2000).

Psychological therapy vs. medication

Evidence suggests that, once treatment comes to an end, many psychological therapies offer a better prognosis for clients than medication (Gould et al., 1995). For example, a comparison of the efficacy of cognitive behavioural therapy (CBT) and medication found that around 57 per cent of clients relapsed after drug treatment compared with only 27 per cent after receiving psychotherapy (De Maat et al., 2006). Patients treated with antidepressants did, however, recover more rapidly than those who received counselling (Chilvers et al., 2001), implying that medication is able to make a difference more quickly than talking therapies.

Counselling is embedded in a *therapeutic alliance* between therapist and client, which comprises both a *bond* between the counsellor and the client and an *agreement* about the goals of the treatment and the tasks to achieve the goal. It has long been acknowledged that successful psychological therapy is grounded in a strong, genuine therapeutic relationship, without which no techniques are likely to be effective. The therapeutic relationship makes substantial contributions to clients' success in all types of counselling, and the therapeutic relationship appears to account for why clients improve, or fail to improve, as much as the particular choice of therapy (Norcross, 2011).

The psychodynamic approach

Psychodynamic psychotherapy is one of the most commonly practised forms of talking therapy and yet one of the least researched (Vaughan et al., 2000). It focuses on the psychological roots of emotional suffering, and its main features are self-reflection, self-examination, and the use of the relationship between the therapist and client. The goals of psychodynamic therapy are to improve a client's self-awareness and help them understand the influence of past experiences on their present behaviour, and it is recommended for people experiencing depression alongside other complex illnesses.

Research indicates that clients receiving psychodynamic psychotherapy make substantial progress and maintain such change over time. Patients with a range of common mental disorders who received short-term (40 hours) psychodynamic therapy were compared with controls, and it was found that their symptoms had improved. Further improvements were found at follow-up. This suggests that psychodynamic therapy lays the groundwork for ongoing change (Shedler, 2010).

The aim of most psychodynamic therapies is for the therapist to help the client to acknowledge the existence of unconscious conflicts that may be causing symptoms of psychopathology, bring them into conscious awareness, and develop strategies for change. Psychoanalysis is a form of psychodynamic therapy devised by Sigmund Freud and may include the *techniques* of free association, transference, and dream analysis and dream interpretation. There is an emphasis on the linking of the 'there and then' with the 'here and now' within the 'transference' dynamics. *Transference* refers to the tendency of human beings to transpose aspects of earlier experience into current functioning. Psychoanalysis fell from favour in social work as it became associated with a middle-class, male-dominated view of the world that did not take account of systems theory and the fast-moving social environment of modernity. Psychoanalysis has also become associated with private paying customers and is not commonly used by clients of social workers. The influence of psychodynamic approaches is so far-reaching, however, that social workers should know the essence of the theory, which continues to provides much food for thought.

The cognitive-behavioural approach

In the cognitive-behavioural approach, the emphasis is on the different aspects of a person's thoughts, feelings and behaviours with a view to understanding the implications of thinking patterns on how they feel, and how they consequently behave. It was originally thought of as a 'collaborative empiricism', which captures a way of working with the client to identify issues and decide together how to monitor these (e.g., through 'homework' assignments or the use of diaries).

According to the cognitive model, mental health problems are attributed to irrational beliefs, dysfunctional ways of thinking and processing biases. For instance, according to the emotional cognitive perspective, anxiety can be explained by individuals making unrealistic demands on themselves. When these impossible aims are not met then individuals can feel distress. The behavioural model, however, proposes that mental health problems arise when dysfunctional behaviour is learned.

Cognitive-behavioural therapy (CBT) is a widely used model of treatment in mental health which aims to tackle dysfunctional 'ways of thinking' by challenging them and replacing them with more functional cognitions. For example, Beck's (1991) model considers that depression is maintained by negative schemas (or beliefs) and argues that successful therapy must challenge these biased, irrational and overgeneralized thoughts. CBT is an intervention for changing both thoughts and behaviour by using techniques such as keeping a diary of events and associated feelings, moods and thoughts in order to identify and challenge those that are irrational, dysfunctional or biased and develop new more adaptive ways of thinking.

Cognitive-behavioural therapy suits people who work towards solutions with clear goals using practical techniques. It falls under the umbrella of talking therapies, which can help an individual to manage their problems by changing the way they think and behave. While it is most commonly used to treat anxiety and depression, it can be useful for other mental and physical problems. CBT is adaptable to self-help programmes, including those interactive ones available online (Christensen et al., 2009).

In a comparison study of non-directive counselling, CBT and non-specialized GP care for patients with depression, CBT showed an advantage compared with non-specialized GP care after four months, but this effect was not maintained at twelve-month follow-up (Ward et al., 2000). A comparison of the computerized CBT package 'Beating the Blues' with treatment as normal reported benefits at both three months and six months, highlighting the success of such programs. Research aiming to compare the efficacy of eight weekly sessions of self-administered online CBT to a therapist-assisted email treatment found that there were no significant differences between the two (Richards et al., 2013).

The humanist-existentialist approach

The humanist-existentialist tradition (Kaslow and Massey, 2004) comes from a constructivist and social constructionist position which focuses on meaning and on human aspirations for belonging, including the ways in which meaning is a co-constructed phenomenon. The focus is on empathy and the acceptance of the client on their own terms, exemplifying the shared approach and values of both psychology and social work.

Humanistic therapies take a whole-person approach focused on developing the individual's full potential and were developed to offer an alternative to psychodynamic therapies. Meta-analysis data from fifty-two studies of person-centred therapy suggests that it is as effective and efficacious as other humanistic and non-humanistic therapy. Further research also suggests that person-centred therapy is an effective intervention for common mental health disorders. The percentage of clients who showed reliable improvement and reported feeling better about their problems was very significant (Gibbard and Hanley, 2008).

As detailed above, there are a variety of mental health problems, and everyone who presents with a mental health problem is different. Moreover, successful therapy is about tailoring the approach to the individual, their particular problem and its severity. How to measure quality of the therapist–client relationship remains contentious, as does the question regarding the extent to which any specialized psychological input can be successful if a person's home and social environment are dysfunctional and distressing.

Controversies in contemporary clinical practice

Over-diagnosis of mental disorders?

The advent of the DSM in the 1950s was followed by an increase in the number of mental health diagnosis categories. This led to a rise in concerns about diagnosis inflation – the potential for anyone to be diagnosed with a mental disorder – and the over-diagnosis of normal life experiences. The risks that over-diagnosis may bring are related to clients receiving unnecessary medication, leading to harmful side effects, or the use of unnecessary therapy, which could potentially undermine coping skills and further add stigma to issues surrounding mental health.

Evidence-based practice and 'manualized therapy'

The recent demand for evidence-based practice has seen the rise of so-called manualized therapy – therapy or intervention delivered according to a strict set of steps and procedures in order to ensure uniformity (Griffiths and Steen, 2013). When outcome data indicates a positive impact on an individual through the use of a manualized therapy, the treatment is described as 'evidence based'.

Such manualized therapy, supported by outcome data, has certain empirical or scientific legitimacy, decreases reliance on clinical judgement, and improves training by establishing minimal levels of competence. However, among its disadvantages is that it can be quite restrictive in practice and prohibit customized approaches to treatment.

The influence of new technologies: cybertherapy

In recent years, clinical practice has increasingly employed technology in the direct delivery of psychological services, including assessment and treatment. So-called cybertherapy can be used to replace or supplement face-to-face meetings and might include online psychotherapy programs, email or text psychotherapy, and computer-based self-instruction. Among its benefits are accessibility and anonymity. An example in the UK is the Big White Wall (www.nhs.uk/Conditions/online-mental-health-services/Pages/big-white-wall.aspx), offered by the NHS as an anonymous digital service that supports people experiencing common mental health problems such as depression and anxiety. While such advances may well be suitable for individuals with ready access to computer technology, it should be borne in mind that poverty is a defining characteristic of many people who make use of social work services, hence such developments may exclude many potential beneficiaries; financial charges are applicable for the Big White Wall in some health regions.

In terms of effectiveness, early research is beginning to demonstrate that psychotherapy delivered via the internet and new technologies can work as well as in-person psychotherapy, but success depends on a series of factors such as the presenting condition, the setting and the availability of live support (Richards et al., 2013). Comparative evaluations indicate that internet programmes are especially effective in the case of CBT for anxiety disorders (Christensen et al., 2004), and in health psychology they are effective in treatment of certain pain disorders.

However, the use of technology in therapy is producing several professional dilemmas, such as how to ensure confidentiality across electronic transmission, how to confirm the identity of the client, and how to make interpretations in the absence of non-verbal cues that would be present in face-to-face situations.

Cultural issues in clinical psychology

The UK population is increasingly diverse, particularly in certain geographic areas. Culture shapes how clients understand their problems, and there can be great cultural differences in the way clients understand and define mental illness, the impact of illness on individuals and their views on treatment. It is therefore vital that the therapist assesses at the outset the client's understanding of such issues by asking pertinent questions, such as 'What do you call your problem (illness, distress)?', 'What do you think your problem does to you?', 'What do you think the natural cause of your problem is?' and 'How do you think this problem should be treated?' It is critical that the practitioner possesses the awareness, knowledge and skills needed to function effectively in a pluralistic democratic society. Part of developing cultural competence is the acquisition of appropriate clinical skills and knowledge. Through self-awareness and examining their own culture, effective practitioners will come to the realization that differences are not deficiencies. Culturally sensitive practice means modifying treatments through the use of empirical evidence for members of different groups – for example, 'talk therapy' may work better for some groups than for others, and some cultural groups may respond more positively to 'action' than to 'insight'. It is a great challenge for social workers and psychologists to demonstrate cultural competency when dealing with people with different ways of life to their own. To show an interest in another's culture is a sign of respect, and every effort should be made to ask open questions, to be honest about any lack of knowledge, and to read up on different societies and their normative behaviours. One can never be 'of' a society other than one's own, but to empathize and try to understand issues from a cultural perspective can only lead to deeper understanding.

Focus: parenting and mental illness – the experiences of children and young people caring for a parent with a mental health problem

The presence of certain serious mental health conditions in adults has been linked to poor or even unsafe environments for children. Several serious case reviews (e.g., Torbay SCB, 2010; Summerfield, 2011) where children have been killed or seriously injured have identified unaddressed mental health issues as significant factors in the outcomes. Cleaver et al. (1999) found that parenting capacity is significantly affected by the 'toxic trio' of mental illness, substance abuse and domestic violence. The *Framework for the Assessment of Children in Need and their Families* (Department of Health, 2000) is a key tool for social workers which emphasizes the need for holistic assessments that assess parenting capacities, social networks and the wider environment alongside a child's developmental attainment. Untreated mental illness can lead to parents and carers neglecting or even harming their offspring because of their inability to prioritize children over their own mental health needs. Drug and alcohol abuse can lead to similar outcomes (e.g., Herefordshire SCB, 2009; Radford, 2010) if the level of abuse clouds judgement and responsibility to such an extent that children are neglected or abused. Research such as that of Mullender et al. (2002) and Cummings and Davies (2010) also tells us that children witnessing domestic violence as a regular part of their upbringing are likely to suffer in the long term in relation to their ability to form relationships and in respect of their own mental health problems.

A research briefing by Roberts et al. (2008), undertaken for the Social Care Institute of Excellence (SCIE), found that, of the estimated 175,000 young carers in the UK, over a third cared for an adult, often their mothers, with a serious mental health problem. It was noted that considerable stigma was attached to young carers, whose behaviour could be misinterpreted, particularly by school staff. This report urged practitioners to take a more holistic approach to family assessment and to strike a balanced course: 'issues of "safeguarding" pose undoubted challenges to practitioners, but the potential for the caring role to provide benefits to parent, family and child should not be ignored' (2008: 8). Recommendations were that professionals should recognize and celebrate the experiences and skills of young carers, whose roles often meant they were unnecessarily socially isolated.

Summary

In considering counselling and clinical psychology we have discovered much common ground between psychology and social work, based often on a shared humanistic view of the world (Harrison and Ruch, 2007). Equally, we have found differences, and social work has taken on a more politicized, cultural and environmental world view than has most psychology. Both disciplines can learn from each other, and a good starting point is to understand and be inquisitive about respective training, research, terminology and success rates. Having the basic knowledge to start such conversations can only be of benefit, both among professionals and to clients (often shared), who will have the reassurance that all those involved in their situation understand what is happening. The challenges of austerity face both professions, particularly social work, and it is likely that self-help programmes, CBT and cyber-type therapies will attract further government interest on account of their cost-effectiveness. Professionals must always keep sight of their client's particular needs and be able to advocate and lobby for a counselling or clinical intervention that may be lengthy and expensive. Such advocacy is all the more likely to achieve success if it is based on knowledge of specific interventions and their outcomes (Knott and Scragg, 2013). To end this chapter we return to the Brightwells and consider how clinical and counselling interventions might be able to alleviate some of their distress and unhappiness.

Case study

There would appear to be much scope within the Brightwell family for counselling and clinical interventions, but all we know is that Susan Brightwell has been prescribed antidepressants, presumably connected with her feelings towards the drudgery of her life as she cares for an ever dependent mother, a learning-disabled daughter who is being bullied at school, and an adult son who is abusive in ways that evoke memories of her ex-husband. What interventions might work in this family, presuming the respective members were willing to accept such input? Is Susan to stay on antidepressants for ever when so many of the issues she is dealing with seem to relate to her environment? Or are there other possible reasons for her depression? Might there be scope for a family-based intervention? Or will a succession of professionals – GPs, social workers, education welfare officers, the police, drug counsellors – dip in and out of this family's life for ever without there being a concerted attempt at tackling underlying problems? Is there a role perhaps for both individualized and family interventions? Would cost play a part in your thinking? Would you consider using cybertherapies? How much might this family cost the state if different approaches are not even tried? How 'bad' do a family's problems have to be before there is some kind of intervention? Discuss these dilemmas with colleagues, particularly those from different backgrounds and cultures, and try to come up with a holistic plan to improve the mental health of the Brightwell family.

Further reading and resources

(For full bibliographic details, see the References.)

On scientist-practitioner and the emotional intelligence practitioner model:

Blair, A critical review of the scientist-practitioner model for counselling psychology.
Corrie and Callahan, A review of the scientist-practitioner model: reflections on its potential contribution to counselling psychology within the context of current health care trends.
Howe, *The Emotionally Intelligent Social Worker*.
Morrison, Emotional intelligence, emotion and social work: context, characteristics, complications and contribution.

On reflective and relationship-based practice:

Ixer, There's no such thing as reflection.

Knott and Scragg, *Reflective Practice in Social Work.*

Ruch, Relationship-based practice and reflective practice: holistic approaches to contemporary child care social work.

Ruch, Reflective practice in contemporary child-care social work: the role of containment.

On safeguarding:

Brandon et al., *New Learning from Serious Case Reviews: A Two Year Report for 2009–2011.*

The National Society for the Prevention of Cruelty to Children (NSPCC) has set up an online repository for Local Safeguarding Children Boards to place their serious case review findings in the interest of achieving greater nationwide learning. If the NSPCC does not hold an electronic copy of a particular case review, it will direct to the specific LCSB site. Access is via the following hyperlink: www.nspcc.org.uk/preventing-abuse/child-protection-system/case-reviews/national-case-review-repository/.

On theories, models and effectiveness of interventions in mental health:

Baldwin, Interview with Carl Rogers on the use of the self in therapy.

Beck, Cognitive therapy: a 30-year retrospective.

Larsson et al., Counselling psychology and diagnostic categories: a critical literature review.

NHS Choices, Talking therapies explained – stress, anxiety and depression, www.nhs.uk/Conditions/stress-anxiety-depression/Pages/Types-of-therapy.aspx#mindfulness.

Richards et al., A comparison of two online cognitive-behavioural interventions for symptoms of depression in a student population: the role of therapist responsiveness.

On stigmatization and impact of mental health on families and children:

Care Quality Commission, *Right Here Right Now: People's Experiences of Help, Care and Support during a Mental Health Crisis.*

Crisp et al., Stigmatisation of people with mental illnesses.

NHS Choices, *The stand up kid* – campaign against mental health stigma, www.nhs.uk/Video/Pages/the-stand-up-kid.aspx [this short video is part of a wider NHS Choices website which gives a range of practical information about physical and mental health problems].

Roberts et al., SCIE research briefing 24: Experiences of children and young people caring for a parent with a mental health problem.

Mental health organizations:

The mental health charity MIND (www.mind.org.uk) offers a range of guidance and personal narratives from clients of UK mental health services.

The Helen Bamber Foundation, which works with 'survivors of human cruelty', has published a document entitled *Addressing Mental Health Needs in Survivors of Modern Slavery*, www.bond.org.uk/sites/default/files/resource-documents/addressing_mental_health_needs_in_survivors_of_modern_slavery.pdf.

4 Perspectives from Social and Community Psychology: Understanding Values, Attitudes, Diversity and Community Change

The following are the key relevant capabilities and standards in this chapter for social workers.

Professional Capabilities Framework (BASW, 2015)	Standards of Proficiency (HCPC, 2012)
3 Diversity – Understand how an individual's health is informed by factors such as culture, economic status, family composition, life experiences and characteristics, and take account of these to understand their experiences, questioning assumptions where necessary.	**2 Be able to practise within the legal and ethical boundaries of their profession**
4 Rights and Justice – Understand, identify and apply in practice the principles of social justice, inclusion and equality.	**5 Be aware of the impact of culture, equality and diversity on practice** 5.1 Be able to reflect on and take account of the impact of inequality, disadvantage and discrimination on those who use social work services and their communities
5 Knowledge 5.1 Demonstrate a critical understanding of the application to social work of research, theory and knowledge from sociology, social policy, psychology and health 5.4 Recognise the short and long term impact of psychological, socio-economic, environmental and physiological factors on people's lives, taking into account age and development, and how this informs practice	

Introduction

Among the academic branches of psychology, social psychology and community psychology are the most closely related to social work. The domains of the PCF and the HCPC Standards of Proficiency cited above both emphasize the centrality of diversity, anti-discriminatory practice and a commitment to social justice. This chapter will introduce social psychology as the 'scientific' (empirical) study of how people's thoughts, feelings and behaviours are influenced by the actual, imagined or implied presence of others (Allport, 1985). Social work remains a champion of anti-oppressive practice, and it can be more effective in its challenges to racism, ageism, sexism and disablism if a clear understanding is developed regarding the causes of discriminatory behaviour. Appropriate strategies of intervention at individual, family, group and community levels will be considered in the chapter, and the social psychology around institutional care and around new initiatives such as the adult personalization agenda will be illuminated.

Community psychology is a relatively recent branch of psychology that looks beyond social psychology's concerns with the relationships between individuals. The values at the heart of community psychology – inclusivity, social justice and improvement of health and well-being – are held in common with social work. This chapter will explore the contribution of community psychology to the understanding of communities, their contexts, relationships within them and people's attitudes about them. A critique will also be given from the perspective of more radical community psychologists who view traditional psychological interventions as forms of individualistic control that perpetuate the social and economic injustices of neo-liberal societies such as the UK.

Case study

The Brightwell family have been used in this book to explore the applicability and likely success of a range of psychologically based theories and interventions. This chapter provides the opportunity to consider the wider context around the family and introduces the socio-economic background of the Mossford housing estate on which they live. Community psychologists will have a role to play alongside social workers and other professionals in regenerating the estate, which has been granted funding to bring about a transformation in its socio-economic status. The chapter will culminate in an exercise whereby you are asked to decide on suitable priorities and interventions.

Mossford, where the Brightwell family live, is a large ex-council estate in the English Midlands which now consists of 50 per cent owner-occupiers with the remaining 50 per cent of the housing stock having been transferred out of council ownership to Roofways Housing Association; the part of Mossford where the Brightwells live is owned mainly by the housing association. There is a problem with crime, and there is a large population of young single parents and little recreational or local work opportunities. The local primary and secondary school are in special measures, while the GP surgery has relocated away from the estate after a series of break-ins. The relevant adult and children's social care teams work from a large office on an industrial estate some 5 miles away.

There is a high incidence of domestic violence in Mossford, and health and social care agencies have noticed that the victims of this violence are becoming younger, often in their teens. Many of the young people see such violence as the norm. Tensions have risen recently through several refugee families from Syria having been resettled on the estate. UKIP locally has spoken out against this resettlement, saying that local houses should go to local people in need. 85 per cent of the population of Mossford is white British and approximately 10 per cent is Pakistani in origin. Several Syrian families have had windows broken at their homes, and teenagers have had running battles in the streets, necessitating a stepping up of police patrols.

Understanding values, attitudes, prejudice and stereotypes

Values

The core of social psychology theory and its application is that people's attitudes and behaviour are greatly influenced by their situation, whether at home, among friends or at work. Social psychology-based interventions make use of situational knowledge to try to bring about improvements in people's functioning, while acknowledging the role played by individual differences and that not all people in a certain social situation are similarly affected.

Social psychology rose to prominence in the 1960s, a time of much social change and unrest, particularly in the USA, where civil rights movements, race riots and the Vietnam War led to a wide-scale questioning of societal values (Ross et al., 2010). These changing times called for psychology to take on a more socially relevant role rather than confine the majority of its enterprise to laboratory-based environments. Myers, Spencer and Jordon (2009) define social psychology as the science concerned with understanding how people think about, feel about, relate to and influence one another.

Such understanding is critical for effective social work, and criticism has been made in child death reviews in particular about the ways in which social workers and other professionals did not create effective working relationships with families to enable them to challenge behaviours and lifestyles that were harmful to children. Among the values prominent to community psychology are those of commitment to prevention, social change, building on existing community strengths, citizen participation, promoting social justice via the equitable distribution of resources and opportunities, and advocating for the rights of the least privileged members of the community (Sanborne, 2002).

Social psychology is vitally interested in inter-group attitudes and shares social work's commitment to anti-oppressive practice, although social psychologists are less present in the field than social workers. Both disciplines have an interest in attitude formation, and social work in particular has always been a champion of equal opportunities. As outlined in the Health and Care Professions Council's Standards of Proficiency (HCPC, 2012), practitioners need to acknowledge what gives rise to oppression and discrimination in order to fulfil their duty to challenge and address their impact. The PCF

(BASW, 2015) reflects commitment to anti-discriminatory practice, and BASW's Code of Ethics (BASW, 2012) champions social justice as a key social work value.

The International Federation of Social Workers (2014) provides a global definition of the social work profession as:

> a practice-based profession and an academic discipline that promotes social change and development, social cohesion, and the empowerment and liberation of people. Principles of social justice, human rights, collective responsibility and respect for diversities are central to social work. Underpinned by theories of social work, social sciences, humanities and indigenous knowledge, social work engages people and structures to address life challenges and enhance wellbeing.

BASW reflects this global definition and states its explicit commitment to the promotion of social justice in relation to society generally and in relation to the people with whom social workers engage. The principles of social justice are articulated as follows:

- *Challenging discrimination* Social workers have a responsibility to challenge discrimination on the basis of characteristics such as ability, age, culture, gender or sex, marital status, socio-economic status, political opinions, skin colour, racial or other physical characteristics, sexual orientation or spiritual beliefs.
- *Recognising diversity* Social workers should recognise and respect the diversity of the societies in which they practise, taking into account individual, family, group and community differences.
- *Distributing resources* Social workers should ensure that resources at their disposal are distributed fairly, according to need.
- *Challenging unjust policies and practices* Social workers have a duty to bring to the attention of their employers, policy makers, politicians and the general public situations where resources are inadequate or where distribution of resources, policies and practice are oppressive, unfair, harmful or illegal.
- *Working in solidarity* Social workers, individually, collectively and with others have a duty to challenge social conditions that contribute to social exclusion, stigmatisation or subjugation, and work towards an inclusive society. (BASW, 2012: 9)

Attitudes and stereotypes

This subsection will use a series of case studies to explore social psychology perspectives on processes of attitude, prejudice and stereotyping that often lead to discriminatory behaviour. Attitudes are states of mind that affect behaviour, and their formation is a complex mix of emotions, intellectual understanding and experience (Ajzen, 1988). Prejudice can be seen as a pattern of learned attitudes and behaviours, some forms of prejudice being acquired through actual contact with groups and other forms coming about because of portrayals or stereotyping of groups by others or in the media.

Attitudes

An attitude in social psychology is defined as a positive or negative evaluation of an object person, thing, event or issue (Schuman, 1995). Examples of issues that trigger strong attitudes in social work are the ethical ones such as the rights of refugees, gay adoption, discrimination against young black men, and the privatization of care for vulnerable adults and children. Attitude formation occurs through different processes. One of these is repeat exposure to certain objects, events or individuals, which tends to facilitate a more positive outlook and opinion towards them, even in the absence of any action or interaction. Another is learning by association, when a neutral stimulus is paired with a stimulus that naturally evokes a particular attitude. Association is particularly influential in attitude formation when limited knowledge is available about the object in question; in the case of different ethnic groups, for example, association can contaminate attitude formation. Individuals can also attribute their own behaviour as being caused by certain attitudes.

However, the relationship between attitudes and behaviour is less clear, and research has shown that attitudes predict behaviour only when certain conditions are satisfied, such as when the attitude is *specific* to a particular behaviour, in which case it has a greater influence on the behaviour. It is the case that private attitudes predict private behaviours and public attitudes predict public behaviours. Furthermore, the strength of an attitude is determined by the amount of information about the object and the personal involvement and direct experience with it. The stronger the attitude, the stronger the association with behaviour.

Social workers are often seeking to bring about attitudinal change in the families, individuals and communities in which they work. In a case of adult or child neglect, it would be critical to any care plan that the people involved can explain why they acted a certain way and how they might act in future. Cognitive dissonance theory (Festinger, 1957) describes the feeling of discomfort caused by performing an action that is inconsistent with or against one's attitudes. Such discrepancy can cause the attitude to change through a motivational rather than a cognitive approach.

Persuasion is attitude change via an external message – for example, from the media or from expert opinion. The likelihood of changing an attitude through persuasion depends largely on the credibility of the source – i.e., a source is perceived as credible if it is seen to be knowledgeable or trustworthy. However, persuasion has been observed even in the case of non-credible sources, where a message has an impact but its effect is delayed – a phenomenon called 'the sleeper effect'.

Stereotyping

Adorno et al. (1950) believed that personality types, particularly 'authoritarian personalities', are closely associated with prejudice; having been brought up to view the world in a hierarchical way, they defer to people of higher status and discriminate against individuals or groups deemed to be of lower status. Stereotyping occurs when people attribute certain characteristics that they perceive in some people to be representative of all people in that category. Many stereotypes are negative – 'All Romanians are beggars' or 'All young black men are criminals' – whereas others can be positive – 'All nurses are caring' or 'Church-going parents do not harm their children'. Stereotypes can be theorized as helping individuals make sense and giving order and categorization to an ever more complex society. The danger for social workers is that stereotypes prevent critical analysis of specific individuals and circumstances. For example, the inquiry into the Mid Staffordshire Hospital NHS Foundation Trust (Francis, 2013) found that some nurses were certainly not caring, and some religious beliefs would appear to condone practices that can harm and even lead to the deaths of children. The inquiry into the death of Victoria Climbié (Laming, 2003) revealed that her carers believed in spirit possession, and a recent case involving the beliefs of members of the Apostolic Church of God led to the neglect and subsequent death of a baby girl, Rebecca Kandare (BBC News, 2015b).

Social workers will come up against stereotypes regarding their own career – 'You are all sandal-wearing lefties' or 'You're the child snatchers'. Such attitudes do add to the stress of social workers, aggressive use of stereotyping sometimes being used by clients and their families to divert attention from the issues that have brought the social worker to their door. Prejudice and discrimination also cause problems for many of the clients with whom social workers are involved. The majority of clients are from lower socio-economic strata and are often looked down on by others and variously stereotyped in the media as scroungers or ethnic minorities choosing to live off the state. Children can be particularly discriminatory, partly because they lack fully developed cognitive and reflective maturity and partly because of peer pressure. In an ever more materialistic world, the occurrence of serious bullying, often involving social media, can take place if a child does not have the latest trainers or if their body image does not fit with the type promoted by the media.

Social workers can also fall into the trap of not seeing beyond a stereotype. Recent cases of abuse and even the death of children have come about when social workers appeared not to challenge the authority of professional middle-class families (e.g., Cheshire East LSCB, 2011). Social workers read newspapers, watch television and internet videos, and overhear conversations that promote values and moral panics that are alien to their values. Like any other people, they have their own prejudices, but they also need to be reflective and self-critical in their approach to clients, colleagues and friends if they are to accord with the values of the profession (e.g., BASW, 2012). For example, the issue of immigration has recently been particularly contested in the UK, a nation with a proud history of granting asylum over the centuries. Fuelled by right-wing fears about the country being over-run by migrants under the EU's freedom of movement rules, there has been a rise in discrimination against Eastern Europeans, led by the tabloid press and TV. The documentary series *The Romanians are Coming* (Channel 4, 2015) portrayed a very negative image of Romanians, including generalizing about cases of alcoholism and child abuse and neglect in ways that will undoubtedly have a negative effect.

How to combat discrimination is a core challenge for social workers and society as a whole. Social psychologists have challenged the view that contact with individuals and groups from discriminated populations alone cannot change views. Finding common ground, as presented by the opportunities in the Mossford case study at the end of this chapter, would provide a fertile environment in which misunderstandings and prejudice might be lessened. However, many sections of society are never exposed to this type of opportunity because, even in a multicultural society, people tend to live and socialize among the same ethnic and socio-economic groups, where the only messages and images about people who are different are those portrayed in the media. The following case studies provide the opportunity to reflect on issues of attitude, prejudice, discrimination and diversity.

Case studies: attitudes and stereotyping

Case study 1

James, a man in his forties, has moderate learning disabilities, lives in a housing association flat, and enjoys a considerable level of welfare benefits. Local youths have started using his flat for parties and have often 'invited' themselves to stay over. Money often goes missing from the flat, and the police have become involved following concerns about drug dealing from the premises.

Discussion

An awareness of the social psychology at play within such a scenario might lead a social worker to consider society's attitude towards people with learning disabilities, who are often excluded from mainstream society and who, as a community, might be all too likely to view any offers of friendship as welcome and valued opportunities. From an individualistic perspective, the degree to which James is vulnerable is clearly important, but too narrow a focus would fail to take in the other important factors having a bearing in this case. James might be counselled and helped to develop more one-to-one friendships or, alternatively, a youth worker or other professional with an understanding of group and social dynamics might work with these youths to try to ameliorate any negative behaviours and perhaps channel their interests elsewhere. A particular strength of social work is its ability to link professionals and community members together to help form a shared view of a problem, taking a strengths-based overview of a situation (Saleebey, 1996).

The *Care and Support Statutory Guidance* (Department of Health, 2014) provides case examples of scenarios such as the one above, many of the suggestions being put forward to better safeguard individuals being based on an understanding of the social psychologies surrounding an individual. For example, the case of Miss P, also taken from the guidance, describes risks present from sexual exploitation and involved the social worker contacting Miss P's family and working with other professionals, all of whom had different perspectives on the social dynamics around the client and explanations for why she had become prey to exploitation: 'Miss P's family were crucial to the success of the plan as they had always supported her and were able to advocate for her needs. They also had a trusting relationship with her and were able to notify the police and other professionals if they thought that the risk to Miss P was increasing' (ibid.: 14.55).

The social worker in the case of Miss P carried out a co-ordinative role and also initiated individualistic interventions to complement the social/community interventions, such as liaising with a domestic violence worker on safe behaviours and a personal support worker to help her build resilience. Common ground, based on social psychology insights, was found in the cases of James and Miss P and used as a platform from which to plan effective interventions.

Case study 2

Returning to the Brightwell family, Susan Brightwell's mother, Mary, aged seventy-seven, has recently been admitted to hospital after having been found wandering in the street at night. Susan has approached you as the hospital social worker to ask if you will assess Mary for residential care. She advises you that she is rather stubborn and may need 'persuading' to leave her home.

Discussion

The social psychologies within families are deep-seated and complex. Susan devotes a lot of her time to caring for Mary and may well believe she is asking for appropriate and necessary help. However, an inquisitive social worker would want to explore the nature of relationship between mother and daughter as well as those among other family members. Susan may have an ageist view that everyone with dementia in their late seventies should be in residential care, whereas her mother may well be young at heart and determined to stay in her own home for as long as possible. Techniques such as interviewing the daughter and mother alone as well as together are likely to lead to the most empathic outcomes, and, if a trusting relationship can be built all round, any outcome is likely to be more satisfactory to all parties. Such an inclusive approach would take into account Susan's psychological needs and her other caring responsibilities.

Case study 3

A young family with two pre-school-age children have recently moved into Mossford. The mother, aged nineteen, has twice presented at her GP for the children's health appointments and staff have noticed her facial bruising. On one occasion she said she had fallen over on a night out with her sister, and on the last occasion said she had walked into an open bedroom door when going to one of her children in the night. The GP felt that the mother was very withdrawn and has asked you, the GP-attached social worker, to visit the mother at home and explore whether there might be problems involving domestic violence.

Discussion

How could a knowledge of social psychology help your understanding of this scenario, and what approaches to the issues presented might be most effective? Your first point of contact will be critical in forming an effective working relationship with this young mother. You will need to be aware of the nature of abusive relationships, particularly the denials and collusions involved. If you explore the mother's position from a social psychological stance that takes into consideration the nature and pattern of her supportive relationships, as well as her internal coping mechanisms, you will establish a sound intelligence base on which to establish any intervention.

In the above three scenarios, it might be argued that an approach that dealt simply with the individuals' feelings and perceptions and failed to consider wider relationships would have constituted only a partial picture of their lives. As will be demonstrated below, a community psychology approach would have looked at such situations using a wider lens, exploring the parts played by disability, ageism and sexism respectively.

Stigma, diversity and community change

While community psychology has been a field of knowledge neglected in social work education and practice, there has recently been a renewed interest in community-based approaches. Such renewed interest, as espoused in the neo-liberal policy 'The Big Society' (Cameron, 2009), has led to most local authorities investing in community-based approaches to well-being alongside traditional, statutory-based approaches to the problems of social work. A grasp of the complex psychology of diversity within communities will help social workers understand the perspectives taken by others and hopefully lead to better practice in the pooling of ideas and resources, all communities having their hidden strengths that just need to be tapped. A critical community psychology approach to such understanding would include the political view that many of the problems faced by communities such as Mossford were actually the direct result of government policy. Walker (2009) critiqued the UK government's drive to increase the take-up of psychological therapies such as CBT, stating that the need of so many individuals for such therapies was directly attributable to the government having cut public expenditure, deregulated markets and abandoned policies of full employment.

Reflective point

Is it ethical for social workers and psychologists to be trying to solve individual problems by various therapeutic methods when the whole background against which some individuals, families and communities live their lives is oppressive?

Diversity, prejudice and stigmatization

As stated previously, community psychology focuses on relationships between individuals. Its values are those of inclusivity, social justice and improvement of health and well-being, and its aims are to effect positive change in society. It recognizes that many problems which individuals face originate from disadvantage or adverse circumstances and not (only) as a result of their individual features or deficits (Rappaport, 1987). Thus, apart from enhancing an individual's ability to cope with adversity, effective interventions must include change at community and societal levels. This represents a shift from traditional perspectives in psychology, where the majority of interventions are aimed at treating the individual in ways that facilitate a better fit with social norms.

For example, individuals with serious mental health issues tend to encounter difficulties in their lives not only because of their behaviour, perceptions and thoughts but also because society discriminates against them. The origins of community psychology can be traced back to the 1960s movement of deinstutionalization, when it became apparent that the restrictive and dehumanizing environments of large psychiatric hospitals were major contributing factors to the poor outcomes of mental health patients. Moreover, the labelling of persons as 'mental patients' had negative and stigmatizing effects.

A seminal work that came to influence community psychology was that of Goffman (1961), whose participant observation from his position as janitor in an American mental hospital uncovered the divided world of 'institutionalization', wherein staff and patients inhabited quite distinct spheres. The hospital was seen to be run by the staff for the staff, with the patients' health and well-being having become incidental. More recent evidence from England that has significantly influenced political, public and professional awareness has come from the scandals at Mid Staffordshire General Hospital (Francis, 2013) and Winterbourne View, a private mental health hospital (Department of Health, 2012b). The neglect and substandard care that led to the deaths of 1,200 people at the Mid Staffordshire hospital has been attributed to a dysfunctional management-dominated culture fixated on achieving the necessary financial savings that would enable the hospital to achieve the greater autonomies and financial freedoms associated with the attainment of foundation status. Staff at all levels colluded with this culture and rationalized the neglect of patients as necessary in order to achieve the overall business aim of the organization. It was accepted throughout the hospital that staffing levels were inadequate because that was the means necessary to bring down costs. Some staff tried to 'blow the whistle' but were ineffective in the face of organizational systems, and it took a group of patients' families, rather than professional concern, finally to expose the Mid Staffordshire scandal. The following public inquiry (Francis, 2013) took the view that better recruitment of staff and a concentration on their values would be one way of helping ensure that this situation never reoccurred. There are problems with such a simplistic approach, however, as values are very deep and complex and not measurable in the tangible ways demanded by performance management regimes.

Reader, Gillespie and Mannell (2014) took a community psychological perspective on the Mid Staffordshire situation and looked beyond individual failures, considering these in the wider context of relationships, empowerment, organizational behaviour and the values attributed to some groups in society, such as old people. They noted that patients and health care organizations tend to view good care or neglect differentially – organizations looking to the evidence base of performance management systems and patients seeking reassurances in the form of relationships, consistency of care and kindness. A community psychology approach focuses on the part played in any situation by these and other contextual factors, such as how the various hierarchies within organizations communicate and trust each other – this broader perspective perhaps being helpful in moving away from an individual blame culture and seeking to right systemic wrongs.

The traditional response to poor practice since the introduction of business models into health and social care services in the 1990s has been to establish further performance measures and tighter inspectorial and audit regimes. For example, the Care Quality Commission has 158 individual standards and over 700 measurable substandards that relate to quality of care, and it is questionable whether the time devoted to such types of performance management is really helping patient care. Community psychologists would recognize that awareness-raising and training might play a part in raising standards but also that such initiatives will never bring about significant change if the wider caring environment (staffing levels, resources, communication systems) is not appropriate to the organization's mission. The more critical community psychologist might even suggest that less training, fewer targets and less control are the requirements to bring about cultural change in hospital settings. Such a radical approach would free up staff time to invest in patient and staff relationships.

The abuse at Winterbourne View was of a different complexion to that at Mid Staffordshire and was, again, exposed primarily by patients and carers rather than professionals. Many professionals and members of the public believed that large institutional hospitals for the care of people with learning disabilities had disappeared from the 1970s onwards as part of the move to care in smaller, community settings. The Winterbourne View case revealed that many large-scale institutions had in fact been redesignated as private hospitals whose beds were purchased by NHS commissioners. Minimal regulation of the private sector under successive neo-liberal governments has allowed operators such as Castlebeck Care Ltd to operate without sanctions, despite non-compliance with law and contracts; Winterbourne View did not even have a registered manager for a considerable period of time. Driven primarily by profit, the management of Castlebeck Care Ltd kept costs to a minimum, employing unqualified carers for the majority of their staff. Despite the requirements of the contract, virtually no training was given to these workers, a number of whom were able to perpetuate a culture of emotional, physical and sexual abuse without challenge. New members of staff largely fell in line with this culture of abuse or left their employment. Quite clearly, the behaviour of certain individuals (since sentenced to prison terms) is the domain of clinical psychologists, but the wider causes of the abuse – the commissioning system, the lack of effective regulation and the nature of communication between grass-roots staff and the management – are areas for the community psychologist. The recommendations of the inquiry report (Department of Health, 2012b) concentrate on reviews, audits and other systems rather than taking a community psychology perspective on the roots of the underlying forms of disablism and oppression that led to people with learning disabilities being treated in ways that were wholly unacceptable. The scandal at Winterbourne View occurred approximately fifty years after Goffman (1961) published his work on asylums, yet the similarities in the behaviour and attitude of staff towards vulnerable people remain.

As noted by Coimbra et al. (2012) 'community' has many meanings, relating to geographic communities or communities of interest, and is often presented as an uncritical term associated with belonging and acceptance. Communities can, however, also be hostile and dangerous, particularly to people perceived as different. Bauman (2000) describes modern-day communities as being liquid in nature on account of the contemporary pace of technological and social change, a pace which many social work clients find hard to cope with, especially if they are without social or financial capital. New phenomena emerge all the time in the communities in which social workers operate, sometimes as a result of social change (e.g., new immigrant populations) and sometimes because of technological advances (such as those in social media). A recent example that has attracted particular widespread attention is that of gang or group sexual exploitation in English towns and cities, in which young white girls were groomed, predominantly by Asian men, using gifts, false affection and then coercion. A widespread media and professional debate followed the publication of the Jay Report (Jay, 2014), with Asian males being demonized as exploiting vulnerable white girls. While it would indeed appear that this particular phenomenon was perpetrated by groups of Asian men, this should not be used to detract from the fact that, in the UK, sexual exploitation occurs predominantly between white men and white girls. A number of inquiries (e.g., Laming, 2003; Jay, 2014) have shown that social workers and other professionals have been unsure about how to challenge practices in different cultures, and this demonstrates the need for education to facilitate effective practice across society.

Other forms of discrimination emerged as a result of a number of investigations into the English child sexual exploitation phenomenon, both social workers and the police being criticized for having taken judgemental and derogatory stances towards the girls involved rather than seeing them as vulnerable children (Jay, 2014). Community psychologists and social workers have not made any reported progress in gaining access to the communities where these scandals occurred, and little is known about the motivations of the men who systematically abused the girls. Financial gain did not seem to be the driver for their actions, although money did sometimes change hands as girls were passed from associate to associate.

Reflective point

How might you explain the gang/group behaviour of Asian men in the sexual exploitation of white girls in England?

Discussion
Consider the following potential perspectives.

- Might this abuse be some kind of statement about how vulnerable white girls are valued? Might the sexual availability of white girls be something that Asian men could not access in their own communities?
- Were these crimes committed because of opportunism, in that Asian men ran the taxi companies and fast-food shops around which young people gathered at night, or does a similar kind of abuse exist within Asian communities but is not reported?

There are certainly more questions than answers in this contentious area, and research is ongoing among those Asian men imprisoned for their crimes with a view to providing some answers.

Changing communities: digital communities

Social work is carried out in a fast-changing world of technological advance and social policy initiatives that change the nature of communities. The internet and new communication technologies facilitate the creation of 'new' types of digital communities in ways that were not possible ten years ago, and such communities offer both acceptance and threats to vulnerable people, which will be explored below. The development of online communities also offers new ground for social and community psychology and presents real-life challenges to social workers. Cyber-bullying among children and young people has become an increasing concern for social work, and social media have presented a new environment for sexual exploitation (Jay, 2014). The tracking and threatening of girls by mobile phone and social media was a key feature of the sexual exploitation cases referred to above, and both social workers and carers need to be knowledgeable in the ways in which social media can be used in a damaging manner.

The online community can also bring positive forms of support and help families and friends to keep in contact. The internet can be used to promote caring and support for vulnerable groups, and the It Gets Better Project (www.itgetsbetter.org), set up in 2010 to provide a forum for young lesbian, gay, bisexual and transgender (LGBT) people to share their stories and to provide hope and inspiration, is a good example of a group having positive effects. The site has grown to contain some 50,000 user-created video clips over its five-year lifespan, and it is believed to have had a significant effect in reducing the number of suicides among young LBGT people.

Changing communities: personalization policies

An example of social policy bringing a change to communities is the introduction of personalization into social work with adults. Under this policy, eligible adults who have complex needs are given a budget with which they can design their own care package, including employing their own care staff (Dickinson and Glasby, 2010). The personalization agenda has developed from the humanistic psychology of Carl Rogers (Rogers et al., 1967), which is based on a belief in the individual's ability to make their own life choices given the right conditions. Personalized care packages, utilizing facilities within the wider community rather than relying on state-provided day centres, can be seen in many ways to epitomize social work values of empowerment, but they have also changed disabled communities in ways that some commentators (e.g., Heng, 2015) see as detrimental to the fellowship needs of their members. However, traditional services and day centres were also often seen as labelling and stigmatic, unattractive to the younger generation and serving to further segregate disabled people. The personalization policy is more lightly regulated than traditional care services and, while providing opportunities to disabled people, it brings risk to some vulnerable adults who could be exploited by family and carers. A further challenge to the success of personalization is the extent to which the wider community is ready to accept disabled people; prejudices and even hate crime are still features of contemporary society.

Focus: collaborative research and action

Community psychology is committed to the integration of research and action in aiming to resolve societal problems such as those of hate crime and improving the lives of everyone. Such integration involves collaboration with members of communities as partners and co-producers of research and solutions.

The idea of action research or participatory action research has emerged from community psychology. As both designers and stakeholders, action researchers work together and with others to propose a new course of action to help improve work practices and advocate social change. It is important to note that, unlike traditional positivist research, which aims to be objective, action research acknowledges that it is influenced and shaped by the values of the community in which it takes place. The case study of Mossford (see end of chapter) provides the opportunity for individuals to become involved in owning and helping to solve problems themselves rather than having solutions imposed. A traditional hierarchy exists regarding who has the knowledge to be deemed expert in analysing societal problems, and the establishment has been slow to recognize the value of local input into effecting community change. Glasby and Beresford (2006: 278) ask what is more important – 'an academic commitment to a particular way of knowing and researching the world, or the alleged abuse, extreme boredom and poor quality care that some service users say they experience in mental health hospitals'. They go on to discuss the power inequalities regarding who sets research agendas and make a convincing case that the lived experience of clients and carers can be just as valid a form of knowledge as formal academic research.

Understanding groups in social work training and practice

Groups are a central concern of social psychologists (Tajfel, 1982), and group working is central to social work. Knowledge of groups and their productivity can also help social workers better understand some of the dynamics at work, since much of their time is spent in groups. It can be difficult for newly qualified staff in particular to adapt to such situations. Some people are naturally rather inhibited in groups and others perform better. Allport (1985) observed the tendency for people to perform better when in front of an audience and suggested that some individuals need such social facilitation to perform at their best. This may hold true particularly when performing simple tasks with well-learned responses, though the presence of an audience may lead to social inhibition having detrimental effects on performance when the task is more complex. All groups are different, and personification of 'the group' as a being in its own right is a common theme throughout the literature (e.g., Westergaard, 2009).

The theory of group dynamics falls largely into two distinct areas – the developmental theories around group performance (Tuckman, 1965; Tuckman and Jensen, 1977) and the theories around the importance of the individual impact on groups (Belbin, 2010; Slavin, 1997). Tuckman (1965) theorized that there were five stages of group development – Forming, Storming, Norming, Performing and Adjourning. The Forming stage is when individuals take up a position; Storming is when ideas and opinions pour forth; Norming is when a group decides upon its role and function; Performing is when a group carries out its purpose; and Adjourning (sometimes followed by Reforming) is when the group is able to disband as its original purpose has been achieved.

Belbin (2010) produced a seminal body of work on roles within groups, and his categorization of preferred group roles is applicable across a range of professions. Essentially, effective teams need a balance of different skills if they are to be creative and effective – too many or too few of the different roles in a group will render it dysfunctional. Most people prefer two or three roles and can adapt to some others, though there will be some roles that they do not wish to adopt in any situation. Belbin's core roles are as follows.

1 *Plant* A creative and imaginative person who brings new ideas and concepts to the group
2 *Resource investigator* A networker outside of the group who finds the contacts necessary to make things happen
3 *Co-ordinator* Someone who clarifies the aims and objectives of the group and ensures all parties are working for the same ends
4 *Shaper* A person who works on the Plant's ideas and 'shapes' them up, challenging and seeking consensus as appropriate
5 *Monitor evaluator* An individual who stands back from the group and measures its progress
6 *Teamworker* Any teamworker is concerned with the human factors that keep the team cohesive
7 *Implementer* A practical person who ensures that systems and processes are all in order
8 *Completer finisher* Someone who is concerned with the details and accuracy of the group's function
9 *Specialist* In an increasingly specialized world, groups usually need an expert in the field to keep them abreast of current issues.

Reflective points

- Can you relate at all to Allport's observations above regarding the differences in group performance and the complexity of task?
- Do you perform better or worse in groups?
- Thinking of a group to which you belong, can you conceptualize any of Tuckman's stages and do such insights help you better understand and perform within that group?
- Do you observe colleagues playing any of Belbin's group roles? Can you think of any successful or unsuccessful groups in which you have been involved and whether the mix of roles might had an in   he outcomes?
- Can you identify the key group role(s) which you adopt an   ou avoid?
- Are there any ways in which you want to become compete   nt roles and how might you achieve such change?

Group working

Discussion

What really happens when we are working as a team? Does the presence of others make us work harder? Research suggests that, in fact, this is not the case; in teamwork, people appear to put in less effort – known as social loafing (Williams and Karau, 1995). This occurs as a result of a diffusion of responsibility – people in a group can feel individually less personally responsible for the task and thus their contribution is (literally) 'lost in the crowd'. In high performing groups, a person might take a lesser role, knowing that the group will still function. Equally, in a dysfunctional group a person may keep a low profile as they do not wish to be associated with its poor performance. Chapter 6 considers some of these team-working dilemmas further in relation to the ways in which social work organizations operate, including the unique challenges of multi-disciplinary working.

Preparation for group work

There is a case to be made for social work students to be better prepared for the complexities of group work with colleagues and clients. Group work as both a therapeutic and task-oriented method of intervention has undergone a revival in recent times across a range of human services (Schiola, 2010; Westergaard, 2009), while the need for social workers to be part of effective multi-disciplinary groups is emphasized in numerous inquiries and serious case reviews (Brandon et al., 2012). Knight et al. (2010) emphasize the importance of reflection, both to achieve greater self-awareness and to be able to judge the impact on others within the group. Binks et al. (2013) develop these points further and suggest that, before students become involved in group work with clients, they should first have experienced being part of a forum that discusses their own selves, in order to develop empathy and insight when they are later acting as facilitators.

Payne (2014) identifies three main approaches within group work, including that which takes place in community environments:

- *remedial* – where the group is designed to bring about change in an individual situation, for example with problems of substance abuse or the neglect of an older person
- *reciprocal* – where the emphasis is on self-help and mutual support involving shared experience with peers – e.g., fellow foster carers or children who have been bereaved; the intention is that the group members will support one another with the help of a facilitator
- *social goals or action* – where there is an identified need for change in a community and where group members have a specific goal in mind – e.g., the regeneration of a housing estate.

Social workers may become involved in any of the above types of group, where success is perhaps best guaranteed by adopting the three core conditions of Rogers et al. (1967) – empathy, acceptance and realness. Knowing who we are and the ways in which others experience us is key to success in both group and community settings.

Summary

This chapter has discussed the synergies among social work, social psychology and community psychology and has found a lot of common ground. Traditional forms of psychology have been criticized for not having an explicit value base and of not being concerned with the realities of social environments and communities. The importance of the social and wider environment is seen as critical to social and community psychologists, particularly as community psychology is overtly political about its commitment to social change.

The complexities of group working, particularly in the social work environment, where prejudice and discrimination are often encountered, have been explored and the potential benefits of group and identity theorists discussed. Knowledge of such theories is presented as helpful to social workers in making sense of the professional and client-based settings in which they operate.

Recent phenomena such as the scandals over child sexual exploitation and within institutional care across England have been used to illuminate the dynamic nature of groups and communities in which social workers are charged with bringing about both effective protection of the vulnerable and social and community change. The pressure on meeting managerial deadlines and casework targets can lead to social and community forms of intervention being relegated to the sidelines.

This chapter has demonstrated the importance of social and group approaches, all of which can be seen to be of relevance to the fictional community of Mossford. The case study below provides scope for reflection on all aspects of the chapter and also on how to balance the needs of vulnerable individuals with the long-term needs of the wider community.

Case study

Recent community development funding of £4 million has been earmarked for Roofways to regenerate the Mossford estate, with a particular focus on raising the aspirations of young people (see pp. 72–3 for more detail on the Mossford community).

Task
- What do you see as the potential for social work within this funding? How might the local social work team work with Rooftops, especially using knowledge of community psychology?
- Might social work skills be used to bring together the different interest groups on the estate or to mediate differences?
- Might there be an opportunity to suggest ways of working that kept individuals and their families off the caseloads of both children's and adults' services?
- How might improving the services in Mossford help the life chances of the Brightwell family, especially with regard to Shana and Brandon?
- How might success be measured of any community social work initiatives that are taken up?

Discussion
Social workers and their managers clearly have a key opportunity to play a most useful part in transforming Mossford if they are able to form effective relationships with colleagues in housing, education, police, health and other community organizations. Social work skills are strong in the area of bringing disparate parties together and, using their base of non-discriminatory practice, may be well placed to approach different interest groups and try to find common ground.

Individuals and whole families, such as the Brightwells, will always need some specifically tailored interventions, but if universal services in Mossford can be developed by improving the overall community capacity, preventative and outreach services from youth groups, church groups and others may well have the effect of reducing statutory caseloads. If trust is built up between organizations, this is likely to lead to better sharing of information and a better allocation of resources.

If a more caring community can be created with the various authorities sharing commitment to an action plan, then families and individuals in Mossford should have to deal with less bureaucracy and should be provided with greater opportunity overall. Involving residents, young and old, established and new, in the development of any action plan with the regeneration funding is essential, and statutory authorities should be seeking to develop all potential capacity within the community.

As regards the specific situations of the two younger Brightwells, it might be that Shana could take advantage of assertiveness groups or exercise/sports groups in the neighbourhood to help with any problems of weight and bullying. Brandon, who appears to be doing well, may be able to develop his potential and take a different path to that of his older brother

Wayne if a range of new accessible and affordable opportunities around learning and development for young people appeared on his doorstep.

Community social work and community psychology are closely aligned and could both contribute knowledge and insight into the Mossford project. The pattern of social work in recent decades has been to grow caseloads year by year, and community approaches have fallen from favour, particularly as their effects might take years to materialize, whereas the current world of performance management demands quick and tangible results. The challenge for community psychologists, social workers and residents is to find ways of measuring the success of a large-scale project such as the Mossford estate in ways that reflect the community's priorities yet also make out a case for best use of public money. Working together is far more likely to produce such meaningful measurement than working in separate areas and also offers a rare opportunity for people with different backgrounds and prejudices to come together towards a common good.

Further reading and resources

(For full bibliographic details, see the References.)

Values in social work:

Banks, Integrity in professional life: issues of conduct, commitment and capacity.

Bisman, Social work values: the moral core of the profession.

Gray, Moral sources and emergent ethical theories in social work.

Gray and Gibbons, There are no answers, only choices: teaching ethical decision making in social work.

Hugman, Professional values and ethics in social work: reconsidering post-modernism?

Breaking the Prejudice Habit (http://breakingprejudice.org/teaching/group-activities/) is a resource consisting of a series of classroom exercises covering a range of issues, among them gender stereotyping, physical appearance prejudice, cognitive dissonance, and the role of social media on stereotyping and prejudice.

Values Exchange (www.values-exchange.com) is a web-based tool for social debate which enables in-depth discussion and debate about a range of ethical issues, including those that concern social work and psychology.

Understanding groups:

Belbin, *Team Roles at Work.*

Tuckman, Developmental sequence in small groups.

Diversity, prejudice and stigmatization:

Corrigan, How stigma interferes with mental health care.

Corrigan and Penn, Lessons from social psychology on discrediting psychiatric stigma.

Department of Health, *Transforming Care: A National Response to Winterbourne View Hospital.*

Francis, *Independent Inquiry into Care provided by Mid Staffordshire NHS Foundation Trust, January 2005 – March 2009*, Vol. 1.

It Gets Better Project, www.itgetsbetter.org/.

NHS Choices, *The stand up kid* – campaign against mental health stigma, www.nhs.uk/Video/Pages/the-stand-up-kid.aspx [this short video aims to stamp out the stigma faced by young people affected by mental health problems].

Collaborative research and action:

Fenge, Striving towards inclusive research: an example of participatory action research with older lesbians and gay men.

Glasby and Beresford, Who knows best? Evidence-based practice and the service user contribution.

Healy, Participatory action research and social work: a critical appraisal.

Moffatt et al., Community practice researchers as reflective learners.

Stephens, Beyond the barricades: social movements as participatory practice in health promotion.

Psychologists against Austerity – https://psychagainstausterity.wordpress.com/psychological-impact-of-austerity-briefing-paper/ – gives details of a recent organization set up by psychologists who have combined forces with BASW in marches against austerity. This is believed to be the first time the two professions have come together with a shared political agenda and augurs well for the future.

Service user involvement:

Beresford, Service users' knowledges and social work theory: conflict or collaboration?

Beresford and Croft, Service users and practitioners reunited: the key component for social work reform.

Cowden and Singh, The 'user': friend, foe or fetish? A critical exploration of user involvement in health and social care.

Heffernan, Social work, new public management and the language of 'service user'.

Hodge, Participation, discourse and power: a case study in service user involvement.

Molyneux and Irvine, Service user and carer involvement in social work training: a long and winding road?

Peck et al., Information, consultation or control: user involvement in mental health services in England at the turn of the century.

Community psychology:

Coimbra e al., Rethinking community psychology: critical insights.

Prilleltensky, Value-based praxis in community psychology: moving toward social justice and social action.

Rappaport, Terms of empowerment/exemplars of prevention: toward a theory for community psychology.

Reader et al., Patient neglect in 21st century health-care institutions: a community health psychology perspective.

5 Health Psychology: Understanding Health, Illness, Stress and Addiction

The following are the key relevant capabilities and standards in this chapter for social workers.

Professional Capabilities Framework (BASW, 2015)	Standards of Proficiency (HCPC, 2012)
5 Knowledge 5.1 Demonstrate a critical understanding of the application to social work of research, theory and knowledge from sociology, social policy, psychology and health 5.4 Recognise the short and long term impact of psychological, socio-economic, environmental and physiological factors on people's lives, taking into account age and development, and how this informs practice	**2 Be able to practise within the legal and ethical boundaries of their profession** 2.3 Understand the need to protect, safeguard and promote the wellbeing of children, young people and vulnerable adults 2.4 Understand the need to address practices which present a risk to or from service users and carers, or others **5 Be aware of the impact of culture, equality and diversity on practice** 5.1 Be able to reflect on and take account of the impact of inequality, disadvantage and discrimination on those who use social work services and their communities. **9 To be able to work appropriately with others** 9.2 Be able to work with service users and carers to enable them to assess and make informed decisions about their needs, circumstances, risks, preferred options and resources

Introduction

Social workers are involved in service provision in a variety of health care settings, such as hospitals, rehabilitation centres and hospices, where they make use of psychological principles as part of their endeavours to promote changes in people's attitudes, behaviour and thinking about health and illness. This chapter will explore the application of psychological theories and research to understanding biological, psychological, environmental and cultural factors involved in health and the prevention of illness. It will look in depth at the particular issues of dementia, obesity in children and substance abuse as key concerns of social work that might helpfully be conceptualized and addressed through the lens of health psychology.

Health psychology aims to provide explanations of the links between psychological processes and health. Knowledge of health psychology is important to social workers because health, both mental and physical, is a crucial determinant of many clients' and carers' lives. In the fields of child development, mental health, learning disabilities, physical disabilities and dementia services, health issues and their associated risks are of core concern. An understanding of the psychological phenomena of health conditions will provide a shared knowledge base from which social workers can effectively work with psychologists and other health professionals. Social workers with such knowledge should be more empathic, better able to advocate for services, and be more focused in their views about the appropriateness of a range of interventions. A sound understanding of these principles should also help them engage more effectively with members of the health and psychological professions with whom they often work on shared cases and interventions.

What is health psychology?

Health psychology is devoted to   ng the psychological factors associated with health and   cuses on health promotion and the prevention and treatme.   ide health policy formation. Health psychologists share fie.   social work, nursing and other disciplines aimed towards   hanging health-related behaviour. As health and illness a.   a continuum, health psychology is concerned with the onsu   king, symptom perception, illness cognitions, illness ada   change, social support and health outcomes, all of which are   al work practice arenas as well.

Matarazzo (1982: 4) provided one of the first formulations of a definition of health psychology, as:

> the aggregate of the specific educational, scientific, and professional contributions of the discipline of psychology to the promotion and maintenance of health, the prevention and treatment of illness, the identification of etiologic and diagnostic correlates of health, illness, and related dysfunction, and to the analysis and improvement of the health care system and health policy formation.

The way in which social workers approach the assessment of people's needs involves the individual, their family setting and the wider environment. When a person's circumstances are affected by poor health, social workers must consider ways in which support can be provided, both for the individual involved and for their family.

Applying health psychology to social work practice

Health psychology and social work share many areas of focus and concerns as well as common approaches, as both professions seek to help individuals and families to overcome complex problems. Most social workers deal with families where damaging health behaviours – smoking, lack of exercise, stress, unhealthy relationships, substance abuse, heavy medication regimes – are the reality and are often exacerbated by environmental issues such as poverty, poor housing environment and ill health.

Case study

The Brightwell family live in social housing and are on benefits, their resources being strained by caring for Mary, who has an unspecified form of dementia. The financial and emotional stress of this situation is falling mainly on her daughter Susan, particularly as Mary refuses any other help. Susan has to take two buses each way across town to her mother's house twice a day and, in common with many women of her generation, also has child-care responsibilities at home. Taking a health psychology approach to the Brightwells both as individuals and also as a family unit may produce different perspectives. Holistically, the Brightwells might be seen as a family with poor psychological health overall, yet there are strengths in the family – a family which, despite its many problems, are still together as a unit. Some of these positive behaviours and problems will be explored in this chapter.

A bio-psychosocial model of health

The bio-psychosocial model, initially put forward by Engel (1977), views illness as being a result of biological, psychological and social factors. This approach is far broader than the biomedical model, which historically has dominated the understanding of illness and is based around scientific constructs and aspects of medicine.

The bio-psychosocial perspective draws on an interdisciplinary approach in ways that can enable social workers to understand and appreciate the relationship between biological, psychological and social factors, all of which are core to social work assessment. One of social work's distinguishing features is that it is able to draw from a range of health and social care models and thus is well placed to interpret and assess the complexities in the lives of clients and carers. Such knowledge should also give social workers the confidence to better understand and challenge other professionals and bring them together in shared decision-making.

Health behaviours

Health behaviours interest psychologists, social workers and many other professionals because of their links with mortality, and because many harmful behaviours are avoidable (Conner and Norman, 1996). Being healthy has become increasingly important to many individuals, and we are more and more aware that our behaviours play a role in achieving and maintaining good health. In a seminal study, Belloc and Breslow (1972) investigated a number of different behaviours and found that good practices contributed to health, regardless of an individual's sex, age or economic status. This finding had great significance in health psychology, as it highlights that health behaviours are important in predicting both mortality and longevity in individuals. Many recent initiatives (for example, Department of Health, 2006) have placed great emphasis on personal responsibility for health, partly as a result of pressures on the NHS caused by poor lifestyle conditions such as obesity and smoking. Within adult social care, the personalization agenda (Dunning, 2008) has placed great emphasis on the responsibility of the individual in running their own care services following a needs and financial assessment by a social worker.

Personality and health behaviour

Research across social, developmental and personality psychology has established associations between the way in which people feel, think and behave and various health outcomes. For example, systematic observations indicate that certain personality traits, such as optimism and hostility, as well as certain behaviour patterns, predispose individuals to respond to life stressors in ways that may impact on their health. Optimistic people tend to experience increased psychological well-being and better physical health (Peterson et al., 1988). *Optimism* in this context refers to the expectation that, in the future, good things will happen and bad things will not. Optimistic individuals express confidence in a stable way, across time and across a range of domains. The reasons underlying the link between optimism and health are unclear, although several mechanisms have been suggested – e.g., optimists are more likely to avoid high-risk situations or, alternatively, may employ more effective coping strategies, the use of which may lead to better health by helping them avoid negative outcomes.

The construct of *Type A behaviour* emerged from the work of cardiologists as a result of attempts to understand the causes of heart disease beyond the risk factors related to diet and smoking (Friedman and Booth-Kewley, 1987).

This type of behaviour is characterized by competitiveness, ambition, aggression, impatience and a sense of urgency or hurriedness. Sirri et al. (2012) found that individuals displaying a consistent Type A behaviour pattern were twice as likely to develop coronary heart disease. However, further research suggested that particular aspects of Type A behaviour present more of a risk than others – for example, a small but consistent link has been identified between *hostility* and coronary heart disease (Whooley and Wong, 2011). Hostility refers to a negative attitude towards others, encompassing cynicism about others' motives, mistrust, a tendency to interpret others' actions as offensive, and strong connotations of anger and aggression. For instance, a mechanism through which hostility may increase the risk of cardiovascular disease (CVD) is experiencing more interpersonal conflict, which leads to stress. Similarly, hostile individuals may be more cynical about health warnings and thus be less likely to engage in good health practices. Moreover, hostility may be a feature of particular families' negative interactions, thus suggesting both that individuals sharing similar backgrounds may develop CVD and that hostility may be a personality trait from a young age and therefore difficult to change.

Case study

Consider the case of the Moore family, where the relationship between the mother and father is characterized by regular verbal abuse, including lengthy arguments and sulks which can go on for days. Their teenage son and daughter often 'take sides'. The mother's own mother, Doreen (aged seventy-five), has recently been bereaved and is under pressure from her family to move in with them. She is also obese and takes a variety of medication for her blood pressure. You are the social worker who has managed Doreen's domiciliary care package. During a recent review of this care package, Doreen asks you what you would advise regarding this proposed move.

Discussion
This situation is full of dilemmas, as Doreen has mental capacity and you believe in her right to self-determination. However, you might help her draw up a list of pros and cons about what the benefits and drawbacks might be, especially so soon after her bereavement, and let her decide from there. You might suggest to her that her own health, both physical and mental, is of paramount importance. You would have to find a sensitive way of pointing out to Doreen the potential consequences to her health of moving into what is a very difficult household and let her know the particular risks associated with stress, such as CVD.

Other personality characteristics associated with the risk of developing CVD are *extroversion vs. introversion*. Extrovert individuals tend to be outgoing, sociable and assertive and show high levels of energy. Introverts are individuals who tend to be cautious and serious and avoid over-stimulating environments or activities. Extroversion has been linked to both positive (e.g., exercise) and negative (e.g., smoking) health and is generally associated with positive psychological well-being and better physical health practices. However, the underlying mechanism for this association is unclear – it has been suggested that extroverts have more effective strategies to cope with stress and more social support than introverts, but there is no strong supporting evidence (Hagger-Johnson et al., 2012).

Obesity and child neglect

Turning now to explore some health psychology issues concerning children, the areas in which social workers are usually involved are those of neglect and failure to thrive. Serious case reviews such as that of Daniel Pelka (Lock, 2013) reveal neglect leading to malnourishment and dehydration. Cases that reach the threshold of significant harm under the Children Act 1989 often lead to child protection plans and placements in care. Much recent attention in health psychology, however, has been focused on childhood obesity, and social workers need to have a perspective on the extent to which this condition might be construed as neglect (Viner et al., 2010). This new focus of concern is a good example of how health psychology never stands still and how health behaviours are attributable to many changing social factors. The rise in sedentary habits, the omnipresence of junk food, both parents being in work, and the fear of allowing children out to play in open spaces may all have their part to play in analysing why a child may be so overweight as to attract the attention of social workers (Williams et al., 2014). Psychoanalysts would doubtless come up with different explanations for the rise in obesity across the UK population, and the bio-psychosocial model of health is of further relevance in the above type of scenario, which will be explored further in the following exercise.

Reflective point

Read the excerpt below from an article published in *The Times* and think critically about the issues raised.

> Obesity has played a part in at least 20 child-protection cases across Britain in the past year. Fifty paediatricians were asked by the BBC if they though that childhood obesity was a child-protection issue.
> One doctor spoke of a 10-year-old girl who could walk only a few

yards with a stick. He believed that her parents were 'killing her slowly' with a diet of chips and high-fat food. Some doctors now believe that extreme cases of overfeeding a young child should be seen as a form of abuse or neglect, according to the report. (*The Times*, 15 June 2007)

- Should childhood obesity be treated as child neglect?
- Should obese children be removed from their parents?
- What knowledge and evidence regarding health psychology might you use to support your perspectives?

To assist broader thinking around the topic, the following two academic articles debate whether childhood obesity might be seen as neglect. They reflect a range of arguments from international perspectives:

Goldbas, A. (2014) Childhood obesity: can it really be child neglect?, *International Journal of Childbirth Education*, 29(2): 37–40.
Alexander, S. M., Baur, L. A., Magnusson, R., and Tobin, B. (2009) When does severe childhood obesity become a child protection issue?, *Medical Journal of Australia*, 190(3): 136–9.

Task
After reading these articles, critically analyse the extent to which they may have changed your initial position on the debate. How might you now explain the reasons why Shana Brightwell from our case study has become obese?

Concepts and theories

Models and theories of health beliefs and behaviours have been developed in order to predict behaviours and to lead to interventions designed to promote health and well-being. These different models and theories will be explored throughout this section; different research examples will be highlighted and their relevance to social work made explicit.

The health belief model (HBM)

The health belief model aims to explain why individuals engage in health-promoting behaviours and argues that action (or lack of action) is determined by an individual's perceptions of health problems – i.e., how susceptible they are to illness and the potential severity of illness – together with what is necessary to reduce the threat, also known as the costs and benefits analysis. The HBM suggests that these two core beliefs can be used to predict the likelihood of health-promoting activity (Montanaro and Bryan, 2014). In practice, the HBM is used as a framework for interventions based on motivating individuals to take positive actions resulting in good health and avoiding negative consequences.

However, the HBM model focuses on the conscious processing of information, with no weight being given to emotional factors or the consideration that alternative factors may also be in play. The main strength of the HBM is the holistic view it provides in including key beliefs related to decisions about certain behaviours. The HBM was expanded into protection motivation theory (Rogers, 1975), which attempted to include an emotional component in the understanding of health behaviour, a model that will be explored later in the chapter.

Overall, the HBM provides a 'common-sense' approach and has been successfully used to predict a range of behaviours across a range of different populations. For example, research has investigated the use of sunscreen to prevent skin cancer, which was found to be linked to perceived sensitivity, severity and benefits (Davati et al., 2013). In another study, physical activity among children was found to be significantly influenced by perceived barriers though not influenced by perceived benefits (Ar-Yuwat et al., 2013), which suggests that, to promote children's engagement with healthy behaviours, removal of (perceived) barriers is more effective than highlighting benefits. This may be useful when working with children and young people who may never have taken part in, or have withdrawn from, physical activity because of perceived barriers, such as having a poor body-image or having been bullied.

Case study: the Brightwell family

Shana, who has mild learning disabilities, suffers emotional abuse from her mother, who constantly tells her she is fat, useless and lazy, just like her father (the parents live apart, and Shana has weekend contact with her father). She was told by her mother that she would never get a boyfriend and that she would end up lonely and sad. Shana has begun to eat less and less, throws away her packed school lunch, and never wants any tea or supper. She has lost a lot of weight and refuses to do any PE at school. A teacher noticed she was being bullied and referred her to the school's social worker for assessment of her needs.

Discussion

An understanding of the HBM help could shape the social worker's approach to Shana by attempting to develop her cognitive understanding of the barriers that have led to her eating habits. Shana and her social worker might explore what barriers she perceives as stopping her eating at what times. Alternatives in terms of what food is on offer, who prepares it, where it might be eaten, and whether it might be eaten alone or in company are some examples of 'common-sense' processes that could lead to practical solutions. Shana may well have deeper emotional issues that also need addressing, such as her mother's lack of emotional warmth and her father having left the family, but tapping into her belief systems could help her reach a better state of health from which it may be possible to explore such avenues. While Shana's mild learning disability will present a further obstacle to the use of the HBM, if the social work relationship is strong enough, adaptations can be made to engage her at an appropriate level of understanding.

Protection motivation theory (PMT)

Protection motivation theory (Rogers, 1975; Prentice-Dunn and Rogers, 1986) was originally proposed with a view to expanding the HBM to include emotional factors. The main contribution of the PMT over the HMB was the addition of fear, something that the HBM lacked (Prentice-Dunn and Rogers, 1986). It proposes that self-protection depends on five factors: the perceived severity of a threatened event, the perceived probability of the event, the effectiveness of the recommended preventative action, and self-efficacy and *fear*. This information influences the five components of the PMT, which then elicit either an 'adaptive' coping response or a 'maladaptive' coping response. The PMT provides a model for increasing health-promoting behaviour through persuasive communication, and it has been successfully applied in moves to prevent skin cancer (Baghianimoghadam et al., 2011).

Reflective point

Over recent years the government has launched a series of strong and graphic anti-smoking campaigns, notably:

- Smokefree campaign: worried (2009), www.youtube.com/watch?v=jBt16vVx8BQ
- Health harms – mutations (2015), www.youtube.com/watch?v=v-UrEV89S8Y.

Task
Consider how the PMT explains why such campaigns might work to produce the desired effect (smoking cessation).

Transtheoretical model of change (TMC)

The transtheoretical model of change (Prochaska and DiClemente, 1983) is a model that views change in behaviour across six basic stages: the pre-contemplation stage, contemplation, preparation, action, maintenance and relapse. These stages do not always occur in a linear fashion, and the model describes behavioural changes as dynamic. This model also takes into account how the individual weighs up the costs and benefits of a particular behaviour.

The TMC has been applied in several health-related situations, such as smoking and alcohol use (DiClemente et al., 1991; Cox et al., 2003) – issues familiar to social workers supporting a range of individuals. For example, it is often applied to help people give up smoking, because it can be tailored to individuals at different stages of engagement.

Case study

Imagine that Wayne Brightwell has just been paid in cash for a week's bricklaying – he has £500 in his pocket and a very heavy cocaine habit. Use the six stages of the transtheoretical model of change (pre-contemplation stage, contemplation, preparation, action, maintenance and relapse) to gain insight into how Wayne might decide to spend his wages – on paying off debts, giving rent to his mother or having a week-end blow-out on cocaine and partying.

Task

Consider how an awareness of the transtheoretical model might shape the interventions of social work or psychology professionals if Wayne wanted their help.

Discussion

It would be important to engage Wayne while he was not under the influence of drugs in order to establish a contract with agreed goals. There is no indication that Wayne has any cognitive impairment when not taking drugs, and therefore he could collaborate with his social worker or psychologist in prioritizing the area he wished to tackle first and how the related threats and coping mechanisms might be identifiable at each stage. If, for example, he wanted to address his desire to have a week-end blow-out on cocaine, it might first be established where this drive comes from (pre-contemplation stage) before moving on to discuss the contemplation stage – i.e., how and when does this desire manifest: after a hard day at work, as a result of boredom, or on account of peer pressure to behave in a certain way? The preparation stage would explore how Wayne planned to face or perhaps avoid his mother after work – possibly going straight from work to a friend's house where he can shower and where he has previously taken his casual clothes. The action stage might involve a mutual consideration of what Wayne actually does on these week-end blow-outs and what risks can be identified. The maintenance stage would be concerned with how he gets himself back into the working week and establishes some kind of equilibrium with his mother. The pattern that leads to relapse would then be examined. It would be the goal of a transtheoretical-based approach that a person with cognitive insight, enabled to look at their behaviour with constructive, staged guidance, might go on to change any behaviours that were harmful.

Dementia – a shared concern for health psychology and social work

Dementia is a much misunderstood phenomenon, often seen in a negative or derogatory light: people often joke about 'being senile', which is a most unhelpful and vague phrase. There is also the stereotype that all people with dementia have no lucid moments and thus are incapable of making any decisions about their own lives.

Dementia is the general term for a range of diseases or conditions affecting the brain, in the form of loss of memory, disorientation, loss of reasoning and anxiety (Downs and Bowers, 2014). Alzheimer's disease, often wrongly used interchangeably with the term 'dementia', is in fact one particular disease caused by deterioration in brain cell function (Alzheimer's Society, 2015a). Another subcategory of dementia that many professionals encounter is vascular dementia, where brain damage brought about by episodes such as strokes leads to deterioration in brain function. Other subcategories of dementia are those associated with Parkinson's disease and Huntington's chorea (Alzheimer's Society, 2015b). Mainly, but not exclusively found in the elderly, dementia has been described as the biggest challenge facing the health and social care services in the UK as a result of the growing number of older people who are increasingly receiving dementia diagnoses (Department of Health, 2012a).

Neurological, emotional, social and behavioural processes make a contribution to the understanding of dementia and its associated interventions and therapies. The behavioural symptoms of dementia – aggression, hallucinations and inattention to personal hygiene – can cause immense stress in families, particularly to women (Parker et al., 2015), who are predominant as informal carers (as is Susan Brightwell in the case study). It is very important that clinicians, psychologists and social workers see the dementia sufferer as a whole person with a social context and unique history. A person with dementia may also have physical illness, mental illness and relationship or social problems to contend with. Over-medication, urinary tract infections and medicines which counteract each other, often irregularly and improperly taken, exacerbate the complexities of the disease (Downs and Bowers, 2014).

Behaviours should be systematically assessed by social workers and other professionals before interventions such as nursing home care are put forward. Transfer to a care or nursing home does not necessarily mean that the individual with dementia will have a better quality of life, although their carer might (the reflective point below explores the nursing home issue further). A confident social worker will ask questions about medication and care regimes in order to understand better the sets of dynamics around the dementia sufferer and with a responsibility also towards that person's wider family and community. Blanket diagnoses and attitudes towards 'people with dementia' are not acceptable and go against the individualistic, person-centred principles of social work (BASW, 2012).

Reflective point

Fossey (2012) examined a number of key studies concerned with the types of behaviours associated with the different settings in which people with dementia might receive care. Regimes within residential and nursing home settings are very different to that of a person receiving services in their own home. Behaviours in dementia can exacerbate or ameliorate, depending on a range of factors around consistency of care, medication regimes and levels of stimulation. The task below (based on figure 5.1) asks you to think more critically about the interplay of some of these factors, since social workers often have to deal with the extra complexities of the wishes and views of family members about the appropriateness of some care settings.

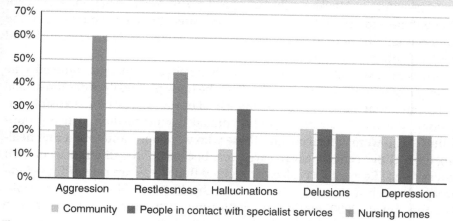

Figure 5.1 Cross-sectional frequency of common psychiatric and behavioural symptoms in people with dementia (percentages)

Source: Data from Fossey (2012).

Tasks

What health psychology theory or interventions might explain the rise in aggressive and restless behaviours noted in nursing homes? What health psychology theory or interventions might explain the fall in hallucinatory behaviours in nursing homes?

Stress, coping and health

Psychologists have defined stress in a variety of different ways, and individuals also have different ways of describing it. Stress refers to a range of negative perceptions and reactions experienced when mental or emotional pressure becomes too much. Contemporary definitions regard stress stimuli from the external environment as *stressors* and the response to them as *distress*. The concept covers biochemical, physiological, behavioural and psychological stress.

How is stress experienced?

The human body is designed to experience stress and react to it in varying different ways. Stress can be *positive*, in keeping the body alert and avoiding danger, experienced both biologically and psychologically. Stress, however, becomes *negative* when an individual faces continued stress without relief, leading to *distress*. When an individual finds themselves in a stressful situation, the hypothalamus, a part of the brain which controls the stress response, is activated. The autonomic nervous system (ANS) has two different branches – the sympathetic and the parasympathetic – which promote opposite effects to stress. The sympathetic branch helps an individual deal with stressful situations by initiating a *'fight-or-flight'* reaction, a concept that will be explored later in this chapter. After the danger has passed, the parasympathetic branch takes over, decreasing heartbeat and relaxing blood vessels (Cohen et al., 2007).

Stress can cause illness *directly* through the physical changes induced. One example of how stress can directly affect the body physically is demonstrated in research that looked at how wounds heal in stressful or non-stressful conditions. Kiecolt-Glaser et al. (1995) studied wound healing in two groups – those who were caregivers and those who were not – and found that healing took 24 per cent longer in caregivers because of the differences in their stress levels. Research has also highlighted that stress can cause illness *indirectly*, through increasing negative or unhealthy behaviours. For example, O'Connor et al. (2008) found that people under extreme stress ate fewer main meals and increased their intake of food high in sugar.

Exposure to intense and chronic stressors during the developmental years has been associated with lasting neurobiological effects, putting individuals *at risk* of anxiety and mood disorders, thus highlighting the impact stress can have on individual psychosocial development (Shaw, 2003; Gunnar and Quevedo, 2007). Moreover, without a mechanism to control stress, people often turn to *self-medication strategies*, such as taking drugs or drinking too much alcohol to calm the nervous system and feel more relaxed. Many addicts self-medicate in order to try and control or decrease their symptoms of negative stress (Khantzian, 2003).

Concepts and theories of stress and coping

The diathesis-stress model

The diathesis-stress model (Goforth et al., 2011) suggests that biological factors interact with environmental stress, which can result in health-related problems. This theory suggests that an individual's predisposition to a particular psychological condition can be triggered by stressful, negative life events. The model provides a means of understanding why some predisposing vulnerabilities seem to result in some individuals developing a condition while the same vulnerabilities do not lead to the same results in others. It also highlights how genetic inheritance and biological factors can have an influence on behaviour, although this impact is moderated by intervening life events which can act as stressors.

The diathesis-stress model has been successfully applied in understanding the onset of major depression in adolescence (Goforth et al., 2011). Having a family history of depression predisposes vulnerability to depression in adolescence; however, the onset of depression was predicted only in combination with other negative life events, such as rejection by peers or bullying.

Reflective point

How could the diathesis-stress model help a social worker make decisions in assessing the suitability of prospective adoptive parents in relation to pre-existing mental health conditions? For example, should prospective adoptive parents be rejected outright if they have a family history of mental illness?

Fight or flight

The fight-or-flight response, also known as 'the acute stress response' (von l... ., 2012), is the physiological reaction that occurs when an individual experiences something that is highly stressful or terrifying. Its aim is to... body either to fight or to flee the threat and is an evolutionary rea... tart of a stress response is signalled by specific physiological... the sympathetic nervous system, triggered by the release of adre... orepinephrine from the adrenal glands. When the fight-or-flight response is activated, individuals tend to perceive everything in their environment as a possible threat to survival.

The transactional model of stress

The transactional approach conceptualizes stress as a transaction between stressor and the environment (Lazarus and Folkman, 1984). The stress experienced by an individual is dependent on their appraisal of the stressor and the coping methods they use. Thus stressful experiences are interpreted as person–environment transactions. There are two main types of stressor:

1 *life events* – positive or negative events which represent a change in a person's circumstances (e.g., marriage, death of a spouse, birth of a child, moving house)
2 *daily hassles* – daily events causing the repeated activation of the stress response system.

In the presence of a stressor, the person evaluates the potential threat. This is the stage of *primary appraisal*, in which an assessment is made as to whether the occurring event is stressful, positive, controllable, challenging or irrelevant. If it is assessed as challenging, the person engages in the stage of *secondary appraisal* – an estimation of their own coping resources and options to bring the situation to a resolution (Cohen and McKay, 1984). This paves the way for actual *coping* actions aimed at resolving the problem.

Coping with stress falls into two broad categories:

1 *problem-focused coping* – processes which involve making plans or taking actions to help change the situation or reduce its impact
2 *emotion-focused coping* – processes focused on regulating the individual's emotions rather than changing the stressful situation.

The problem-focused approach is often considered to be the most constructive way of coping with stress. However, when nothing can be done to alter the stressor – after, say, bereavement or a life-threatening diagnosis – an emotion-focused approach may be the best option. Other strategies of coping with stress have been identified as:

- *positive reappraisal* – cognitive restructuring so that one sees the stressful situation in a more positive light; this has been associated with improvements in mood after stressful events (Moskowitz et al., 1996)
- *benefit finding* – the ability of those who have experienced a major stressor to find the benefits and advantages in the experience; this has been shown to improve mental and physical health in difficult situations (Helgeson et al., 2006).

Reflective point

How could the above models of stress help understand the health of individuals – adults and children – who experience domestic violence? To support your understanding, you may wish to retrieve and read the following articles:

McCrory et al., Heightened neural reactivity to threat in child victims of family violence.

Evans et al., Exposure to domestic violence: a meta-analysis of child and adolescent outcomes.

Holt et al., The impact of exposure to domestic violence on children and young people: a review of the literature.

Discussion

In considering situations of domestic violence, a social worker with an understanding of some of the above models is likely to be better placed to effect constructive interventions. For example, the fight-or-flight response is part of our basic survival instinct. If a person is threatened or pushed to a certain point, then the subconscious response is to prepare to fight or flee from the perceived danger. Being aware of the previous learned experiences of a victim of domestic violence – i.e., how she will react if you act in a certain way – or employing techniques previously learned in dissipating a threat can also help lessen stress levels. However, living with domestic violence, particularly over any extended period, in which the victim is always on edge awaiting the next assault, will take its toll in terms of stress. It may be that models such as problem-focused coping are the most helpful in making positive decisions to effect change in a situation, such as deciding to reappraise and leave an abusive relationship.

Interventions

Health psychology implements and promotes a range of different interventions in which stress can be managed, and social workers may be directly involved in their activation. This section of the chapter will explore two different interventions, cognitive-behavioural therapy and overall stress management techniques. Many individuals who experience stress self-medicate, a behaviour which will be explored later in this chapter with a focus on the impact of addiction on individuals and their families.

Cognitive-behavioural therapy

One of the most common interventions aimed at changing the way individuals think and behave is cognitive-behavioural therapy (CBT), a talking therapy which has become increasingly popular for its effectiveness and low level of cost (NHS Choices, 2013). Research assessing the impact of a CBT intervention on measures of perceived stress and coping strategies (Hamdan-Mansour et al., 2009) highlights a significant improvement in outcomes. For example, following the intervention, the individuals in the sample had lower scores on perceived stress, lower depressive symptoms, less use of avoidance coping strategies, and greater use of approach coping strategies, thus highlighting the positive impact CBT can have when managing and dealing with stress. Social workers may attend further specialist training that would enable them to deliver CBT, but it is more likely that their clients will be offered the therapy by specialist services as part of a wider plan. A major criticism of CBT is that it deals primarily with a person's symptoms and does not take into account the often overwhelming nature of their social and family problems. As part of a wider set of interventions, however, CBT can be helpful to clients who have the motivation and cognitive ability to engage with its structured approach.

Stress management

Stress reduction techniques and interventions aim to alleviate stress, relaxing the body and mind via the neuropsychological pathway involving the parasympathetic nervous system. For example, stress release techniques include meditation, relaxation, guided imagery and positive self-suggestion. Many physical and emotional issues are directly or indirectly caused by stress, and therefore practising effective management techniques may improve an individual's emotional and physical well-being.

Social support

Being part of a social network, such as having an extended family or belonging to a church group, can act as a resource in coping with stress (Feeney and Collins, 2015). Several types of social support have been identified, including emotional, instrumental and informational. Health psychology research is attempting to identify which types of support are most helpful in different situations, whether the quality is more important than the quantity, and what are the mechanisms through which social support operates. An early review of eighty-one studies found that it was related to beneficial effects on cardiovascular, endocrine and immune functioning (Uchino et al., 1996)

However, despite consistent research findings over thirty years that have reinforced the relationship between social support and health outcomes, relatively little remains known about the mechanisms through which such support operates (Thoits, 2011). Stress-buffering processes have been linked to self-esteem, a sense of control, belonging and companionship. An important role is played by two categories of supporters: significant others – who offer empathy and instrumental help – and experientially similar others, who offer, in addition to empathy, role modelling in coping. In order to be beneficial, social support has to be perceived as helpful by the recipient. Recent studies have explored the use of the internet as a potential source – e.g., in providing sources of information or virtual support groups.

Research indicates that social support can have benefits for the giver, with the giving, rather than the receiving, of support generally being perceived as beneficial for health (Brown et al., 2003). However, this will only happen where the provision of support is not so demanding as to become a stressor in itself, as may be the case for a carer of someone with dementia or where those living with people suffering from PTSD suffer from secondary traumatization. The harsh reality for many social work clients, however, is that social networks are scant or non-existent and that material resources, such as internet access, limited.

Loneliness in old age has recently been recognized as a significant factor leading to poor physical and mental health and to increased usage of state medical services. Not all older people will want support that might be deemed institutional, such as day centres and old age clubs, but may desire different types of social support. An individualized, psychological approach might explore a person's needs and customize a package of care. For example, a bereaved older man who enjoyed golf but stopped playing after his wife's death might choose to visit the golf club once a week with support to get there rather than use local day centres where he has no opportunity to rekindle old networks and his hobby. The English government's personalization agenda (Sealey, 2015) is designed to offer such individual choice. Opponents of this practice and policy say that the parallel loss of state-funded day-care facilities deprives older and disabled people of a unique type of fellowship and mutual support.

The impact of addiction on individuals and families

Families where addiction is present are often difficult for any family member, and are particularly challenging for children. Living with an addict puts the entire family under stress, as normal routines are being interrupted by unexpected or even frightening experiences. The all-pervasive presence of drugs and the readily availability of cheap alcohol across the UK means that problems of dependency are now common across all strata of society, although social workers tend to work mainly with dependency problems in families at their lower end of the socio-economic scale, where the consequences are often greater in terms of poverty and neglect of children.

Social workers play a key role in assisting individuals, families and communities to address addiction, and they encounter people with addictions or impulse control disorders in a variety of different settings. It is therefore important for them to understand the wide range of health issues associated with addiction, both biologically and psychologically. The health behaviour models outlined above may help a social worker's understanding, assessment and plan of action when providing intervention for individuals with addictive behaviours. The way in which society has traditionally understood addiction has changed over recent decades (White, 1998), although there is still no single theory or intervention to explain the complexities of addiction. The following section will explore approaches to issues of substance abuse and domestic violence as they pertain to the well-being of children and young people.

The impact of family substance misuse on children

It has been forty years since foetal alcohol syndrome (FAS) was first identified in a number of children who had been born to chronic alcoholic mothers (Jones and Smith, 1973). Prenatal exposure to alcohol can result in a range of neurobehavioral disabilities, now known as foetal alcohol spectrum disorder (FASD). However, during the last decade, following a failure to detect any negative neurodevelopmental effects on babies, an increasing number of reports suggest that mild to moderate drinking of alcohol in pregnancy is acceptable (Chan and Koren, 2013). Whereas Jones and Smith (1973) identified FAS in the babies of chronic alcoholic mothers, it should not be extrapolated that all mothers who drink some alcohol are placing their unborn babies at risk.

Dearden and Becker (2000) found that families in which substance misuse was present in the parents often experience multiple social stressors – poverty, housing, homelessness, long-term unemployment and discrimination (specifically for the child) – that can affect parental capacity and in turn impact on the child. Family disharmony has been found to be a key indicator of increased risk to poor outcomes for children, especially when this disharmony is paired with parental substance misuse. Cleaver et al.'s (1999) seminal work emphasizing the very high levels of risk present for children's safety and development when the 'toxic trio' of substance abuse, mental illness and domestic violence are found in a family setting still holds true today, as illustrated by many serious case reviews of child deaths (see Brandon et al., 2012).

The effects of substance misuse on families can continue through generations. For example, a child of an addict may grow up to be an overprotective and controlling parent who does not allow his or her children sufficient autonomy (Kaufman et al., 2005). Those who are consistently lied to will become untrusting of others. Their thinking begins to change, expecting the worst out of every situation. Dealing with addiction will affect not only their home life but also how they behave and interact with other individuals and in different social situations. The anxiety and stress of an individual affected by addiction can have a range of different health effects and implications for other family members, including loss of appetite, headaches, and even heart problems brought on by stress.

The outcomes of the risk of domestic violence on the child are clearly demonstrated in the study by Abrahams (1994), where the most common experiences of the children are those of seeing a parent upset (usually the main caregiver), witnessing violence, being aware of the atmosphere, and overhearing attacks and/or being attacked by a parent who was misusing. Sher et al. (1991) conducted a study comparing children of alcoholic parents and children of non-alcoholic parents, testing them on psychopathology, cognitive ability and personality. The findings suggested that children with alcoholic parents were more likely to have stronger alcohol expectancies (the cognitive, affective and behavioural outcomes an individual expects to occur due to drinking) and more psychiatric distress. Conclusions were also that such children had lower academic and verbal ability and, further into adolescence, were at higher risk of substance misuse themselves.

Kroll (2004) set out to examine a number of studies relating to the experiences of children who endure parental substance misuse. The main themes that emerged from these qualitative studies were:

1 denial, distortion and secrecy or the 'don't talk' rule: children were told not to tell about their parents' problem.
2 attachment, separation and loss: loss covered the loss of a reliable and consistent adult, the child's loss of their self-esteem and the loss of normality; children felt that there were barriers between them and their parents and that attachment to the parental figure was limited because of their obsession with the substance. The accounts of the participants portrayed a sense of their becoming invisible.
3 role reversal and the child as a carer: the process of the child becoming the adult and the adult becoming 'child-like' was explored.

The research suggested that adults who misused substances appeared to step out of their role as parents and their children became 'young carers', a responsibility that can hijack childhood (Becker et al., 1998).

There is considerable evidence that parental substance abuse is a significant feature in many of the contemporary cases known to social workers in the UK. For example, a study carried out by Forrester and Harwin (2008) found that a third of all children's social worker cases involved parental substance misuse, a figure that rose to 60 per cent when children were involved in care proceedings. Outcomes for children with substance-misusing parents were poor, whether they were taken into care or whether they remained at home. However, little evidence exists regarding what models of intervention are most effective in this complex area of practice. Forrester et al. (2016) evaluated an intensive family service and found that, six years after referral, fewer children were being taken into care and there had been overall reductions in parental substance abuse. Parents were said to have engaged well with this service and reported improvements in well-being, despite a context of intergenerational abuse and poverty. The service worked in a very structured way, building on the strengths of families and on issues of confidence and self-esteem. While little is known about the views and experiences of children living with parental substance abuse, Hill (2015) found that such children and young people were able to articulate their issues. This research supports that of Fraser et al. (2009), whose small-scale case study found that children were both knowledgeable and resilient in the face of their parents' problems, despite high levels of emotional turmoil.

Cultural factors in health psychology

It is crucial that health psychologists and social workers appreciate fully the impact of cultural factors on the health and illness-related experiences of their patients as well as the disparities in health care between ethnic groups, in terms of both quality of care and attitudes towards caregivers. Lord Laming has carried out a series of reviews into child protection practice in England and has emphasized, since the death of the African child Victoria Climbié in Haringey, London (Laming, 2003), that the welfare of the child must come first, regardless of any sensitivities regarding race or ethnicity. Other cases, such as the deaths of Daniel Pelka in Coventry (Lock, 2013) and Khyra Ishaq in Birmingham (Radford, 2010), have similarly exposed a range of misunderstandings about how much weight should be given to cultural issues when the safeguarding of a child is the core concern. The Rotherham inquiry into child sexual abuse (Jay, 2014) found that the abuse of vulnerable white girls by groups of Asian men was systematically ignored over a ten-year period. Professionals and politicians were criticized for having placed too much importance on cultural sensitivities and the need to avoid racial conflict rather than on safeguarding vulnerable children.

Case studies: Applying theory in practice

1) A local nursery reports that a mother of young twins is increasingly stressed and looking thin and dishevelled. Other parents have told the nursery manager that the mother's partner is a heroin addict who physically abuses her and emotionally abuses the twins, who have a different father. When asked after her welfare, the mother has always been very chatty and says that everything is fine. Her partner is always extremely pleasant and courteous when he visits the nursery.

Task

How might knowledge of health psychology and addiction be helpful in understanding this situation?

2) You are aware that many of the young children in your London borough are being pressurized by their parents to be high fliers, and the children's days are packed with extra-curricular activities to such a degree that the local child guidance clinic has become overwhelmed with referrals about self-harming as well as young people presenting with symptoms of stress and reporting feeling of worthlessness.

Task

How might a social worker approach such 'high achieving families' with concerns about a child's welfare because of stress? What knowledge might help them to prepare for a parent's response in this situation?

3) A 60-year-old daughter has been caring for her 85-year-old mother at home for five years, but now, concerned at the daughter's mental state, the local practice nurse has made a referral to adult social care. The daughter is very unkempt, sleeps in her mother's room in an armchair, and appears to be existing on a diet of toast, cigarettes and coffee. The nurse is concerned that the daughter's seeming inability to care for herself is beginning to impact on the mother, who is often cold and hungry when the nurse visits.

  You visit in your role as social worker to suggest a range of interventions, including respite sitters so that the daughter can have some time to herself and maybe visit old friends and go out socially. Despite your concern at the amount of stress and the isolation the daughter is under, you find her resistant to all suggestions. She has insight into the worsening situation at home but continues to be isolated and exhausted and to partake of a poor diet, and concern remains about mother's well-being.

Task

How might a bio-psychosocial approach to this case help professional understanding and guide any interventions that might be effective?

The Brightwell family

Where do you think the sources of stress are in the Brightwell family? What theories from health psychology might best help a social worker understand these stresses and plan any interventions for their amelioration?

Summary

Health psychology is a relatively new branch of psychology that shares many of the concerns of social work. It acknowledges the various biological, psychoanalytical, behavioural and environmental factors that impact on the psychologies of individuals and their families and, as such, can helpfully blend some of these approaches in ways that lead to a fuller understanding of the causes of problems.

The chapter looked particularly at key contemporary concerns around dementia, at obesity as possible neglect in children, and at the dynamics and theories around substance abuse. The concerns of social work and health psychology are very wide-ranging, and there are many other areas that could be similarly explored. These examples have hopefully encouraged wider thinking about social work issues, often presented as 'facts of the case' needing swift and cost-effective resolutions. Having the knowledge and taking the time to reflect on and analyse the complex health psychologies around cases that management are anxious to close will lead to better and possibly even more cost-effective solutions, valued by the clients and their families. The following chapter will pick up on some of these issues around the psychologies of management, the rapidly changing workplace of social work, and the psychologies of organizational and political behaviours.

Further reading and resources

(For full bibliographic details, see the References.)

On personality and health behaviour:

Friedman and Booth-Kewley, Personality, type A behavior, and coronary heart disease: the role of emotional expression.

Hagger-Johnson et al., Neuroticism and cardiovascular disease mortality: socioeconomic status modifies the risk in women.

Sirri et al., Type A behaviour: a reappraisal of its characteristics in cardiovascular disease.

Whooley and Wong, Hostility and cardiovascular disease.

On models and theories of health beliefs and behaviours and their applications:

Bui et al., Protection motivation theory and physical activity in the general population: a systematic literature review.

Marcus and Simkin, The transtheoretical model: applications to exercise behaviour.

Norman et al., Understanding binge drinking among young people: an application of the theory of planned behaviour.

Prentice-Dunn and Rogers, Protection motivation theory and preventive health: beyond the health belief model.

Prochaska and DiClemente, Stages and processes of self-change of smoking: toward an integrative model of change.

On social support:

Brown et al., Providing social support may be more beneficial than receiving it: results from a prospective study of mortality.

Feeney and Collins, A new look at social support: a theoretical perspective on thriving through relationships.

Thoits, Mechanisms linking social ties and support to physical and mental health.

Uchino et al., The relationship between social support and physiological processes: a review with emphasis on underlying mechanisms and implications for health.

On cultural factors in health outcomes:

Williams and Mohammed, Discrimination and racial disparities in health: evidence and needed research.

On childhood obesity:

Alexander et al., When does severe childhood obesity become a child protection issue?

Goldbas, Childhood obesity: can it really be child neglect?

Viner et al., Childhood protection and obesity: framework for practice.

Williams et al., Can foster care ever be justified for weight management?

On children living with parental substance misuse:

Forrester and Harwin, Parental substance misuse and child care social work: findings from the first stage of a study of 100 families.

Forrester and Harwin, Parental substance misuse and child welfare: outcomes for children two years after referral.

Forrester et al., Helping families where parents misuse drugs or alcohol? A mixed methods comparative evaluation of an intensive family preservation service.

Fraser et al., Exploring the impact of parental drug/alcohol problems on children and parents in a Midlands county in 2005/06.

Hill, 'Don't make us talk!' Listening to and learning from children and young people living with parental alcohol problems.

Kroll, Living with an elephant: growing up with parental substance misuse.

Kroll, A family affair? Kinship care and parental substance misuse: some dilemmas explored.

On the effect of domestic violence on children – some of the seminal reviews:

Evans et al., Exposure to domestic violence: a meta-analysis of child and adolescent outcomes.

Holt et al., The impact of exposure to domestic violence on children and young people: a review of the literature.

Kitzmann et al., Child witnesses to domestic violence: a meta-analytic review.

Wolfe et al., The effects of children's exposure to domestic violence: a meta-analysis and critique.

6 Organizational Psychology: Understanding the Individual and the Organization in the Social Work Structure

The following are the key relevant capabilities and standards in this chapter for social workers.

Professional Capabilities Framework (BASW, 2015)	Standards of Proficiency (HCPC, 2012)
5 Knowledge 5.4 Recognise the short and long term impact of psychological, socio-economic, environmental and physiological factors on people's lives, taking into account age and development, and how this informs practice **8 Contexts and Organisations** 8.1 Recognise that social work operates within, and responds to, changing economic, social, political and organisational contexts 8.2 Understand the roles and responsibilities of social workers in a range of organisations, lines of accountability and the boundaries of professional autonomy and discretion 8.3 Understand legal obligations, structures and behaviours within organisations and how these impact on policy, procedure and practice 8.4 Be able to work within an organisation's remit and contribute to its evaluation and development 8.5 Understand and respect the role of others within the organisation and work effectively with them 8.6 Take responsibility for your role and impact within teams and be able to contribute positively to effective team working 8.7 Understand the inter-agency, multi-disciplinary and inter-professional dimensions to practice and demonstrate effective partnership working **9 Professional Leadership** 9.1 Recognise the importance of, and begin to demonstrate, professional leadership as a social worker	**4 Be able to practise as an autonomous professional, exercising their own professional judgement** 4.1 Be able to assess a situation, determine its nature and severity and call upon the required knowledge and experience to deal with it 4.2 Be able to initiate resolution of issues and be able to exercise personal initiative **9 Be able to work appropriately with others** 9.1 Understand the need to build and sustain professional relationships with service users, carers and colleagues both as an autonomous practitioner and collaboratively with others 9.6 Be able to work in partnership with others, including those working in other agencies and roles **13 Understand the key concepts of the knowledge base which are relevant to their profession** 13.1 Recognise the roles of other professions, practitioners and organisations 13.2 Be aware of the different social and organisational contexts and settings within which social work operates

Introduction

Social work is a highly stressful occupation, with practitioners currently staying in the profession only for an average of eight years (Curtis et al., 2010), which is far less than the average career lengths of fellow health professionals such as nurses and GPs. Working conditions and the inability to strike an appropriate work–life balance are often cited as reasons for social worker burnout (Webb and Carpenter, 2012). An understanding of the ways in which organizations behave and of ways to 'look after yourself' in social work's ever changing landscape is of vital importance to the profession and to the health and well-being of individuals. Healthy practitioners are also far more likely to carry out their work in ways that lead to more successful outcomes for service users and carers, and it is vital to recognize the 'healthy worker effect', whereby people who are more psychologically robust tend to remain employed in high-strain jobs (Li and Sung, 1999). The role of resilience is much debated in social work, and a key question is whether one is born resilient – an innate trait – or whether resilience is a learned set of skills and adaptations to changing environments – resilience as a process.

Organizational psychology – also known as occupational or work psychology – is concerned with the performance of people at work and with how individuals, small groups and organizations behave and function. It is relevant for social work practice in providing understanding of social workers' roles and the ways in which their organizations are led and managed, as highlighted by the Social Work Reform Board (SWRB, 2010) and the Munro Report (Munro, 2011).

This chapter will explore the relevance of organizational psychology to the social work profession and social work organizations. Using the employee's life cycle as a framework, issues around performance management will be scrutinized from the employee's perspective. Interruptions to the employee's life cycle, such as work stress, leaving, high turnover, retiring and redundancy, will be discussed alongside considerations of the role of continuing professional development, feedback and supervision. Links will be made with current issues in professional practice resulting from recent changes in social work as a profession (SWRB, 2010). From an organizational behaviour perspective, issues such as motivation, teamwork and leadership, and organizational change will also be explored within the context of contemporary social work. The need to return to a model of working centred on relationship-based practices (Ruch, 2007) which enable deep-seated psychological issues to be properly explored as part of social work intervention is seen as critical to the future welfare of clients and the job satisfaction levels of social workers.

The organizational context of social work

Organizational psychology applies psychological theories – for example, social, developmental and health – to employment and work settings. Although traditionally focused exclusively on employment as paid work and its associated processes such as recruitment and motivation, occupational psychology has recently been extending its reach to concerns such as the interface between employment and spheres outside formal work environments – such as the work–life balance, health in the workplace and stress at work.

Change is constant within social work. After an initial period of stability, the generic social services departments that had been set up in England after the Seebohm report (Seebohm Committee, 1968) were split into children's and adults' specializations following the implementation of the Children Act (1989) and the NHS and Community Care Act (1990), partly in recognition of the need for further specialization but also because of the need to control expenditure. The government White Paper *Modernising Social Services* (Department of Health, 1998) brought in very significant changes to social work which drew heavily on the principles of business, markets and managerialism, leading to an environment preoccupied with systems and conformity (Jones, 2001; Harris, 2003). The role of the state has been gradually lessened since this period, and councils have increasingly become the commissioners of services rather than simply being the organizations that deliver services. Continued failings, particularly with regard to inter-agency communication and child deaths (Laming, 2009), led to children's social work becoming part of integrated children's services, which were largely dominated by education services. Adult social work became more closely aligned with health authorities under the care management model, gaining a focus on assessment and reviewing. Changes such as direct payments and personalization policies have increased choice for some individuals but at the cost of a reduction in the provision of community services such as day centres.

The changes since *Modernising Social Services* (Department of Health, 1998) have seen the role of managers become dominant over professionals. Harris (1998, 2003) noted how managerialism increasingly removed professional social workers' discretion and control by introducing systems designed to achieve conformity and compliance. Team leaders became managers concerned primarily with the attainment of targets, particularly financial targets, in an environment where public services were being cut. The previous styles of supervision within social work which concentrated on supporting professional decisions and encouraging personal and professional growth have gradually been replaced by supervision that concentrates on target attainment within increasingly computerized systems (Harris 1998, 2003).

Reflective point

What are the arguments for and against managerial control over professional decision-making?

Discussion

You might consider that, once trained, a professional such as a social worker or psychologist should need to rely only on their own judgement. However, this does not encourage parity of performance across teams, and idiosyncratic approaches might reflect an individual's preferred way of working rather than on the real needs of the client. Also, some interventions and subsequent packages of care are very costly, and it might be argued that managers are necessary to control budgets and make sure best use is made of public money.

The debate about discretion within social work is ongoing (Evans and Harris, 2004; Ferguson 2008), but the reality is that performance management has taken away from social workers' fieldwork roles, estimates being that some 80 per cent of their statutory time is taken up by office-based systems tasks (Munro, 2011). Governments have to be accountable for public expenditure, and there is a need perhaps to ensure some equity of service across authorities, but do the business world's models of economy and efficiency really translate into the moral world of social work? Many of the 'customers' of social work teams are not 'willing' customers of the commercial sector but have come to the attention of social workers as a result of problems of abuse or neglect. They are often vulnerable and in need of protection in complex ways that have no parallel in the business realm.

Regulation and reform in social work

Social work in the UK is now a degree-level profession and one which is ever more tightly regulated. Admission criteria for master's and undergraduate degree courses consist of a mix of academic qualifications and work experience. Driven by the findings of the Francis report (Francis, 2013) into the lack of compassion and professional standards at the Mid Staffordshire hospital in England, recruitment has become 'values-based' in an attempt to underpin the selection of candidates with a series of core social work values. Values are complex, and it is difficult to confirm the authenticity of responses on application forms and interviews. However, by using a variety of assessment methods and bringing in service users and carers as part of the interview process, serious attempts are being made to guarantee the quality of entrants to what is a demanding profession.

Many of the applicants applying for social work training courses express such admirable desires as wanting to 'give something back', 'to change society for the better', 'to challenge inequality' and to 'champion the plight of vulnerable adults and children'. However, although it pays reasonably well, social work is not a career in which riches and wealth will be found; statutory social work, in particular, has increasingly become preoccupied with issues of risk and the rationing of resources across both adult and children's services. Carey (2003) noted that the emancipatory aspirations of many of those completing social work courses quickly disappeared in the daily grind of the office and its systems, which kept social workers away from both the 'social' and the 'community'. Evans (2010) identified the style of management within adult social work teams as one of 'remote control', whereby managerial decisions are made and communicated by electronic means without personal contact with the social worker on the ground.

Social work is certainly a stressful profession which calls for a resilient approach, and achieving a work–life balance is difficult when cases seem never ending and the systems surrounding them grow increasingly complex. Social work has a 'daily diet' of demanding situations, many of which will evoke deep feelings and ambivalence within social workers. Additionally, unlike psychologists and nurses, social workers also have to cope with a hostile press and an unsympathetic public who see only bad news about social work practice, which makes it all the more imperative that social workers are well supported in their immediate workplace by colleagues and management. This need is all the more difficult to meet given the reality of constant reorganizations, interim senior management posts, and the increasing usage of agency workers (Unwin, 2009). Resilience and finding the space to be a busy yet reflective practitioner who can keep a healthy perspective on their own self and the pressures of the workplace are essential if a social worker is going to be effective within their organization.

A supportive workplace should be able to provide much of what social workers need to make their job more fulfilling, but the move towards mobile and flexible working, often meaning that social workers are home-based and reliant on electronic forms of communication with peers and managers, has taken away much personal and professional support. Social workers might usefully explore ways to keep support systems alive, such as holding regular Skype discussions, ensuring that their own professional portfolio is up to date by attending courses, and by looking at innovative ways to share knowledge and contacts within professional communities. Online discussion groups, the British Association of Social Workers (BASW) and the Social Work Action Network (SWAN) are also sources of support and offer different visions of social work. Trade union membership is also highly recommended as helping give peace of mind in an increasingly litigious culture that receives mixed messages from government regarding its value.

The social work profession has been increasingly regulated by a series of neo-liberal governments, beginning with the establishment of the General Social Care Council (GSCC) in 2002. The GSCC, replaced in 2012 by the Health

Care Professions Council (HCPC), was intended to boost accountability and public confidence by the establishment of a Social Worker Register in line with the teaching and medical professions. In 2002 the New Labour government also established the Social Care Institute for Excellence (SCIE), which was designed to raise standards of knowledge and practice across the profession. Despite such initiatives, however, the image of social work throughout the 1990s and early part of the millennium remained poor and vacancy rates were high, especially in inner-city areas. In 2009, the average vacancy rate in England for qualified social workers was over 10 per cent, and social work departments had the worst sickness levels across local government (Morris, 2009; Curtis et al., 2010).

The Social Work Task Force was instigated by the New Labour government in 2009 as a result of a series of inquiries into the failings of social work across all services. Its brief was to produce new systems, models and training provision for social work in England that would produce a better quality social worker and better working conditions and therefore hopefully lead to a culture wherein the profession is valued and appreciated for the good work it does. The recommendations of the task force were adopted by the Social Work Reform Board (SWRB, 2010) and were intended to raise the calibre of entrants to the profession, to improve the standard of qualifying courses, and to offer better support to individuals throughout their careers, starting with an assessed and supported year immediately after qualification, which should be characterized by a protected caseload. In addition, the Social Work Reform Board led to the establishment in 2011 of the College of Social Work, which was seen as a way of raising the standards and the professional status of social workers, who also had to register with the HCPC.

Unfortunately, the College of Social Work was closed by the Conservative government shortly after its election in 2015 as part of its commitment to wide-ranging cuts in public expenditure. The government can be accused of giving mixed messages to the social work profession – for instance, in setting up and then abolishing the College of Social Work and in referring to social work as a noble calling (Mason, 2013) yet introducing mandatory reporting of child abuse in response to a public outcry when Daniel Pelka (Lock, 2013) was killed by his parents after a series of mistakes in communication by a range of agencies. Mandatory reporting makes it a crime not to report suspected or actual child abuse, placing extra pressure on social workers and other professionals already trying to make complex decisions in situations that are never straightforward.

Reflective point

What might be the psychological effect on a social worker of the mandatory reporting legislation?

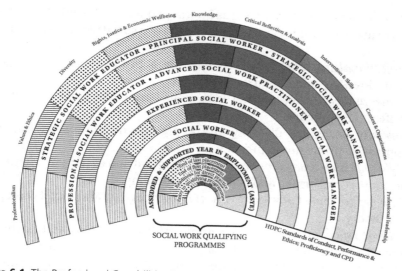

Figure 6.1 The Professional Capabilities Framework

Source: © The College of Social Work. Correct at the time of going to press. The PCF is subject to regular updating, and is now managed and delivered by BASW.

Discussion

Might the mandatory reporting legislation bring about improved efficiency and lead to fewer children being at risk, or might it lead to overly defensive practice in which children are unnecessarily brought into the child protection system?

A social worker might feel less likely to use their professional judgement and to rely instead for decision-making on checklists and templates that omit factors such as relationship and professional instinct. Such legislation is also likely to add to the stress already felt by the social work profession and could possibly lead to fewer people entering or more people leaving the profession at a time when vacancies, especially in children's services, are already at a critical level.

Professional Capabilities Framework for Social Workers in England

The main legacy of the College of Social Work was the development of an overarching standards framework, the Professional Capabilities Framework for Social Workers in England (see figure 6.1 above). This was designed to support and inform the national career structure and is relevant for all levels of social work. The term 'capabilities' has been used in a dynamic way to demonstrate that learning and development is a continuous process, and this model is seen as a positive development for social workers and their developmental aspirations.

Within its nine domains, the Professional Capabilities Framework contains specifics about how a social worker might evidence their capabilities in practice. These domains are seen as interdependent and overlapping, building up to make a complex and holistic picture of a social worker's career path:

1 *Professionalism* Identify and behave as a professional social worker, committed to professional development.
2 *Values and ethics* Apply social work ethical principles and values to guide professional practice.
3 *Diversity* Recognize diversity and apply anti-discriminatory and anti-oppressive principles in practice.
4 *Rights, justice and economic well-being* Advance human rights and promote social justice and economic well-being.
5 *Knowledge* Apply knowledge of social sciences, law and social work practice theory.
6 *Critical reflection and analysis* Apply critical reflection and analysis to inform and provide a rationale for professional decision-making.
7 *Intervention and skills* Use judgement and authority to intervene with individuals, families and communities to promote independence, provide support and prevent harm, neglect and abuse.
8 *Contexts and organizations* Engage with, inform, and adapt to changing contexts that shape practice. Operate effectively within own organizational frameworks and contribute to the development of services and organizations. Operate effectively within multi-agency and inter-professional settings.
9 *Professional leadership* Take responsibility for the professional learning and development of others through supervision, mentoring, assessing, research, teaching, leadership and management.

These domains have been welcomed by the social work profession as helpful and positive, and they suggest the need for a learning and supportive culture if work satisfaction and career longevity and progression are to characterize social work of the future. The framework provides a very positive model that locates social work alongside other professions and communities, while recognizing its distinct values and knowledge base. Custodianship and development of the framework has passed to BASW since the demise of the College of Social Work, and hopefully it will continue to raise aspirations and standards within the profession. The working lives of all employees should benefit from this framework being operationalized as a live and dynamic tool, whose domains are owned and shared by all in the profession.

Individuals in the organization: the employee life-course cycle

In contemporary Western societies, the world of employment is characterized by constant change, and adapting to this is a constant challenge to both the individual and the organization. Social work across statutory, charitable and private sectors is a prime example of a profession dealing with constant change in response to society's values and expectations, influenced particularly by variations in government policy. From the perspective of the individual, taking a life-course perspective (discussed in chapter 2) offers the advantage of allowing a time-span dimension to capture such complexities. The individual's career is placed in the context of their life by mapping out the different stages in employment. For example, a person enters a job though being attracted to a role and then being selected for that role. They probably then transition into a different role(s) and participate in continual professional training and development. In this journey, an employee might experience various interruptions in the employment cycle – such as through illness or maternity/paternity leave – which, if prolonged, requires a process of integration back into work.

Work stress can lead to interruptions in or bring an end to the employment cycle, the end coming when the employee leaves the organization, whether voluntarily or not, through taking up a new position, retirement or redundancy. It is vital, however, to understand the employment cycle as embedded in the individual's own life course, as this will have an effect on their performance. Additionally, if a social worker has knowledge of such psychological constructs as the life-course cycle, they can be more empathic, and therefore perhaps more effective when dealing with colleagues from a range of disciplines in the field.

For example, children's social workers work closely with foster carers, whose own position is a rather particular one, both psychologically and organizationally. They are not employees but they work for social work organizations; they are not professionally recognized but are expected to work in a professional manner; they are asked to provide a homely environment for vulnerable children but are also asked to adhere to rules around safeguarding (such as not having the children in their bedroom and not ever being seen naked by them) as well as to keep records of the children's progress in ways that would not be part of a normal home environment. The complex psychologies at play here are brought even more sharply into focus when considering the situation of kinship carers. Kinship care is becoming increasingly popular in the UK and is the term used when family members or friends offer to look after a child needing a home; this often means that a child's trauma can be lessened, as they already know their new carer, and it is also less expensive than mainstream foster care. The life-course perspective is an interesting one to apply to foster care, particularly in respect of kinship care.

The general public's image of foster care remains distorted. Despite years of campaigns promoting foster care as being for anyone with a spare room, a flexible attitude towards children and having committed no serious offences, the myth persists that carers have to own their own home, be married, and to have led a trouble-free life. The average age of foster carers in England is mid-fifties, and there is an estimated shortage of 8,000 foster carers nationally (Fostering Network, 2015). Young people in their twenties, whether single or partnered, might be at a stage in their life course where they have time and energy to devote to foster children, whereas a couple in their fifties whose children had left home might offer experience and wisdom even if they have less physical energy. Both would have a lot to offer, and an assessing social worker should be aware of life-course dynamics. Consider the following case examples of a couple in their thirties who have no children and a kinship assessment of a grandmother and grandfather in their sixties. In life-course, the young couple are at the beginning of their fostering career and are uncertain and unproven. However, they are likely to have great commitment and energy as well as an open mind. They may also be viewing foster care as a short-term commitment – say, for the next two or three years. The kinship application is by the grandparents of the child in question. Although they will have strong emotional bonds, they may not have the energy and commitment to work with social work systems regarding safeguarding in terms of their son's terms of access. Many of their peers will be winding down from working lives and not likely to be able to offer a great deal of support.

Case study 1: Mainstream foster care

John and Sandra Streathers are a couple in their late twenties. Sandra has worked in children's nurseries and John has an accountancy background. Both had quite disruptive childhoods and were brought up by single parents with low levels of material provision. They have not fully decided whether they would like their own children and have agreed to apply to become foster carers for children aged up to ten, believing they are not experienced enough with teenagers. Fostering, as compared to adoption, is often about rehabilitating children so that they may return to their parents, although it is not unusual for 'short-term' placements to become permanent, especially if adoption is not the agreed plan for a child.

Task
What considerations might a social worker need to take into account in assessing the Streathers, particularly looking at their propensity to become attached to younger children? How might future plans to have their own family impinge on the well-being of any foster children who had been in placement for some length of time and for whom the plan was a permanent foster placement?

How might a fostering organization with a fixed outlook view the potential of these applicants, and how might a more open organization regard them? Consider the benefits of a life-course approach in the above situation.

Case study 2: Kinship care

Mary Jones and her husband Ken are aged sixty-four and sixty-seven respectively. Both have retired from local government positions and have a good level of pension income. They own their own house and have applied to become kinship carers for their only son's child, Amy, aged nine months. Their son, Jerry, has a heroin habit, and his partner died shortly after Amy's birth due to a heroin overdose. Jerry had been investigated for neglect of Amy when he tried to raise her alone, supported by Mary and Ken. Mary generally has good health apart from some arthritis and Ken has been well since a triple heart bypass two years ago. Social workers have become increasingly concerned about the number of heroin users at Jerry's flat, and the police removed Amy under an emergency protection order when they recently raided the flat and could find no adult able to take care of the infant.

Amy was taken to temporary foster carers, as social workers did not believe that Mary Jones in particular would be able to comply with a care plan that meant Jerry could have only supervised access to Amy. Jerry is the Jones's only child, and Mary is said to dote on him, despite his lifestyle. The plan for Amy turned into one of adoption, to which Mary and Ken have objected, putting themselves forward as kinship carers.

In terms of their life course, Mary and Ken had envisaged a life of holidays and quality time on their own. They were surprised and delighted to have a grandchild and say they are happy to devote the rest of their retirement to looking after Amy. They have a small network of friends, all retired.

Task

How might a fostering organization with a fixed outlook view the potential of these applicants and how might a more open organization regard them? Consider the benefits of a life-course approach here.

Managing performance: training, feedback and supervision

Understanding and managing performance are key issues that concern occupational psychology. The business models of performance management have increasingly come to dominate professional discretion and decision-making in social work, unlike the case in psychology, where professionals largely still make their own decisions with a minimum of managerial scrutiny. Performance management is normally carried out via appraisals, which from the organization's point of view aims to improve current performance and remedy under-performance. From the individual's point of view, an appraisal can result in being rewarded for good performance, being engaged in further development programmes or, in the case of under-performance, lead to disciplinary action(s).

Professional issues of concern or celebration should be raised in supervision – supervision being a traditional quality hallmark of social work, despite some evidence (SWRB, 2010) of its being patchy on a nationwide basis, with a quarter of children's social workers not receiving monthly supervision. McGregor (2013) found that this situation had worsened, with almost one-third of all UK social workers not receiving any supervision. Social workers who received supervision reported that the focus had become more managerialist, moving from reflection, support and looking at personal development towards a dominance of targets, case discussion and action plans. Performance management should play a part in supervision, but appropriate supervision should enable issues of concern to be raised by the social worker regarding practice alongside development planning in regard to their professional career, including skill development, abilities and understanding. A further function of supervision is offering a restorative or supportive environment in which employees can reflect upon their reactions to work (Wilson et al., 2011). Munro (2011) has also identified the need for good supervision and sees it as the opportunity to provide space for critical reflection and professional reasoning, thus facilitating better assessments and decision-making. Therapeutic styles of supervision, such as those in the psychological professions, can help well-being and the ability to cope with stress. In ever busier social work teams, it is too easy for supervision to be cancelled when operational pressures run high, and this should always be challenged.

Reflective point

Workplaces are increasingly busy, and often staff shortages and illness add to the pressures on remaining staff. Regular supervision is often one of the first things to be dropped in such environments. Are there ways in which your workplace might be able to ensure that the above situation does not occur? For example, might you be able to arrange peer or group supervision? Might you be able to cover an extra session of duty to enable a colleague to attend their supervision? If your team carries out flexible and mobile working, might you be able to conduct some sessions by Skype? Are you sufficiently sensitive to the support and supervision needs of newly qualified staff, particularly in teams using mobile and flexible working?

The new National Framework for Supervision, promoted by the SWRB (2010), sets out minimum standards, including that sessions should last for at least an hour and a half and that they should occur weekly for the first six weeks of qualification, fortnightly for the next six months and stabilize at monthly. This framework stated that all social workers should receive supervision from a registered social worker, but the extent to which these standards will be adopted nationwide remains unclear.

The role of learning and development

Psychologists, social workers and other professionals should all have the opportunity to develop their practice in a continual manner, social work's commitment to post-qualifying practice having been noted by the SWRB (2010) as disappointing and not supported consistently by management, especially when caseloads were heavy. Some recent policy developments do offer the hope of a return to social work as a learning culture, based on the types of relationship-based practice that service users seem to value. The SWRB (2010) offered an alternative vision of social work to the marketized and managerialist model and, together with the Munro report (Munro, 2011), presented its future as one characterized by supportive, learning environments. The Hackney Council initiative entitled *Reclaiming Social Work* (Cross et al., 2010) promoted a learning culture and established posts of consultant social workers to promote best practice while at the same time supporting and developing staff, as a result of which significant reductions in sickness levels and the use of temporary agency social workers was reported. Other councils have since adopted or adapted this model, which augurs well for the realization of a learning culture across social work.

Organizational behaviour

The relationship between the individual and the organization is a complex one, often conceptualized as a psychological contract (Rousseau, 1995) binding people through various social influences. Commitment is an example of such a social influence, deriving from fulfilling a motivational goal. Compliance derives from the presence of rewards and punishments and models extrinsically motivated behaviour. Motivation is a crucial aspect of performance, and it is therefore important to understand how to motivate people in the workplace. When a person's individual and organizational goals are aligned, then motivation is enhanced. In order for this to happen, organizations need to understand the emotional intelligence needs of their employees, as individuals perform at their best when their jobs are in harmony with both their emotional and their material needs. Goleman (1995) defined emotional intelligence as the ability to stay positive and empathic in the face of frustration and distress. The development of emotional intelligence is critical for social workers, who are faced with other people's distress on a daily basis and will encounter frustrations both within and outside of their own organization. Negative public and political perspectives of the social work role increase frustration in ever more managed environments which emphasize performance in relation to empirical targets rather than the well-being of the worker. Relationship-based practice is an approach that facilitates in-depth work, but this approach has become less valued in the increasingly proceduralized world of social work, despite evidence from studies such as that by Brandon et al. (2012), which clearly linked the quality of the worker–family relationship with competent outcomes for children at risk. Social workers cannot operate in a vacuum and need to be able to work in a relationship-based way with clients and colleagues across agencies if they are to be effective and stay in their career for any length of time. Ruch (2007) argued that relationship-based practice is an effective way of challenging oppression because it operates from a more egalitarian basis of recognizing power and agency within both the client and the social worker. However, the performance management drivers that dominate in social work largely call for cases to be opened and closed as rapidly as possible, making even the briefest of relationships and trust that much harder to effect.

Leadership as motivation and influence in the workplace

The term 'leadership' is both a popular and a contested notion of influencing the activities of a group towards achieving a goal. Initial ideas saw leadership as an innate personality trait and leaders as more intelligent, self-confident and achievement-oriented than others. However, subsequent formulations propose a dynamic and transactional view. For example, the path–goal theory (House and Mitchell, 1974) argues that leader behaviour is motivational to the degree it makes the satisfaction of employees' needs contingent on effective performance and to the extent it provides guidance, coaching, support and rewards necessary for this. Alternatively, the situational leadership theory proposes that optimal leadership style is dependent on the level of maturity of the followers – i.e., low follower maturity requires a high level of task-oriented leadership and high follower maturity requires a supervisor low on both task- and relationship-orientation.

Leadership in social work has been addressed at the national level as a result of the recommendations of the SWRB (2010). The College of Social Work was established in 2011 to raise the level and profile of social work and improve standards but was then abolished in 2015, partly because of criticism that it had not proved effective. Chief social worker posts for children and for adults were also established as a result of the SWRB, but these posts are compromised as they are essentially the voice of government rather than champions of the profession. BASW continues to grow as the independent voice of social work and has taken on some of the responsibilities of the College of Social Work, such as the Professional Standards Framework.

Leadership in social work teams was traditionally carried out by team leaders – experienced social workers who supported and developed the work of their colleagues. However, since the advent of business models (Harris, 2003), such traditional leadership has been supplanted by management, and social work organizations have been dominated by managerialism. Senior managers often now have backgrounds in business rather than social work. A lack of leadership at all levels (political, senior management and team), combined with the rapid turnover in senior managerial posts, has been identified as a cause for concern in recent inquiries into social and health care scandals. For example, the sexual exploitation of children and young people in the Rotherham area (Jay, 2014), where groups of men, largely of Asian origin, systematically sexually abused vulnerable white children over a period of some ten years, was seen to have been prolonged through a combination of a political cover-up, managerial ineffectiveness and professional incompetence. The Mid Staffordshire NHS Foundation Trust Inquiry (Francis, 2013) is an extreme example of how a managerialist agenda – i.e., to put the hospital on a financial footing that would bring with it the business advantages of foundation trust status – led to neglect, substandard care and, ultimately, the death of some 1,200 patients. Social workers were hardly mentioned in the Francis Report, but the question remains as to why social workers did not blow the whistle on practice that was clearly contradictory to their values and ethical base.

Reflective point

Although the Mid Staffordshire Hospital was primarily a case of neglect by managers and health professionals, why do you think that the social workers at this hospital did not speak out? Was it perhaps fear of losing their jobs (as happened to certain health personnel who spoke out) or was it that social workers were so busy with procedural tasks that they missed the suffering and neglect all around them? Or was it that social workers were too small a voice in the health-dominated culture of a hospital?

Do you know the whistleblowing policy in your organization? What steps would you have taken had you been a social worker at the Mid Staffordshire Hospital when patients were openly neglected?

Multi-agency working

An important source of motivation in the workplace is a group of co-workers – supportive work groups being critical to employee motivation and satisfaction. Self-categorization theory (Hornsey, 2008) suggests that members who identify with a group will think, feel and act in pursuit of group goals and interests. Groups represent a way of structuring roles and activities to achieve a goal, though it is important to note that groups do not always operate as teams. A team is an interdependent way of working to achieve a particular goal. For example, in the multidisciplinary teams in which social workers are increasingly expected to operate, the situation relies on the complementarity of skills and expertise. Multi-agency working, despite the many arguments in its favour – such as fewer professionals being required per family, keeping costs down, understanding each other's language and sharing skills (Farrell et al. 2006; Payne, 2014) – is not always successful, and many tragedies, particularly in respect of children, can be partly attributable to poor and ineffective multi-disciplinary working (Brandon et al., 2012). Atkinson et al. (2007) examined a range of multi-agency activity in which education authorities were engaged and found significant evidence of confusion regarding responsibilities and roles, differing priorities, varying funding arrangements, and elements of competition between agencies regarding whose authority should take prominence. Working relationships can closely reflect the typically messy lived experiences of the families they support. Furthermore, confusion regarding confidentiality and information-sharing can be exacerbated by professionals working under different mandates. Cultures can also develop between agencies which are 'conflictual, bureaucratic, and consumed by complaining, disputing and dumping' (Morrison 2000). Such cultures can lead to defensive practice and an increase in anxiety. Munro (2008) suggested that the single most important factor in lessening error in children's safeguarding would be for a professional to admit they are in the wrong. Unfortunately there is little evidence that the outcomes of practice from working together across human services have improved, despite structural and process changes (Sloper, 2004; Brown and White, 2006).

Consider the micro-example below which involves different professionals working under a new structure and poses questions about power differentials and different values that affect the psychology of a multi-disciplinary team.

Case study

You join a multi-disciplinary mental health team that has recently merged with a health trust provider, and you soon realize that the merger has taken place without any team-building and that working arrangements are fragmentary and divisive. You are one of only two social workers in a team dominated by health professionals, and your colleague is rather reticent in personality and seems not to want to form a 'partnership' with you to challenge a health-dominated ethos. The result is a work environment that is very unhappy, with staff battling for positions and a senior management obsessed with proving to their 'political masters' that the new service is value for money. At a recent staff meeting you suggested that an away day or some kind of social event would be a positive way of addressing this problem, but your idea was derided by the team manager (a psychologist) as a waste of time. Sickness levels and stress levels are high in your team.

Task

Should you stay or should you go? What strategies might you employ to bring about change? Consider the short- and long-term psychological implications for your career and personal well-being of the decisions you might make in such a scenario.

Discussion

You might try to get your social work colleague to see beyond her caseload by suggesting that you work on a case together or go out for a drink after work. Gaining her confidence and suggesting a joint challenge may be effective. Alternatively, you might put the topic of stress and sickness levels on the staff agenda and produce some concrete ideas for changing things. It might help if you can place a cost on any planned events or ways of working as you showing an appreciation of the wider concern for value for money. You might, for example, work out the cost (both personal and financial) of staff absence and agency cover and suggest that your idea could prevent such future cost. You might find articles to circulate and discuss that celebrate team-building and effectiveness, particularly ones relating to multi-disciplinary working. Are there other ideas you might have?

On a personal level, your job is probably hard enough without having to work in a non-welcoming environment where staff absence leads to heavier workloads for those still present. If you do find yourself in such a situation, it is all the more important for your own well-being that you balance these work pressures with positive family or social experiences and ensure that you do not end up working excessive hours, even if that is the culture of the team. You might be ambitious and want to move on in your career, but trying to effect change in creative ways is always worthwhile. In the event that your ideas are not accepted, you can move on with a clear professional conscience that you had done your best. A review of the literature undertaken by Cameron et al. (2012) on behalf of the SCIE found that, despite high levels of satisfaction reported by service users involved in multi-disciplinary working, there was a lack of their involvement in what outcomes were expected – hence it was difficult to know what worked for them. Merely placing different professionals together under structures such as those of the integrated children's service model does not guarantee new and better practice. Most existing studies on multi-disciplinary working were noted to be small in scale, and the need for large-scale research to assess the efficacies of joint working from a service-user perspective was recommended.

Case study

Let us now focus down on the likely effects of multi-disciplinary working on the Brightwell family, since it is likely that they are being seen by a number of different professionals with different agendas, different values, different models of intervention and different resources. Some might take a family or community perspective on the issues being experienced the family, whereas others will only ever interact with a single individual. The following is an estimate of how many professionals might have contact with certain members of the Brightwell family in relation to their various problems:

- grandmother, Mary Brightwell – supported housing staff, dementia nurse, hospital social worker
- mother, Susan Brightwell – GP, counsellor
- older son, Wayne Brightwell – drugs outreach worker, counsellor, debt adviser
- daughter, Shana Brightwell – school counsellor, dietician, form teacher.

As can be seen from the multiplicity of issues involved, some professionals are likely to work to a medical model and some more to a social model, but how many will have thought to approach any of the family's problems more holistically? Each professional may have a different understanding of what confidentiality means or see their role as being concerned exclusively with their immediate client. For example, has Mary Brightwell had it pointed out to her by anybody that she might be expecting too much of her daughter? Have the school counsellor or form teacher invited Susan into school to gain another perspective on Shana's issues? Will the advice being given to Wayne be the same from his counsellor as from his drugs outreach worker, and has anybody considered any risks to Susan or to Wayne's siblings from some of his aggressive behaviour? Might Wayne ameliorate his behaviour if he could see the strains on his mother caused by her caring for Mary and on Shana, who has been experiencing bullying at school? Might the children's estranged father, Mick Fuller, be able to play a more supportive role in the family, especially as he still has contact with Shana? Do professionals make the best efforts that they can to engage men in family problems or, as in tragedies such as that of Peter Connelly (Jones, 2014), are the men largely invisible to the professionals?

Group performance

Psychology has taken a lead in the study of group performance. Social workers spend large amounts of their professional time in groups, some of which may work well while others may be dysfunctional. Knowledge of the psychological studies on groups can prove illuminating for the interested social worker. Every social worker will be aware of groups where the whole is less than the sum of the parts, and such team loss can occur because of a number of phenomena, including 'groupthink' and 'social loafing'.

Groupthink is the 'false consensus' generated by pressure to conform (Janis, 1973); unfortunately, it is quite common in organizational contexts and has detrimental consequences (e.g., Griffiths and Luker, 1994). It tends to occur when the desire for group consensus dominates people's desire to present alternatives or voice a critique or an unpopular opinion. Social loafing refers to the tendency of people to fail to do their fair share of work in collective contexts in contrast to when they are working alone; this is particularly evident when the individual is anonymous in the collective context (Latane et al., 1979). Recent research indicates that groups can be productive so long as the task requires genuine co-ordination and members share a meaningful social identity in relation to that task (Hornsey, 2008).

The following case study provides the opportunity to reflect on the roles of personalities within formal group settings such as safeguarding conferences or foster care panels ,where strong personalities, possibly senior professionals, can dominate and sway the opinions of others.

Case study

John and Mary Tweddle applied to foster teenagers for a private foster care agency. Mary had a recent history of depression (still controlled by medication) and found stressful situations difficult. Now in their fifties, this childless couple had a comfortable lifestyle, ran a local scout group and were involved in the local church youth club, which met at their large house. The social worker presenting the Tweddles to the foster carer panel argued that the couple's experience with young people was sufficient to indicate that they would be able to adapt to the needs of young people needing a foster placement.

The panel was chaired by Paul, an ex-senior social worker of many years' experience who summed up his reservations before asking the views of the rest of the panel, all of whom were younger and less experienced. His views were rather negative and, some might say, patronizing. He talked about other cases of religious foster families with whom he had previously worked who had tried to 'force religion down the necks' of foster children, saying that God wil[...]al them. He also talked about his work within the field of ment[...] stated that, in his experience, people who still needed med[...]be with depression were not mentally fit to care for foster childre[...]he extremely rejecting and abusive behaviours of many foster c[...]ld only make Mary Tweddle's depression worse. After Paul ha[...]p, he asked the other five panel members to comment, all [...]of whom followed his line of argument and did not recommend approval. The exception was Jane, a 45-year-old ex-foster child who had suffered from depression herself. Jane's view was that the couple had a lot to offer; she stated that they said they would not necessarily 'force' religion on anybody, that they could relocate the church youth club meetings away from their house, and that proper supervision should ensure they would always put the needs of foster children first. She also pointed out that a significant percentage of the population suffered from various types of depression yet still performed a wide range of family and work responsibilities.

The panel decision recommended to the foster agency decision-maker that the Tweddles should not be approved. This recommendation might be seen as an example of groupthink because Jane's arguments were the better ones, based more on fact than on conjecture. The eventual outcome of this case was that the agency decision-maker, a senior manager in the foster agency who has to scrutinize panel recommendations for their fairness and legality, overturned the 'groupthink' decision, and John and Mary Tweddle went on to have a successful fostering career, helping many troubled adolescents.

Reflective point

What might the foster agency do vis-à-vis Paul's role and way of chairing the panel that would avoid such similar occurrences in the future?

Focus: work stress, work–life balance and high turnover in social work

What is work stress?

It is now largely accepted that the workplace is a major source of stress. Occupational health psychology is concerned with the application of psychology to protecting and promoting the safety, health and well-being of those in the workplace. There are various models that conceptualize how work stress may occur.

The demand–control model (Karasek, 1979) proposes that workplace stress depends on the combination of demand and control in the job. Demand refers to how challenging a job is and includes factors such as heavy workload, fast pace of work, and conflicting requirements, while control refers to the extent to which an employee has a say in decisions about what they do and is able to develop their abilities. According to the demand–control model, jobs characterized by high demand and low control (known as high-strain jobs) lead to increased workplace stress, as do jobs that are low in demand and high in control (also known as low-strain jobs). Jobs that are high in demand and high in control (also known as active jobs) are less stressful than high-strain jobs because they offer the individual the opportunity to develop protective behaviours. Jobs that are low in demand and low in control (known as passive jobs) may be boring and lead to learned helplessness and reduced activity.

High-strain jobs have been linked to heart disease and negative health behaviours (e.g., Hellerstedt and Jeffery, 1997; Van der Doef and Maes, 1998), but having low job control may also be particularly detrimental, and this may explain the link between high levels of cardiovascular disease in low-level jobs (e.g. Marmot et al., 1991).

The effort–reward imbalance model (Siegrist, 1996) is based on the principle of social exchange and argues that negative health outcomes arise from an imbalance between the efforts the employee puts in at work and the rewards they receive. There is mounting evidence to support this model (e.g., Van Vegchel et al., 2001). Experiencing high efforts and low rewards will be more stressful for someone who is extremely committed to their work, something that is known as 'over-commitment' in the model.

While both these models contribute to our understanding of the emergence of work stress, an approach which integrates the two may be more appropriate. For example, Tsutsumi et al. (2001) suggested that effort–reward imbalance, together with low job control and over-commitment, was associated with depression. Social work is a very diverse career that, although carried out predominantly in statutory organizations, also takes place in charitable organizations and in the private sector. Each sector carries with it different workplace challenges: the charitable sector is prone to the 'over-commitment' model; the increasing dominance of managerialism over professional discretion in the statutory sector might result in social workers suffering from low morale as they lose more control; and social work in the private sector might be characterized by healthier levels of effort–reward balance on account of the generally higher levels of reward and better working conditions. The recent increase in agency social work is essentially a private-sector phenomenon in which social workers receive higher pay rates and are able to avoid office politics, as they move through a series of contracts with different organizations before perhaps finding a longer-term personal fit.

Work–life balance

Work–life balance refers to the equilibrium between a person's working life and their other responsibilities, such as family life, community engagement or other interests (Clark, 2000). The boundary between work and home life has become increasingly blurred in recent years (Grzywacz and Marks, 2000). There are two directions in which conflict between work and family operates. Work-to-family conflict occurs when work interferes with family life. This is the most common. Family-to-work conflict occurs when family interferes with work life.

There is increasing evidence that pressure arising from potentially conflicting work and family roles (Clark, 2000) is harmful, and some research suggests that there are links between work-to-family conflict and poor physical and psychological health (e.g., Allen and Armstrong, 2006; Emslie et al., 2004).

The following case study might be approached by considering the effort–reward imbalance model (Siegrist, 1996) and the work–life balance theory (Grzywacz and Marks, 2000). It is typical of a situation you may encounter in the workplace, where professional responsibilities and personal relationships can be difficult to manage.

Case study

Your social work friend and colleague is finding the target-driven culture of adult statutory social work a great strain. She is behind with her paperwork, and she has confided in you that she is drinking very heavily, sometimes a bottle of whisky at night as well as 'secret' drinks throughout the day. You are aware that she is driving to see service users, but she has begged you to keep her confidence. She is a popular member of the team and is well respected by all her peers. She has tried to raise the issue of being overworked with her team manager, who has said that her workload is no greater than that of her colleagues and that she should prioritize her systems work over spending time with clients.

Task
Consider the relevance of the effort–reward imbalance model to the above situation. What courses of action are open to you as a friend and as a colleague? How would you differentiate between these roles in choosing your option?

Summary

The organizational contexts in which contemporary social workers operate are challenging in all aspects. The nature of the work is stressful, the timescales and caseload logistics are stressful, and the changing nature of the workplace in relation to technological innovations presents challenges, especially to relationship-based ways of working. Social workers need to know themselves and how they can become more resilient while retaining enthusiasm and empathy.

Social workers need a deep understanding of organizations, how they work, and how to use theory and challenge to bring about change. Such challenges are most likely to be met where organizational psychology is embedded in their knowledge and practice. There is hope on the horizon, with a recent series of reports promoting learning cultures for social work-ers and a commitment, despite some mixed messages from government, to raising the status and profile of the social work profession. Renewed commit-ment to continuing professional development and supervision are in their early days, and BASW has stepped into the breach left by the closure of the College of Social Work, determined to lobby government as the independent and strong voice of the profession (BASW, 2015). There is a long way to go before the wider world understands the complexities of social work organiza-tions, but indications are that the profession is beginning to understand and champion its own position through a national voice that is increasingly able to challenge injustice and oppression.

Further reading and resources

(For full bibliographic details, see the References.)

Multi-agency working:

Brandon et al., *New Learning from Serious Case Reviews: A Two Year Report for 2009-2011.*

Brown and White, *Exploring the Evidence Base for Integrated Children's Services.*

Cameron et al., *SCIE Research Briefing 41: Factors that Promote and Hinder Joint and Integrated Working between Health and Social Care Services.*

Carpenter et al., Working in multidisciplinary community mental health teams: the impact on social workers and health professionals of integrated mental health care.

Francis, *Independent Inquiry into Care provided by Mid Staffordshire NHS Foundation Trust, January 2005 – March 2009,* Vol. 1.

Griffiths and Luker, Intraprofessional teamwork in district nursing: in whose interests?

Jones, *The Story of Baby P: Setting the Record Straight.*

Lymbery, United we stand? Partnership working in health and social care and the role of social work in services for older people.

Sloper, Facilitators and barriers for co-ordinated multi-agency services.

Work–life balance:

Clark, Work/family border theory: a new theory of work/family balance.

Curtis et al., The expected working life of a social worker.

Edwards and Rothbard, Mechanisms linking work and family: clarifying the relationship between work and family constructs.

Grant and Kinman, 'Bouncing back?' Personal representations of resilience of student and experienced social workers.

Grzywacz and Marks, Reconceptualizing the work–family interface: an ecological perspective on the correlates of positive and negative spillover between work and family.

Siegrist, Adverse health effects of high-effort/low-reward conditions.

Team-working and leadership:

Evans, *Professional Discretion in Welfare Services: Beyond Street-Level Bureaucracy.*

Latane et al., Many hands make light the work: the causes and consequences of social loafing.

Lent et al., Toward a unifying social cognitive theory of career and academic interest, choice, and performance.

NHS Choices, 'Transformational managers' may be bad for workplace health.

Norris and Vecchio, Situational leadership theory.

Rousseau, *Psychological Contracts in Organizations: Understanding Written and Unwritten Agreements.*

Contemporary work environment: hot-desking

Millward et al., Putting employees in their place: the impact of hot desking on organisational and team identification.

Unwin, Modernisation and the role of agency social work.

7 Forensic Psychology: Understanding Criminal Behaviour and Working with Victims of Crime

The following are the key relevant capabilities and standards in this chapter for social workers.

Professional Capabilities Framework (BASW, 2015)	Standards of Proficiency (HCPC, 2012)
5 Knowledge 5.1 Demonstrate a critical understanding of the application to social work of research, theory and knowledge from sociology, social policy, psychology and health 5.4 Recognise the short and long term impact of psychological, socio-economic, environmental and physiological factors on people's lives, taking into account age and development, and how this informs practice	**2 Be able to practise within the legal and ethical boundaries of their profession** 2.3 Understand the need to protect, safeguard and promote the wellbeing of children, young people and vulnerable adults 2.4 Understand the need to address practices which present a risk to or from service users and carers, or others **5 Be aware of the impact of culture, equality and diversity on practice** 5.1 Be able to reflect on and take account of the impact of inequality, disadvantage and discrimination on those who use social work services and their communities **9 Be able to work appropriately with others** 9.2 Be able to work with service users and carers to enable them to assess and make informed decisions about their needs, circumstances, risks, preferred options and resources

Introduction

Across the fields of child care and adult services, many social workers encounter situations where knowledge of forensic psychology can prove invaluable. Forensic psychology is placed at the intersection between psychology and the criminal justice system and aims to apply psychological theory both to the understanding of criminal behaviour and to working with perpetrators and victims of crime.

Forensic social workers may be involved with adults and young people who have committed serious offences, who might be experiencing severe forms of mental illness, or who may be victims or survivors of abuse and violence. Forensic knowledge about causes of behaviour, assessment, predictability and intervention underpins daily practice in this area of social work and provides a shared platform of information from which to share and debate issues with colleagues from different backgrounds.

Forensic social work is very demanding on its practitioners on account of working daily with adults and children who have experienced or perpetrated the most serious crimes and forms of abuse. Much of the work involves multidisciplinary settings across high, medium and low secure provision within both community and hospital settings. Forensic social work was promoted in 1975 by the Butler report (Rapaport, 2009), a government-commissioned report concerned with improving the ways in which mentally disordered people were treated in the criminal justice system. The role of the forensic social worker involves assessment of risk to individuals, their families and the community, and their subsequent recommendations are often presented in a legal setting such as a court or tribunal. Monitoring and aftercare of offenders and their social networks also constitute a key part of a forensic social worker's duties. Rapaport (2009) reports the complexities of assessing the benefits and dangers of contact after an individual had been responsible for the serious harm or death of another, these complexities being all the more fraught when that individual had been undergoing a psychotic episode at the time and may have no recollection of the event.

The chapter will explore contemporary contributions from forensic psychology and social work towards understanding criminal behaviour, attitudes to crime and the effects of criminal victimization. It will then discuss some current psychological approaches in working with child and adult victims.

Psychosocial theories of criminal behaviour

Understanding criminal behaviour has been and continues to be the focus of many disciplines – biology, psychology, psychiatry, sociology, history – and each one offers a particular point of view to explain the emergence and manifestation of criminal behaviour. Historically, criminal behaviour has been interpreted via a combination of biological and psychological factors gravitating around the nature vs. nurture debate – criminality as inherited vs. criminality arising out of social and environmental factors.

Evidence from family studies, including twin and adoption studies, supported the idea that there are genetic influences on antisocial behaviour (Kendler et al., 2014, 2015). Based on observations such as delinquent individuals being more likely to have convicted parents or delinquent older siblings, initial ideas about criminal behaviour put forward the hereditary component. However, families also share similar socio-economic factors, ethnicities and environments – therefore any aggregation of criminal behaviour is also an effect of the shared environment. Research findings from large population studies in Sweden found that there is a strong family risk factor in violent crimes which encompasses both genetic and environmental elements, although these can be moderated by individual variables such as gender, socio-economic position, age at first criminal conviction, and sub-type of violent crime (Frisell et al., 2011).

Research has also documented the phenomenon of *intergenerational transmission of criminal behaviour*, which is an association or correlation between the criminal behaviour of parent and child. For example, among some of the well-established explanations based on this idea is that parents are abusive because they have been abused themselves as children. Indeed, findings support such association across generations in violent offending. In particular, exposure to paternal violence has been shown to play an important role in the violent offending of offspring (Weijer et al., 2014). Moreover, physical and verbal aggression in the family of origin were associated with similar patterns of aggression in young adult couples (Cui et al., 2010), supporting the idea of intergenerational transmission of aggression towards intimate partners.

The negative effects of abuse on children's later adjustment, including violence, aggression, health risk behaviour and poor mental health, have been well documented (Øverlien, 2009). Recent longitudinal research reinforces this and further shows that the combined effects of abuse and exposure to domestic violence predict antisocial behaviour during adolescence (Sousa et al., 2011). These findings have important implications for practice, supporting the idea that early intervention and prevention of abuse and exposure to domestic violence could reduce the risk of antisocial behaviour during adolescence. However, the notion of intergenerational transmission should be used with caution in practice and not in a deterministic way, as research also shows that there is considerable variation in individuals' responses to early experiences with violence. Not all child victims of abuse or those exposed to early violence will become violent and abusive adults.

Applying theory to practice

Case study 1: Intergenerational transmission of criminal behaviour

Johnny Macintosh and David Thompson were adopted two years apart as three-month-old babies by Eric and Rosemary Cavendish. The Cavendish family had a middle-class lifestyle: Eric was a bank manager and Rosemary gave up a teaching assistant job to care for her adopted boys, both of whom were from different family backgrounds about which little had been shared, were in good physical health, and developed well in terms of motor and cognitive abilities. Johnny, the elder of the two, was never very affectionate and from the age of six or seven began to display violent tantrums and to assault fellow children at school, leading to his eventual expulsion and transfer at the age of eleven to a pupil referral unit. Through their secondary school years, David continued to develop and thrive intellectually, whereas Johnny got more and more uninterested in learning and became withdrawn from family and peers. He began to steal cigarettes when he was thirteen and to steal money and property from his adoptive parents on a regular basis from this age onwards. Any shows of affection had ceased in respect of his adoptive parents and adoptive brother by his early teens. After an escalation in his offending behaviours (stealing from neighbours, taking a car without consent, and a sexual offence against a neighbour's adult daughter), Johnny left home at sixteen to join a passing fair. He had very little contact with his family from that point on, and the last they heard of him was that he had been arrested for dealing drugs while on the road with the fair. David was in his first year of university when the news arrived that Johnny had been found dead in his caravan from a heroin overdose.

Discussion
How might the theory of intergenerational transmission of criminal behaviour be relevant in helping explain the different paths taken by the two boys? Might it be that Johnny's genetic inheritance was one that predisposed him to violence or might there have been nurturing issues in the Cavendish family that favoured David over Johnny, leading to the latter's rejection of a stable family for a life of crime? Might it be that both genetic and environmental factors played a part?

Case study 2: Breaking the cycle of violence and abuse – the role of resilience

Chris was born into a family where domestic violence had been present for several generations. His paternal grandfather had served a long sentence for the manslaughter of a previous partner, her death having occurred as a result of a blow to the head after a heavy night's drinking. Chris was a well-built lad and was always being encouraged by his father to 'stick up for himself' and to retaliate with his fists should any other young person show him aggression or disrespect. Chris was also told that women were lesser beings than men and had to be obedient or else be beaten. Chris, however, felt increasingly uncomfortable with the 'macho' role into which he had been nurtured and, from the age of twelve, began to disassociate himself from all such behaviours.

Unlike previous male members of his family, Chris attended school and studied hard. Inspired by a newly qualified teacher and the role models of successful young celebrity chefs, he took a particular interest in cooking. At the age of sixteen Chris took a live-in job as a kitchen assistant and moved away from his family and their environment. He has a new circle of friends, none with similar backgrounds to his, and he has resolved to turn his back on his family, preferring only to keep in touch via social media and birthday and Christmas cards. His two older brothers are both in jail for attempted rape.

Discussion

Clearly, Chris found some inner resilience to turn away from a violent and criminalized background. His education, possibly through the influence of the supportive home economics teacher, encouraged him to take a different path. His intellectual ability to perceive the differences in lifestyle options would also have been a factor, and chance too may have played a part – i.e., the live-in position some way from his parents' home.

Chris's older brothers may have been more influenced or fearful of their father and may have had neither the same cognitive ability nor the good fortune of finding a teacher to advocate for them. Are there any other explanations you could think of for Chris's resilience?

Social learning theory: contribution to the understanding of offending behaviour

A seminal explanation for the influence of nurture on criminal behaviour is offered by Bandura's (1978) social learning theory of aggression. Emerging from the alliance between behaviourism and cognitivism, social learning theory maintains that most behaviours are learned through modelling – by observing and reproducing the behaviour performed by other people. Bandura's famous 'bobo doll' experiment demonstrated how children act aggressively by reproducing an adult's aggressive behaviour towards the bobo doll (www.youtube.com/watch?v=NjTxQy_U3ac).

Social learning theory helps explain the association between childhood physical abuse and later violence. Longitudinal research has consistently demonstrated that children who experience aggressive and violent parenting will tend to behave in similar ways (e.g., Moylan et al., 2010). Child maltreatment significantly predicts future offending, and a recent study which examined five types of maltreatment – physical abuse, emotional abuse, sexual abuse, physical neglect and emotional neglect – found that physical neglect had the most significant effect (Evans and Burton, 2013). This suggests that types of maltreatment affect children differently and thus result in different pathways into adolescent offending behaviour. Interventions to deal with offending behaviour should therefore be tailored to target specific types of maltreatment.

Risk and protective factors in the development of criminal behaviour: social, family and psychological development

It is now largely accepted that the pathway into criminal behaviour combines biological predispositions with psychosocial (risk) factors in a life-course developmental perspective (e.g., Farrington, Coid and Murray, 2009). Within the complex interplay of causal factors in criminal behaviour, much research has attempted to establish the risk factors in offending.

Before embarking on an exploration of this question, it is important to understand what is meant by a risk factor. In this context, a risk factor is a variable or a combination of variables that predicts a high level of offending. For example, children who experience poor parental supervision are at increased risk of engaging in criminal behaviour later on. Risk factors should be distinguished from causes of offending – the risk factors may contribute to a higher incidence of criminal behaviour but they do not necessarily cause the offending. For example, poor parental supervision per se does not cause criminal behaviour later on in life; in conjunction with other factors, however, it may contribute to its occurrence.

Understanding the risk factors at play is crucial to designing and implementing interventions to target criminal behaviour. The key risk factors for offending are well documented in the literature (Farrington 1993, 2005; Farrington, Ttofi and Coid, 2009) and can be classified at different levels of influence:

- individual factors – e.g., high impulsiveness, low intelligence
- family factors – e.g., low parental supervision and harsh and inconsistent discipline; aggressive and violent parenting and child abuse; parental conflict, disrupted families, family criminality and being part of a large family
- peer factors – e.g., associating with known offenders
- socio-economic factors – e.g., low income and poor housing
- neighbourhood or community factors – e.g., living in a high crime neighbourhood or attending a school with a large number of offending pupils.

For intervention to be successful, it is not sufficient to target only risk factors; protective factors must also be strengthened. Protective factors should not be understood simply as the absence of risk factors but as independent factors that predict a low probability of the negative outcome or factors that may interact with the risks to cancel its effect. For example, while poor parental supervision is a risk factor in delinquent behaviour, school achievement is a protective factor, as it predicts a low probability of offending.

Critical practice focus: looked-after children in the criminal justice system
Children who have been looked after in the care system, usually because of dysfunction or abuse in their own families, are significantly over-represented in the adult criminal population in the UK (Hart, 2006; Blades et al., 2011). Social and economic factors such as unemployment will play a structural part in this unfortunate reality, but the psychological factors that might lead to a young person ending up in the criminal justice system also have critical influence. Research by Schofield and her colleagues (2012) emphasized that the experience of a child or young person before coming into care must be taken into account when looking at the offending rates, and they found that these were lessened by early entry into the care system, accompanied by stability and multi-agency support. Interestingly, evidence was also produced that appropriately matched placements could serve to help reduce offending in young people who did not enter the care system until their adolescent years. Schofield and other collaborators (2015) further acknowledged the complex interplay of environmental factors as they related to offending behaviours in young people in care and additionally stressed the key role played by the individual's level of social cognition in this area.

The following is based on the work of Blades et al. (2011), who carried out a survey for the Prison Reform Trust of fifteen- to eighteen-year-olds in prison in England using a methodology that involved eliciting the views of young people in care about reasons for offending behaviours. Their lack of any bonding with stable adult figures, both professional and personal, comes through in the testimonies, which also highlight perceptions and experiences of being discriminated against merely by virtue of being in care:

> What I've heard from different police officers when I've been arrested, it's like, 'you're a kid in care, you're never [going to] get out of this way of life. You're in care, kids in care are always on drugs, kids in care always make themselves unsafe, kids in care always self-harm'. So they sort of put a title on kids in care like they're something bad. (Blades et al., 2011: 2 [sixteen-year-old girl with a conviction])

Less than 1 per cent of all children in England are in care; however, looked-after children aged between ten and seventeen are five times as likely to be convicted, or subject to a final warning or reprimand, than other children. Blades et al. (2011) reported that a quater of boys and half of all girls in custody in recent years have spent some time in care. Frequent changes of residential homes or foster placements increased the likelihood of custody for these children.

It was not the aspect of being in care that was put forward by the young people interviewed by Blades and her colleagues (2011) as the only or main reason for their offending or that of others but, rather, a more complex set of circumstances, many of which call for better social work and psychological intervention:

- loss of, or infrequent contact with, family or friends
- poor relationships with carers and social workers
- difficult relationships with peers or peer pressure
- type and number of placements.

The authors put forward a seven-point plan for policy-makers and practitioners designed to promote protective factors to reduce offending by children in care:

1 proactive care planning
2 getting the placement right
3 being aware of family influences
4 nurturing children's aspirations
5 recognizing the importance of relationships with adults
6 working across agencies
7 being a good parent.

It is indeed important that social workers should see the care planning process as an individualized and meaningful process that considers the psychology behind a young person's offending. The need to hear the young person's own voice is all too often overlooked when care planning is seen only as an administrative task. 'Getting the placement right' is a difficult challenge because what may seem a good match on paper does not allow for the idiosyncratic and psychological dynamics that are often the intangible elements leading to successful placements. Family influence is also an unpredictable dynamic that can work against a care setting when trying to raise a young person's aspirations, and hence it is essential that there are adult role models on whom they can rely for emotional and practical support. The high turnover rate of social workers (Laming, 2009) is such that foster carers or residential staff are often the only adults who can provide this stability. Blades et al. (2011) put forward a convincing argument, informed by the voices of children and young people, for staff in care settings to be better trained and aware of the issues surrounding offending behaviours. However, since 2011 the numbers of children in the care system involved with the criminal justice system has remained highly disproportionate, leading to the Prison Welfare Trust (2015) announcing a further review, to be led by Lord Laming.

Parenting style and child criminal behaviour: how upbringing and family relationships contribute to criminal behaviour

One of the early factors that can predispose individuals towards criminal activity later on in life is the style of parenting they have received. There are three main aspects of parenting that have been linked to criminal behaviour: the presence, or absence, of appropriate and consistent discipline, supervision, and parent–child interactions (Farrington, 1993, 2005).

Based on the type and amount of discipline applied, Baumrind (1978) classified parenting styles as authoritarian, permissive (this could be permissive indulgent or permissive neglectful) and authoritative. Authoritarian parents demand obedience and apply punishment to maintain control over the child's behaviour. This often results in harsh and ineffective discipline, such as disproportionate and repeated reprimands for relatively minor behaviours, parent–child interactions being hostile, and supervision being authoritarian rather than nurturing. This style of parenting appears to have the opposite of the desired effect, as children often rebel and are consequently more prone to engage in delinquent behaviour (Bornstein, 2005).

A permissive neglectful parenting style is associated with inconsistent but harsh discipline, while the permissive indulgent parenting style is also inconsistent in discipline but has nurturing interactions. Both can result in children failing to internalize appropriate controls, which can in turn result in antisocial behaviour. The caveat is that the nurturing interactions of the indulgent style moderate the negative effects to some extent, and the behaviours tend to materialize in rebelliousness rather than typically delinquent behaviour.

Authoritative parenting styles balance nurturing interactions with constructive discipline around clear boundaries and proportionate and consistent consequences for unacceptable behaviour. As a result, children learn to take responsibility for their actions and are less likely to engage in criminal or delinquent behaviour than those who have been raised using the other parenting styles.

Although there are other factors in life that influence a propensity towards criminal behaviour, parenting style has been consistently identified as central (Scott et al., 2010).

Discussion

An example of neglectful parenting is shown by a single mother, separated from her abusive partner, who is isolated and trying to bring up two teenage boys, aged twelve and fourteen. Because of the mother's depression and her constant struggle to make ends meet financially, she may find that she does not have the energy constantly to set boundaries for her boys. Consequently she does not discipline them at all, lets them smoke in the house, lets them swear at her and hit her when they do not get their own way, and colludes with their refusals to go to school, especially on cold mornings.

Clearly, it is difficult for any single mother to discipline teenage boys effectively, but not to set any boundaries is not what children want, and the unchecked use of violence in the home and lack of school attendance are likely to lead these two boys into a future career of offending.

However, the association between parenting practices and the aetiology of delinquency needs to be interpreted with caution and not in a simply causal way, as many other factors are at play in the emergence of delinquent behaviour. Scott et al. (2010), in a large-scale English study, found that negative parenting styles involving harsh and inconsistent discipline were directly linked to more severe antisocial behaviour in children, even after a range of family socio-economic factors were taken into account. Schroeder and Mowen's (2014) study investigated the impact of shifts in parenting on juvenile offending and, as acknowledged by Scott et al. (2010), emphasized the importance of taking into account the ways in which parent–child interactions change as children grow. Parenting practices are also affected by certain stressful conditions, such as divorce, and thus it is important to understand that parenting style is much more fluid than suggested, for example, by Baumrind's (1978) typology.

Moreover, the associations between parenting style and later delinquency have to be interpreted with caution, as research has shown that there are significant differences on the effects of harsh discipline across various cultures. For example, physical discipline in childhood was shown to increase the risk of European-American adolescents' externalizing behaviours – such as aggression, violence, and trouble at school and with the police – but decrease that of African-American children (Lansford et al., 2004). While one mechanism for such findings may be children's cognitive interpretations of the experience of physical discipline based on their cultural backgrounds, there are alternative explanations that need to be explored. For example, how are African-American adolescents learning not to use violence to solve problems when their parents use physical punishment to discipline them (Lansford et al., 2005)?

Reflective point

Reflect on your relationship with your parent(s) as a child. Which type of parenting style would it fit into? Did your parents' style change over time as you grew up? If so, what determined the change and what impact did this have on your behaviour? Identify any protective factors that moderated the effects.

Task

Research has shown that there is a link between negative peer experiences and antisocial behaviour and, in particular, suggests that school bullying may act as a strong predictor for later offending.

Retrieve one of the research articles below based on the Cambridge Study in Delinquent Development. Critically evaluate its findings.

- To what extent are later violence and offending linked to school bullying?
- To what extent are other inter-related factors, such as poor education and poverty, linked to offending behaviour?

Farrington, Bullying as a predictor of offending, violence and later life outcomes.

Ttofi et al., School bullying as a predictor of violence later in life: a systematic review and meta-analysis of prospective longitudinal studies.

Working with adult and child victims of crime

The effects of criminal victimization

Being a victim of crime or witnessing criminal behaviour is traumatic. In the immediate aftermath of a crime, the effects of being victim or witness are similar to the effects of other traumas, including physiological reactions such as shock and numbness, and psychological effects, such as severe anxiety or denial. Negative psychological reactions are shown to occur even in cases where the victim did not confront the perpetrator directly – such in the case of a house burglary in the absence of the owners. Individual reactions are dependent on the type of crime to which the person is subjected – e.g., sexual assaults are considered to have the most negative impact – but there are also gender differences. For example, both men and women are severely and negatively affected by rape, but they deal with the effects differently: male victims are more likely to feel hostile, anxious and depressed than female victims (Frazier, 1993). A potential explanation for such differences may be found in the way that gender roles are stereotyped in our society, with men being expected to retaliate to violence with hostility and not to show their emotions, thus leading to internalizing and eventual depression (Chapleau et al., 2008). Similar gender stereotypes may be at play in reporting rape – for instance, it has been documented that men are less likely to report rape as they feel it may impact negatively on their masculinity (Pino and Meier, 1999). Being aware of such gender differences is important in practice, as dealing in the same way with male and female victims of rape may not be effective.

A large part of the cognitive process of coming to terms with being a victim of crime consists of the attempt to understand its causes – why it happened and 'why me?' – and this also holds true for witnesses and people hearing about a crime from a third party. Among psychological perspectives, attribution theory (Seligman, 1972) postulates that there is a human propensity to seek the causes of events and to explain both their own or others' behaviours, especially when these are unexpected or unusual. People's thinking in making sense of victimization has been shown to contain certain cognitive errors or judgements about why the event occurred, and these may interfere with their coming to terms with the trauma experienced. For example, attributional errors such as counterfactual thinking ('if only') and hindsight bias, while helping the victim in making sense of the event, are related to self-blame, which may hinder their progress towards recovery. In the case of rape – which is essentially an event over which a victim has no control – thinking along the lines of 'If only I had not accepted that drink from a stranger' or, 'In hindsight, I did wear a short skirt that day' is inducing self-blame and is counterproductive to their recovery. Cognitive therapy attempts to change such attributions.

In the long term, the impact of crime can induce post-traumatic stress disorder (PTSD) in victims. PTSD is diagnosed around the manifestation of three clusters of behaviour: re-experiencing the traumatic event via flashbacks, nightmares and intrusive thoughts; suppression and avoidance of trauma reminders; and experiencing general anxiety. Research in this area has been inconclusive, pointing to multiple factors that are involved in the development of PTSD, and it is important to note that not all individuals experiencing trauma will develop the condition. Rape is one trauma that commonly induces PTSD symptoms (Mezey, 1997).

A contemporary example of the effects of victimization – the Jimmy Savile case

The UK has recently seen a spate of celebrities (e.g., Jimmy Savile, Gary Glitter, Rolf Harris) being found guilty of historical rapes and sexual abuse of children. The victims (predominantly women) who have come forward with allegations, often after several decades, have variously been portrayed both as brave and as 'gold-diggers'. The fact that so many cases have been found proven favours the 'brave school', and it is difficult to imagine what the psychological effects of living with such abuse might be in terms of the victims' feeling of self-worth and distorted perceptions of sexual relationships. The report *Giving Victims a Voice* (Gray and Watt, 2013) into the Jimmy Savile case found that abuse caused psychological problems such as mental ill-health and substance abuse throughout victims' lives. The words of one woman are illustrative:

I was too embarrassed because he was Jimmy Savile. You don't want to get him into trouble. He was Jimmy Savile and I couldn't say a bad word against him. I was scared what the repercussions would be if I did scream, so I just let it go. I went from being a quiet person and an innocent person at that age, and I went the opposite. I became quite promiscuous in my 20s. I tended to gravitate towards older men for some reason or other, I don't know why. (BBC News, 2015a)

This victim kept her abuse hidden for over ten years, before confiding initially in her husband. It is also important to note that those close to a victim may also be negatively and significantly affected by the event, a phenomenon known as secondary traumatization. For example, in social work practice is important to consider that non-offending parents of a child victim may be affected by the trauma of the abuse. Moreover, in cases of crimes against children, family members may be suspects, thus adding great complexity to the social workers' difficulties.

Attitudes towards crime

Many people who have been victims of crime do not tell anyone about their experience for a variety of reasons – including fear of not being believed or being blamed, or feeling ashamed. In particular, victims of rape and sexual assault are not likely to report what has happened to them, and this is linked to the negative societal attitudes about rape, rape victims and rapists (Suarez and Gadalla, 2010). Many people do not report sexual crimes from fear of being negatively evaluated and may instead internalize such attitudes and blame themselves, which in turn affects their recovery.

Unfortunately this holds true in cases involving children, and in certain situations victims are being negatively evaluated after sexual abuse and rape (Finkelhor and Browne, 1985). For example, the age of the child has an influence on how they are viewed: in the case of young children, the blame tends to be attributed to the perpetrator, whereas some responsibility for the abuse may be attributed to older children (Olafson, 2011).

Focus: childhood sexual exploitation (CSE) and victim blaming

Much political and professional attention in recent times has been focused on child sexual exploitation (CSE), a form of abuse involving children and those under eighteen in exploitative situations, contexts and relationships, where young people (or a third person or persons) receive 'something' (e.g., food, accommodation, drugs, alcohol, cigarettes, affection, gifts, money) as a result of their performing, and/or another or others performing on them, sexual activities (National Working Group Network on Tackling Child Sexual Exploitation, 2015).

Among particular CSE scandals to have received wide media attention are those in Rotherham, Derby, Oxford and Peterborough. Most of these have centred on 'gangs' of Asian male abusers preying on vulnerable white girls, although CSE across the UK is a far more diverse and complex problem, and white males are statistically its main perpetrators. Large-scale abuse such as that in Rotherham has been characterized by political and professional cover-ups and an unwillingness to admit the scale of the problem, especially where cross-racial sensitivities are involved. Particularly relevant to this chapter are the experiences of young victims who were not believed by professionals and who were pathologized as knowing what they were getting into rather than being viewed as vulnerable young people whose welfare should have been paramount. The Jay Report (Jay, 2014: 4.14) stated that

> In just over a third of cases, children affected by sexual exploitation were previously known to services because of child protection and child neglect. There was a history of domestic violence in 46% of cases. Truancy and school refusal were recorded in 63% of cases and 63% of children had been reported missing more than once.

Despite the clear vulnerability of children and young people from such backgrounds, the Jay Report found examples of staff and politicians blaming and disbelieving them:

- The Police had responded reluctantly to missing person reports, as a 'waste of time'. Some young women had been threatened with arrest for wasting police time;
- The young women concerned were often seen by the Police as being deviant or promiscuous. The adult men with whom they were found were not questioned;
- Some Police said that if young people were not prepared to help themselves by making complaints against their abusers and giving evidence, they would take no further action on the case.

Similar blaming behaviours are reported elsewhere in the literature on CSE. For example, the report *If Only Someone Had Listened* (Berelowitz et al., 2013) found that some key players, who should have been the champions of vulnerable children, displayed beliefs that further victimized the victims. One chair of a local children's safeguarding board is reported as saying of the young people involved: 'They are just prostituting themselves.' Reports on missing children, so often linked to sexual exploitation risks, have also shown discriminatory attitudes by professional social workers and residential care workers, who view these young people as wasting their time (Ofsted, 2013).

Case study

The Jay Report (2014: 36) provides some illuminative examples of children involved in CSE, such as the case of Child O.

> Child O (2013) was 13 when concerns about sexual exploitation emerged. She was wandering around Rotherham late at night, often in the company of an older girl who was a known victim of sexual exploitation. She was found in Sheffield on one occasion. She was often angry and violent towards family members, and they did not seem able to protect her. She was very active on social media sites and had acquired many adult associates whom she perceived to be her friends. She posted information online about a video she had seen of another child being sexually assaulted. The suspected perpetrator made contact with her and threatened if she said anything she would be the next victim. She was beaten up but neither she nor her parents were willing to disclose this to the Police. The risks to Child O were understood and documented by the CSE team, and a programme of preventive work was put in place. Nevertheless, Child O remained secretive about where she was when missing and whom she associated with. She continued to be at risk of exploitation.

Task
Consider how you might explain this behaviour on behalf of Child O. You might take into account any issues of self-esteem or the need to feel 'loved', or whether Child O might be a victim of post-traumatic stress. What kind of relationships might she have witnessed in her own home background? Had she ever received any counselling or other forms of psychological support to help her keep safe?

Discussion
Very little psychological support has been offered to victims of CSE across the country. Of the few psychological assessments carried out into cases where children had continued to have a relationship with their perpetrator, this was often diagnosed as a result of psychological damage rather than wilfulness on behalf of the young person. Many victims never recognized that they had been groomed and exploited and often blamed themselves. The Crown Prosecution Service (CPS) has drawn up some helpful guidance for professionals designed to look beyond the presenting behaviours and attitudes of children and young people involved and to guide prosecutors towards dispelling stereotypes and myths in an attempt to change the culture regarding CSE and criminality. This guidance (CPS, 2013: Annex C) challenges the following stereotypes and myths:

- the victim invited sex by the way they dressed or acted
- the victim used alcohol or drugs and was therefore sexually available

- the victim didn't scream, fight or protest so they must have been consenting
- the victim didn't complain immediately, so it can't have been a sexual assault
- the victim is in a relationship with the alleged offender and is therefore a willing partner
- a victim should remember events consistently
- children can consent to their own sexual exploitation
- CSE is only a problem in certain ethnic/cultural communities
- only girls and young women are victims of child sexual abuse
- children from BME backgrounds are not abused
- there will be physical evidence of abuse.

Guidelines such as these offer a proactive step forward in challenging mind-sets regarding CSE, and it is important for those working with victims to reflect on and understand their own, often automatic or subconscious, negative evaluations towards certain victims. Practitioners need to be aware that certain victims may have been subject to specific and strong negative attributions and to work towards overcoming their self-blaming to facilitate their recovery.

Repeat and multiple victimization: the cycle of abuse

At the beginning of the chapter we considered the intergenerational transmission of criminal behaviour – the observed tendency of offending behaviour to be clustered within families and to be passed on from generation to generation. A similar phenomenon was noted in respect of criminal victimization, with some people appearing more susceptible to becoming a victim of crime. An initial explanation for such 'proneness' is that certain activities in which people are routinely involved make them more susceptible to becoming a target.

Through a process of *repeat victimization*, a person is preyed on again by the same perpetrator, and this is the case in situations of domestic violence and child abuse. Repeat victimization appears where it is difficult for the injured party to protect themselves and/or to escape from the situation without external intervention. For example, due to a multitude of factors, it is notoriously difficult for adult victims of domestic violence to escape the abusive environment.

However, some people can be subject to repeat victimization by different perpetrators over a period of time. For instance, someone who has been subjected to physical or sexual abuse as a child becomes a victim as an adult of domestic violence or rape. Such vulnerability to *multiple victimization* has been explained by the 'traumatogenic model' (Finkelhor and Browne, 1985), which suggests that the negative effects of child sexual abuse – traumatic sexualization, powerlessness, stigma – can make the victim psychologically vulnerable in turn to further victimization as they grow older. However, the traumatogenic model fails to explain the variability in the effects of child sexual abuse and the fact that not all affected children go on to become victims as adults.

Indeed, much recent research has focused on understanding the factors and mechanisms that protect childhood victims from being revictimized as adults. Such resilient individuals appear to show effective coping strategies, have high self-esteem, and experience positive outcomes from the disclosure of their abuse (Robboy and Anderson, 2011). Nevertheless, there is an interplay of a variety of factors, related to the individual, the abuse itself and the environment, in shaping the recovery of the victim and the risk of revictimization. It is important that practitioners are aware of the risk of revictimization and work together with their clients towards breaking the cycle of abuse. Thus interventions, while focusing on developing effective coping strategies, increasing self-esteem, and reducing symptoms of depression, need also to consider the personal circumstances both of the victim and of those close to them.

Working with offenders

Perpetrators of domestic violence and behavioural change programmes

While the perpetrators of domestic violence (DV) are predominantly men, there are very few programmes designed to help change such offenders, and social workers have been criticized for failing to engage with men involved in domestic violence and child protection cases (Cameron et al., 2014).

There is an ethical perspective that the voice of men, even those who perpetrate domestic violence, should be heard, and there is both a moral and an economic argument to be made for investment in trying to change such behaviour if it leads to men's partners and families being freed from violence and to less public spending on social care and the criminal justice systems. However, most outcome evaluations of DV programmes for male abusers are not encouraging. Tollefson et al. (2009), for example, report that most studies regarding such programmes have reported official recidivism rates in the 20 to 40 per cent range. Cessation of violence towards a partner has been criticized by Westmarland and Kelly (2013) as too restrictive a measure of success to be useful, while Stewart et al. (2013: 494) argued that DV programmes needed to 'adapt a paradigm shift, shed ideology, and determine how the maximum impact can be realized from work to reduce intimate partner violence.' They identified issues such as substance abuse, poor communication skills, and lack of motivation to change as being areas needing to be more fully considered in courses, which they recommended should also more fully embrace solution-focused and strengths-based approaches.

Reflective point

What is your personal perspective on working with men who abuse their partners?

How might you design a programme that genuinely engaged men in behavioural change?

What signs of 'disguised compliance', where men just give the expected 'right' answers to a social worker or psychologist, might you look out for?

Young offenders and ASBOs – a badge of honour?

Antisocial behaviour orders (ASBOs) were introduced in England and Wales by the Crime and Disorder Act 1998 and have been available since April 1999. Their minimum duration is two years (although they can last indefinitely), and they contain prohibitions considered necessary to prevent a repetition of a person's antisocial behaviour. Initially a modest number of ASBOs were imposed on children and young people. However, numbers have since grown rapidly.

Research conducted by the Policy Research Bureau and crime reduction charity NACRO looked at ASBOs given to under-eighteens between January 2004 and January 2005 in ten areas of England and Wales. Of 137 young people, sixty-seven had breached their order at least once, forty-two more than once, and six on six occasions or more. Among the findings of the study were that

- high levels of breach had led some sentencers to question how much impact ASBOs were having on the behaviour of individual young people
- parents (like some professionals) commonly argued that ASBOs functioned as a 'badge of honour' for the young people involved, rather than addressing the causes of the behaviour.

A summary of the study is available at http://news.bbc.co.uk/1/shared/bsp/hi/pdfs/02_11_06_asbo_summary.pdf.

Task

In light of various theories of criminal behaviour, consider why ASBOs appear to have failed in their aim to curb young people's antisocial behaviour and even to have had the opposite effect.

Focus: the hidden victims of crime – families and children of prisoners

A significant number of children are affected by their parents being in prison (Lewis et al., 2008). Over recent years there has been an interest in understanding the effects on such children's development (Geller et al., 2012), as they are more likely to face significant disadvantages and to come from families with complex needs. The experience of parental imprisonment per se can result in children undergoing loss, confusion and trauma, leading to increased mental health problems. The separation places a significant strain on parent–child relationships, and children have reported feelings of abandonment and alienation and difficulties communicating with their imprisoned parent (Sharratt, 2014). Moreover, they may experience stigmatization and bullying at school, bringing about poor school attendance and attainment. The family may experience an increase in poverty, and the remaining parent or carer has more caring responsibilities and more stress. In line with the intergenerational transmission of criminal behaviour, children of imprisoned parents are also at greater risk of offending (Murray and Farrington, 2008).

Children can have varying reactions to parental incarceration, as with any other change in family dynamics. Murray et al. (2012) suggest the quality of the relationship between parent and child before the imprisonment, the prior living arrangements, the child's age, the length of the sentence, and contact with the incarcerated parent are all factors influencing the child's response.

As a result of this increased 'vulnerability' to a variety of outcomes, it has been suggested that children who have a parent in prison are likely to need additional support and provision.

Paradoxically, such children are often not a priority for statutory services, leading to their being labelled 'a hidden group of children' (Morgan et al., 2014). This is problematic given the extent of the issue and the poorer educational, social and behavioural outcomes for the individuals concerned (Clewett and Glover, 2009). Barnardo's (2013) took a rights-based approach to working with the children of prisoners and produced a guidance document for practitioners based around eight practice messages:

- A response that can combine practical assistance (around visiting, benefits, etc.) with work around relationships and children's understanding of imprisonment is particularly valued.
- There is a need wherever possible for a prompt (that is, at the point of imprisonment) response to the family affected by imprisonment.
- Talking directly to children about prison and its impact is crucial.
- Parents often need help and support to talk to their children about imprisonment.

- Parents at home may struggle with separating their own needs from their children's in terms of relationships with the imprisoned parent.
- Not all crimes are the same in terms of the impact of parental imprisonment. Sex and serious violent crimes add to the complexity of the work with the children of prisoners.
- Workers with children of prisoners need to engage with wider family networks – particularly grandparents.
- It will often be necessary to liaise very closely with schools to support the children.

Reflective point

Do you think that these practice messages are appropriately child-centred?

In what ways would your interventions strive to promote children's best psychological health when faced with having a parent in prison?

Case study – the Brightwell family

Wayne Brightwell was described in chapter 4 as having a cocaine habit. This habit has developed to such an extent that Wayne is now spending some £200 a month on the drug and has not paid rent to his mother, Susan, for the past three months. Susan has been rather wary of Wayne, as he has been very moody lately and has snapped at her each time she has asked for the rent. He recently called her a 'dried up old hag' and said his estranged father should have hit her about more than he did, as she needed to show the men in the family more respect. Wayne also called his mother a 'waste of fuckin' space'. When she told him not to use that language, he slapped her across the face and shoved his fifteen-year-old sister Shana, who had intervened to protect her mother, into a table, causing her extensive bruising. Wayne has since refused to apologize, and Susan is unwilling to go to the police. Furthermore, Wayne has told her she will get a bigger beating next time if she 'nags' him for the rent.

Task

Looking back over this chapter, how might you account for the behaviour of Wayne and his mother in this violent development? What interventions might you suggest as most appropriate for this family situation?

Summary

Forensic knowledge is essential to the underpinning of social work practice with perpetrators and victims of crime. Psychosocial theories have been found to be helpful in reflecting on genetic and socio-environmental influences on behaviour, and there have been warnings that too deterministic an approach does not take into account the resilience of individuals and families in changing their behaviour. There are some persuasive studies, however, such as that of Weijer et al. (2014), which illustrate links between exposure to familial violence and the intergenerational transmission of criminal behaviour, as explored in the case studies of the Cavendish boys and Wayne Brightwell.

The need for early interventions in families where domestic violence is present has been a key message in the chapter, which has also given perspective to the issues around young people in care who offend, stressing the complex interplay of a range of factors involved. Parenting style has been presented as a critical factor in affecting an individual's likelihood of offending, and the provision of appropriate models has been seen as having a mediating effect even for adolescents entering care placements for the first time. Some standard typologies of parenting (e.g., Baumrind, 1978) have been critiqued for not taking sufficient account of individuals and families whose behaviours challenge such theories. The complexity of all these preceding factors in enabling criminal behaviour to be predicted has been acknowledged and the case studies have provided much opportunity for debate.

Social workers will often have contact with individuals who see themselves as victims, and recent cases have been highlighted to share media portrayals of this phenomenon. Victims' feelings of worthlessness and self-blame are very difficult for both psychologists and social workers to deal with. Investment in consistent and authentic professional relationships are presented in the chapter as being the most appropriate platform from which to effect any change, whether in offenders or victims. Regrettably, the reality of cutbacks and the consequent lessening of face-to-face contact between caring professionals and their clients make this all the harder to achieve. Some positive messages about ways forward in the field of forensic social work have been illuminated, and the core claims of social work to believe in human potential, resilience and the capacity to change have been emphasized as needing to guide all practice in this complex and challenging field.

Further reading and resources

(For full bibliographic details, see the References.)

On genetic and family influences on criminal behaviour – recent evidence from large cohort family studies:

Farrington et al., Family factors in the intergenerational transmission of offending.

Frisell et al., Violent crime runs in families: a total population study of 12.5 million individuals.

Kendler et al., The etiologic role of genetic and environmental factors in criminal behavior as determined from full- and half-sibling pairs: an evaluation of the validity of the twin method.
Kendler et al., A Swedish national adoption study of criminality.

On intergenerational transmission of aggressive and criminal behaviour:

Cui et al., Intergenerational transmission of relationship aggression: a prospective longitudinal study.
Weijer et al., The intergenerational transmission of violent offending.

Child maltreatment and later aggression and criminality:

Evans and Burton, Five types of child maltreatment and subsequent delinquency: physical neglect as the most significant predictor.
Norman et al., The long-term health consequences of child physical abuse, emotional abuse, and neglect: a systematic review and meta-analysis.
Øverlien, Children exposed to domestic violence: conclusions from the literature and challenges ahead.
Sousa et al., Longitudinal study on the effects of child abuse and children's exposure to domestic violence, parent–child attachments, and antisocial behavior in adolescence.

Looked-after children and offending behaviour:

Blades et al., *Care – a Stepping Stone to Custody? The Views of Children in Care on the Links between Care, Offending and Custody.*
Schofield et al., Looked after children and offending: an exploration of risk, resilience and the role of social cognition.
Schofield et al., *Looked After Children and Offending: Reducing Risk and Promoting Resilience.*

Childhood origins of antisocial behaviour:

Farrington, Childhood origins of teenage antisocial behaviour and adult social dysfunction.
Farrington, Childhood origins of antisocial behaviour.
Schroeder and Mowen, Parenting style transitions and delinquency.
Scott et al., *How is Parenting Style Related to Child Antisocial Behaviour? Preliminary Findings from the Helping Children Achieve Study.*

A classic article on the early conceptualizations of child sexual abuse:

Finkelhor and Browne, The traumatic impact of child sexual abuse: a conceptualization.

An up-to-date consideration of child sexual abuse and its impact on victims and coping:

CPS, *Guidelines on Prosecuting Cases of Child Sexual Abuse.*
Olafson, Child sexual abuse: demography, impact, and interventions.
Robboy and Anderson, Intergenerational child abuse and coping.

Child sexual exploitation in the UK:

Berelowitz et al., *'If Only Someone Had Listened': Office of the Children's Commissioner's Inquiry into Child Sexual Exploitation in Gangs and Groups: Final Report.*

Children and parental imprisonment:

Morgan et al., 'A hidden group of children': support in schools for children who experience parental imprisonment.
Murray and Farrington, Parental imprisonment: effects on boys' antisocial behaviour and delinquency through the life-course.
Murray and Farrington, Evidence-based programs for children of prisoners.
Murray and Farrington, Parental imprisonment: long-lasting effects on boys' internalizing problems through the life course.

8 Conclusions

This book has covered a wide range of psychological theories, models and methods that are relevant to contemporary social work, a profession which has moved away from its psychological roots in recent years. The importance of remaining close to those roots has been a core theme, and the chapters have outlined key psychological theories and interventions and related them to contemporary social work concerns and practice. Each chapter has been designed in an interactive way that encourages reflection on personal and professional development, using key psychological theories and ways of approaching individuals, groups and communities. The reflective points and case studies can be used for the purposes of self-reflection, paired reflection or group reflection.

The book has been co-written by experienced authors from the respective fields of psychology and social work and has considered a wide range of perspectives on the issues of domestic abuse, institutional abuse, fostering and adoption, child sexual exploitation, substance abuse, mental health and dementia. Discussion of group work, teamwork, employee life cycles and managerialism, and the challenges they present to the workforce, have taken account of the psychological needs of social workers. These complex topics have been theorized and then applied via a series of case studies which reflect the reality of modern social work. Serious case reviews and national matters of concern, such as the abuse at the Mid Staffordshire Hospital (Francis, 2013) and Winterbourne View (Department of Health, 2012b), have been analysed alongside the effects on victims of celebrity sex scandals. The lives of the fictitious Brightwell family have been interwoven in case studies throughout the book, exploring the applicability of psychological constructs and interventions to their individual, group and community needs.

The psychological issues discussed have been clearly placed within the contemporary reality of a hard-pressed social work profession, ever more tightly managed and publicly criticized as it attempts to tackle new challenges brought about by social changes such as immigration, demographic changes such as the rise in numbers of very dependent elderly people, and technological changes such as the exponential growth of social media and their consequences for vulnerable children and adults. Mixed messages from several decades of neo-liberal governments fixated on public-service cut-backs and performance management regimes have dominated social work at the expense of a commitment to relationship- and psychological-based ways of working. Hope for the future of social work and a recommitment to some of its core values of empowerment, anti-discriminatory practice and social justice took a backward step with the government's closure of the College of Social Work (TCSW) in 2015. However, such values have been held aloft by a reinvigorated and increasingly politicized British Association of Social Workers, whose membership as the strong and independent voice of social work has grown rapidly. BASW has also taken over responsibility from the TCSW for the Professional Capabilities Framework (PCF). This is the main legacy of the TCSW and is the framework against which a social worker's professional development is facilitated and measured throughout their career, from pre-qualifying to advanced status. The relevance of the PCF at qualifying level is stated at the beginning of each chapter, as is the corresponding fit of the latter's content with the regulatory demands of the Health Professionals Council (HCPC), the professional body responsible for the conduct and integrity of the social work profession.

Managerialism and the performance-dominated nature of social work have a firm grip on the profession, despite a lack of evidence that these meth-ods of working have actually improved the lives of the vulnerable adults and children with whom psychologists and social workers are involved (Laming, 2009; Munro, 2011; Featherstone et al., 2014). While there is much evidence that the social work profession is in crisis in terms of stress levels and reten-tion of staff (Curtis et al., 2010), the government has largely ignored the messages of reports they have commissioned that declared the need to aban-don many of their performance management initiatives (e.g., SWRB, 2010; Munro, 2011) and return to a knowledge-based learning culture such as that promoted here. The standard response of neo-liberal governments in the face of criticism and professional failings is to blame the staff, commission fur-ther reports, increase audit and inspection, and threaten privatization. This mantra will be a difficult one to change. However, the more that social work-ers and their organizations use knowledge such as that explored in this book to argue for change, possibly together with their community psychology col-leagues, the greater the likelihood that such change will actually come about. The recent Psychologists against Austerity movement is a most encouraging example of social work and psychology uniting in a common cause: its adher-ents recognize that the plight of their respective clients is often the result of government policy rather than individual dysfunction.

A knowledge-based learning culture for social work, informed by the range of psychological information discussed in this book, would better facilitate families such as the Brightwells and would be more likely to lead to estates such as Mossford experiencing positive and healthy outcomes. We have used this particular case study throughout this book to ground some of the psychological theory discussed. Although we do not know how many social workers might have assisted a family such as the Brightwells over the course of a year, there are likely to have been several changes of personnel. Such levels of turnover prevent the development of effective working relationships with clients and colleagues and mean that people are processed through social work systems rather than given the opportunity to explore issues that could lead to transformational change. Greater attention to the messages from organizational psychology might lead to greater stability within social work teams, whose members would be likely to stick around to provide the consistency and continuity desired by their clients.

The involvement of multiple professionals with the same family and the problems that this can bring, especially when different knowledge and value bases are present, have been discussed throughout the book. Psychologists and social workers do not train together in any systematic way as part of their university or post-qualifying training, despite the large amount of common ground they share. The subject matter here is clearly relevant to those training or practising in social work but also of interest to undergraduates or postgraduates in psychology who might be considering a career in social work. While professional psychologists require a doctoral qualification, after which they can specialize in one of the various fields, a social worker can attain professional status after successful completion of an undergraduate course. The higher academic qualification threshold is one reason why the psychology professions have enjoyed superior status and have not been as oppressed as their social work colleagues by managerialism and the performance management culture. Psychologists have greater freedom and professional discretion to use a range of interventions with individuals and families, but social workers who can adapt and apply the knowledge gained through reading this book may find that they, too, are granted greater professional discretion to try different approaches. Coimbra et al. (2012) suggest that now may be the time to abandon the performance management regimes which take up so much professional time and for this lost time to be spent building relationships in ways that are critically informed by psychological theory. Both the quality and the longevity of the working lives of social workers are likely to benefit from such a radical change in direction, but the main beneficiaries are likely to be families such as the Brightwells and estates such as Mossford. Relationship-based forms of working, drawing on a blend of social work and psychological knowledge about families and their social and community environments will lead to authentic and effective interventions rather than the superficial ones that, in recent years, have sometimes led to the neglect and deaths of the vulnerable.

A post-view of the book

Looking back on the individual chapters in this book, the opening chapter, 'The Place of Psychological Knowledge and Research in Social Work Training and Practice', set out the contemporary environment – the managerialism, the media profile and the retention issues – in the face of greater demands and expectations. The loss of many of the social work profession's psychological roots was reflected upon and arguments put forward as to why the interest and knowledge in psychology should be rekindled. The complex nature of social work caseloads and the potential contribution of psychology in helping manage such work were discussed. The research base of different branches of psychology was also explored. The fictitious case study of the Brightwells, a family likely to have much in common with real cases known to social work, was introduced as a core reference point to be used throughout the book.

Chapter 2, 'Signposts from Developmental Psychology on Human Development over the Life Course', explored the main concepts and theories of development, such as attachment, cognitive and moral development, the theory of mind, and theories of the life course. The seminal authorities on human development and socio-cultural development across the fields of psychodynamics, behaviourism and cognitive development were discussed in ways that made them applicable to the world of social work. Case studies on topics such as substance abuse, adoption, fostering and sexual abuse were used to illuminate the benefits of psychological approaches to working with individuals and families. A life-course approach was presented as a most helpful avenue for social workers, whose clients are likely to have experienced discontinuous styles of development in lives often characterized by stress and trauma. It was acknowledged how difficult it is for social workers, who practise in more generic ways than most psychologists, to be able to have a deep knowledge of all developmental theories, but the importance of a sufficient understanding of other approaches was emphasized. Knowledge of psychological theory and interventions concerning issues of human development were positioned as critical for social workers assessing risk and vulnerability in adults and children.

Chapter 3, 'Perspectives from Clinical and Counselling Psychology on Mental Health and Illness', placed its focus on mental health, a core concern for both adult and children's social workers. A spectrum of psychological approaches to mental health was covered, from medical models that seek to cure to counselling-type models that empower clients to determine their own mental health. The importance of raising the profile of individual therapies within a performance-managed world of social work was emphasized and the need to reinvest in relationship-based practice was again championed. The theoretical models that explain a range of mental health problems, such as anxiety, depression, mood disorders and eating disorders, were related to practice interventions. It is important that social workers appreciate what type of help their clients may be receiving from other professionals and agencies, and the knowledge gained from this chapter should also encourage social workers to be inquisitive and find out more about clinical and counselling interventions and their likely outcomes. A specific focus of the chapter was the effect of poor mental health in parents on the well-being of children and on cultural considerations within the complex field of mental health.

Chapter 4, 'Perspectives from Social and Community Psychology: Understanding Values, Attitudes, Diversity and Community Change', emphasized how closely these disciplines relate to social work in their commitment to operating from explicit value bases and in their focus on behaviours in social and community settings respectively. The values and aims of community psychology were shown to have particular synergy with social work in their respective commitments to social justice and social change. Issues central to social work, such as tackling discrimination and working in anti-discriminatory ways, were highlighted and further explored in reflective points and case studies concerned with issues such as child sexual exploitation, disablism and domestic abuse. The social psychology that surrounds institutional abuse, with specific reference to the scandals at Winterbourne View (Department of Health, 2012b) and Mid Staffordshire (Francis, 2013), was examined, as were new initiatives such as the adult personalization agenda. Stereotyping and prejudice and the effect that such behaviours have in the working lives of social workers were also explored, together with strategies for community development, culminating in the case study of Mossford, the fictional housing estate where the Brightwell family lives.

Chapter 5, 'Health Psychology: Understanding Health, Illness, Stress and Addiction', provided analysis of the links between psychological processes – knowledge that is very relevant to social workers, who deal with cases of mental and physical health across a range of age groups. Research findings and a series of different health psychology theories, such as the health belief model and the trans-theoretical model of change, were examined to provide social workers with greater insight into work with clients and the ways of fellow health professionals. Health psychology also shares much common ground with social work, and practitioners can relate in particular to the bio-psychosocial model when they look in any depth at the complexity of factors that have shaped the health and welfare of their clients. Case examples around dementia, obesity and neglect were used to illuminate the issues of health psychology.

Chapter 6, 'Organizational Psychology: Understanding the Individual and the Organization in the Social Work Structure', provided insights into the contemporary social work environment that are helpful in enabling professionals to step outside of their everyday environment and to try to achieve that much talked about work–life balance. Retention rates are low in social work, stress levels are high, and burnout is common in a profession where staff should be highly esteemed and rewarded for the most difficult job they carry out on behalf of society. Techniques for combating work-based stress were explored and models of the employee life cycle employed to help conceptualize the stresses and strains at various stages of employment. Better understanding of organizations, better ways to effect multi-disciplinary working, and how to gain support in challenging policies and practices were all offered in this chapter. The mixed messages from government about the role and value of social work were noted in terms of their wider psychological effect, but hope for better days is seen in the growing strong and independent voice of BASW and the consensus among a wide range of academics, inquiries and government-sponsored reports that the current domination of performance management systems at the expense of person-centred work must change.

Chapter 7, 'Forensic Psychology: Understanding Criminal Behaviour and Working with Victims of Crime', discussed the relevance of forensic psychology to much of social work, placed as it is at the intersection between psychology and the criminal justice system. Psychosocial theories were presented as helpful ways of looking at genetic and socio-environmental influences on behaviour, with notes of caution being sounded about taking too deterministic an approach in this area. There was discussion of individual capacities to change behaviour and break cycles of violence and abuse, as well as resilience in terms of resisting criminal tendencies. The theories of genetic influence and intergenerational transmission of criminal behaviours were considered before being applied to case studies concerned with both risk and protective factors. Particular areas of focus in this chapter were the effects on the families and children of prisoners, the influence of parenting styles, the need for early intervention in situations involving domestic violence, and professional attitudes towards young people who are looked after or at risk of criminalization. The effects of victimization on psychological well-being, using testimony from recent celebrity sex scandals, highlighted the types of trauma, self-blame and feelings of worthlessness which many people have to endure for a lifetime. Again, investing in relationship-based work and recognizing individual potential to change offered positive ways forward in this most challenging area of social work.

Final reflections

Overall, this book has captured the essence of the modernized social work environment and argued for a return to a skills- and relationship-based profession that makes use of psychological knowledge to inform assessments and interventions. No single psychological approach is going to solve the complex problems of a family such as the Brightwells or an estate such as Mossford, but drawing on a number of psychological fields offers greater chance of successful outcomes. Measures of self-esteem, resilience and well-being are difficult to determine convincingly in a performance-managed world, but these are the measures that matter to the foster child, the patient with dementia and the overworked social worker. Giving greater attention to all psychological concerns in the workplace and communities of practice is a positive way of improving social work, and we hope that this book will play a part in such a turn of direction.

References

Abrahams, C. (1994) *Hidden Victims: Children and Domestic Violence*. London, NCH Action for Children.

Adorno, T. W., Frenkel-Brunswik, E., Levinson, D. J., and Sanford, R. N. (1950) *The Authoritarian Personality*. New York: W. W. Norton.

Agras, W. S. (2001) The consequences and costs of the eating disorders, *Psychiatric Clinics of North America*, 24: 371–9.

Ajzen, I. (1988) *Attitudes, Personality and Behaviour*. Maidenhead: Open University Press.

Alexander, S. M., Baur, L. A., Magnusson, R., and Tobin, B. (2009) When does severe childhood obesity become a child protection issue?, *Medical Journal of Australia*, 190(3): 136–9.

Allen, T. D., and Armstrong, J. (2006) Further examination of the link between work–family conflict and physical health: the role of health-related behaviors, *American Behavioral Scientist*, 49(9): 1204–21.

Allport, G. W. (1985) The historical background of social psychology, in G. Lindzey and E. Aronson (eds), *Handbook of Social Psychology*. 3rd edn, New York: Random House, Vol. 1, pp. 1–46.

Alzheimer's Society (2015a) What is dementia?, www.alzheimers.org.uk/site/scripts/documents_info.php?documentID=106.

Alzheimer's Society (2015b) Rarer causes of dementia, www.alzheimers.org.uk/site/scripts/documents_info.php?documentID=135.

Ar-Yuwat, S., Clark, M. J., Hunter, A., and James, K. S. (2013) Determinants of physical activity in primary school students using the health belief model, *Journal of Multidisciplinary Health*, 6: 119–26.

Atkinson, M., Jones, M., and Lamont, E. (2007) *Multi-Agency Working and its Implications for Practice: A Review of the Literature*, www.nfer.ac.uk/nfer/publications/MAD01/MAD01.pdf.

Baghianimoghadam, M. H., Mohammadi, S., Noorbala, M. T., and Mahmoodabad, A. M. (2011) An intervention based on protection motivation theory in reducing skin cancer risk, *Journal of Pakistan Association of Dermatologists*, 21(3): 141–8.

Baldwin, M. (1987) Interview with Carl Rogers on the use of the self in therapy, *Journal of Psychotherapy & the Family*, 3(1): 45–52.

Baltes, P. B. (1987) Theoretical propositions of life-span developmental psychology: on the dynamics between growth and decline, *Developmental Psychology*, 23(5): 611–26.

Baltes, P. B., and Smith, J. (2004) Lifespan psychology: from developmental contextualism to developmental biocultural co-constructivism, *Research in Human Development*, 1(3): 123–44.

Baltes, P. B., Staudinger, U. M., and Lindenberger, U. (1999) Lifespan psychology: theory and application to intellectual functioning, *Annual Review of Psychology*, 50(1): 471–507.

Bandura, A. (1978) Social learning theory of aggression, *Journal of Communication*, 28(3): 12–29.

Banks, S. (2010) Integrity in professional life: issues of conduct, commitment and capacity, *British Journal of Social Work*, 40(7): 2168–84.

Barnardo's (2013) *Working with Children with a Parent in Prison: Messages for Practice from Two Barnardo's Pilot Services*, www.barnardos.org.uk/working-with-children-with-a-parent-in-prison.pdf.

Barnett, E. (2006) *Serious Case Review: In Respect of the Death of Case No. 1.* Birmingham: Birmingham Safeguarding Children Board,

BASW (British Association of Social Workers) (2012) *The Code of Ethics for Social Work: Statement of Principles*, http://cdn.basw.co.uk/upload/basw_112315-7.pdf.

BASW (British Association of Social Workers) (2015) Professional Capabilities Framework, www.basw.co.uk/pcf/.

Bauman, Z. (2000) *Liquid Modernity*. Cambridge: Polity.

Baumrind, D. (1978) Parental disciplinary patterns and social competence in children, *Youth and Society*, 9(3): 239–67.

BBC News (2015a) Stoke Mandeville nurse: Jimmy Savile took my innocence, 26 February, www.bbc.co.uk/news/uk-31506266.

BBC News (2015b) Rebecca Kandare death: parents jailed for malnourished baby killing, 10 November, www.bbc.co.uk/news/uk-england-birmingham-34781044.

Beck, A. T. (1991) Cognitive therapy: a 30-year retrospective, *American Psychologist*, 46(4): 368–75.

Becker, S., Aldridge, J., and Dearden, C. (1998) *Young Carers and Their Families*. Oxford: Blackwell Science.

Beijersbergen, M. D., Juffer, F., Bakermans-Kranenburg, M. J., and van IJzendoorn, M. H. (2012) Remaining or becoming secure: parental sensitive support predicts attachment continuity from infancy to adolescence in a longitudinal adoption study, *Developmental Psychology*, 48(5): 1277–82.

Belbin, M. (2010) *Team Roles at Work*. London: Routledge.

Belloc, N. B., and Breslow, L. (1972) Relationship of physical health status and health practices, *Preventive Medicine*, 1(3): 409–21.

Berelowitz, S., Clifton, J., Firmin, C., Gulyurtlu, S., and Edwards, G. (2013)

'If Only Someone Had Listened': Office of the Children's Commissioner's Inquiry into Child Sexual Exploitation in Gangs and Groups: Final Report, www.childrenscommissioner.gov.uk/sites/default/files/publications/If_only_someone_had_listened.pdf.

Berelowitz, S., Firmin, C., Edwards, G., and Gulyurtlu, S. (2012) 'I thought I was the only one. The only one in the world': The Office of the Children's Commissioner's Inquiry into Child Sexual Exploitation in Gangs and Groups: Interim Report, http://dera.ioe.ac.uk/16067/1/FINAL_REPORT_FOR_WEBSITE_Child_Sexual_Exploitation_in_Gangs_and_Groups_Inquiry_Interim_Report__21_11_12.pdf.

Beresford, P. (2000) Service users' knowledges and social work theory: conflict or collaboration?, *British Journal of Social Work*, 30(4): 489–503.

Beresford, P., and Croft, S. (2004) Service users and practitioners reunited: the key component for social work reform, *British Journal of Social Work*, 34(1): 53–68.

Bifulco, A., and Thomas, G. (2013) *Understanding Adult Attachment in Family Relationships: Research, Assessment and Intervention.* London: Routledge.

Binks, C., Jones, F. W., and Knight, K. (2013) Facilitating reflective practice groups in clinical psychology training: a phenomenological study, *Reflective Practice: International and Multidisciplinary Perspectives*, 14(3): 305–18.

Bisman, C. (2004) Social work values: the moral core of the profession, *British Journal of Social Work*, 34(1): 109–23.

Blades, R., Hart, D., Lea, J., and Willmott, N. (2011) *Care – a Stepping Stone to Custody? The Views of Children in Care on the Links between Care, Offending and Custody.* Cambridge: Prison Reform Trust.

Blair, L. (2010) A critical review of the scientist-practitioner model for counselling psychology, *Counselling Psychology Review*, 25(4): 19–30.

Bornstein, M. H. (ed.) (2005) *Handbook of Parenting*, Vol. 4: *Social Conditions and Applied Parenting.* London: Psychology Press.

Bowlby, J. (1951) Maternal care and mental health, *Bulletin of the World Health Organization*, 3: 355–534.

Bowlby, J. (1958) The nature of the child's tie to his mother, *International Journal of Psycho-Analysis*, 39: 350–73.

Bowlby, J. (1982) Attachment and loss: retrospect and prospect, *American Journal of Orthopsychiatry*, 52(4): 664–78.

Brandon, M., Sidebotham, P., Bailey, S., Belderson, P., Hawley, C., Ellis, C., and Megson, M. (2012) *New Learning from Serious Case Reviews: A Two Year Report for 2009–2011*, Department for Education Research Report DFE-RR226, www.uea.ac.uk/documents/3437903/4264977/DFE-RR226_Report.pdf/cfb03bcc-2193-485b-b36d-b8f1c6c1bb35.

Bretherton, I. (1992) The origins of attachment theory: John Bowlby and Mary Ainsworth, *Developmental Psychology*, 28(5): 759–75.

British Psychological Society (2015a) Psychology and the Public, www.bps.org.uk/psychology-public/psychology-and-public.

British Psychological Society (2015b) Developmental Psychology Section, BPS, www.bps.org.uk/networks-and-communities/member-networks/developmental-psychology-section.

British Psychological Society, Division of Counselling Psychology (2005) *Professional Practice Guidelines*, www.bps.org.uk/sites/default/files/documents/professional_practice_guidelines_-_division_of_counselling_psychology.pdf.

Brown, K., and White, K. (2006) *Exploring the Evidence Base for Integrated Children's Services*. Scottish Executive Education Department, www.gov.scot/resource/doc/90282/0021746.pdf.

Brown, S. L., Nesse, R. M., Vinokur, A. D., and Smith, D. M. (2003) Providing social support may be more beneficial than receiving it: results from a prospective study of mortality, *Psychological Science*, 14(4): 320–7.

Bui, L., Mullan, B., and McCaffery, K. (2013) Protection motivation theory and physical activity in the general population: a systematic literature review, *Psychology, Health and Medicine*, 18(5): 522–42.

Cairns, K. (2002) *Attachment, Trauma and Resilience: Therapeutic Caring for Children*. London: BAAF

Callan, S., and Fry, B. (2012) *Commissioning Effective Talking Therapies*. London: Centre for Social Justice.

Cameron, A., Lart, R., Bostock, L., and Coomber, C. (2012) *SCIE Research Briefing 41: Factors that Promote and Hinder Joint and Integrated Working between Health and Social Care Services*. London: SCIE.

Cameron, D. (2009) 'The Big Society', 10 November, http://conservative-speeches.sayit.mysociety.org/speech/601246 [Hugo Young Memorial Lecture].

Cameron, G., Coady, N., and Hoy, S. (2012) Perspectives on being a father from men involved with child welfare services, *Child & Family Social Work*, 19(1): 14–23.

Care Quality Commission (2015) *Right Here Right Now: People's Experiences of Help, Care and Support during a Mental Health Crisis*. Newcastle upon Tyne: Care Quality Commission, www.cqc.org.uk/sites/default/files/20150611_righthere_mhcrisiscare_summary_3.pdf.

Carey, M. (2003) Anatomy of a care manager, *Work, Employment and Society*, 16(1): 121–35.

Carpenter, J., Schneider, J., Brandon, T., and Wooff, D. (2003) Working in multidisciplinary community mental health teams: the impact on social workers and health professionals of integrated mental health care, *British Journal of Social Work*, 33(8): 1081–103.

Chan, J., and Koren, G. (2013) Is mild–moderate drinking in pregnancy harmless? New experimental evidence to the opposite,

Journal of Population Therapeutics and Clinical Pharmacology, 20(2): 107–9.

Channel 4 (2015) *The Romanians are Coming*, www.channel4.com/programmes/the-romanians-are-coming.

Chapleau, K. M., Oswald, D. L., and Russell, B. L. (2008) Male rape myths: the role of gender, violence, and sexism, *Journal of Interpersonal Violence*, 23: 600–15.

Cheshire East LSCB (Local Safeguarding Children's Board) (2011) *Serious Case Review CE001*, www.cheshireeastlscb.org.uk/pdf/scr-executive-summary.pdf.

Chess, S., and Thomas, A. (1977) Temperamental individuality from childhood to adolescence, *Journal of the American Academy of Child Psychiatry*, 16(2): 218–26.

Chilvers, C., Dewey, M., Fielding, K., Gretton, V., Miller, P., Palmer, B., Weller, D., Churchill, R., Williams, I., Bedi, N., Duggan, C., Lee, A., and Harrison, G. (2001) Antidepressant drugs and generic counselling for treatment of major depression in primary care: randomised trial with patient preference arms, *British Medical Journal*, 322: 772–5.

Chisholm, K. (1998) A three year follow-up of attachment and indiscriminate friendliness in children adopted from Romanian orphanages, *Child Development*, 69(4): 1092–106.

Chisholm, K., Carter, M. C., Ames, E. W., and Morison, S. J. (1995) Attachment security and indiscriminately friendly behavior in children adopted from Romanian orphanages, *Development and Psychopathology*, 7(2): 283–94.

Chomsky, N. (1965) *Aspects of the Theory of Syntax*. Cambridge, MA: MIT Press.

Christensen, H., Griffiths, K. M., and Jorm, A. F. (2004) Delivering interventions for depression by using the internet: randomised controlled trial, *British Medical Journal*, 328: 265.

Churchill, R., Khaira, M., Gretton, V., Chilvers, C., Dewey, M., Duggan, C., and Lee, A. (2000) Treating depression in general practice: factors affecting patients' treatment preferences, *British Journal of General Practice*, 50: 905–6.

Clark, S. C. (2000) Work/family border theory: a new theory of work/family balance, *Human Relations*, 53: 747–70.

Clarke, A. M., and Clarke, A. D. B. (2000) *Early Experience and the Life Path*. London: Jessica Kingsley.

Cleaver, H., Unell, I., and Aldgate, J. (1999) *Children's Needs – Parenting Capacity: The Impact of Parental Mental Illness, Problem Alcohol and Drug Use, and Domestic Violence on Children's Development*. London: The Stationery Office.

Clewett, N., and Glover, J. (2009) *Supporting Prisoners' Families: How*

Barnardo's Works to Improve Outcomes for Children with a Parent in Prison, www.barnardos.org.uk/supporting_prisoners_families.pdf.

Cohen, S., and McKay, G. (1984) Social support, stress and the buffering hypothesis: a theoretical analysis, in A. Baum, S. E. Taylor and J. E. Singer (eds), *Handbook of Psychology and Health*. Hillsdale, NJ: Erlbaum, Vol. 4, pp. 253–67.

Cohen, S., Janicki-Deverts, D., and Miller, G. (2007) Psychological stress and disease, *Journal of the American Medical Association*, 298: 1685–7.

Coimbra, J. L., Duckett, P., Fryer, D., Makkawi, I., Menezes, I., Seedat, M., and Walker, C. (2012) Rethinking community psychology: critical insights, *Australian Community Psychologist*, 24(2): 135–42.

Conner, M., and Norman, P. (1996) *Predicting Health Behaviour*. Buckingham: Open University Press.

Corrie, S., and Callahan, M. M. (2000) A review of the scientist-practitioner model: reflections on its potential contribution to counselling psychology within the context of current health care trends, *British Journal of Medical Psychology*, 73: 413–27.

Corrigan, P. (2004) How stigma interferes with mental health care, *American Psychologist*, 59: 614–25.

Corrigan, P. W., and Penn, D. L. (1999) Lessons from social psychology on discrediting psychiatric stigma, *American Psychologist*, 54(9): 765–76.

Cowden, S., and Singh, G. (2007) The 'user': friend, foe or fetish? A critical exploration of user involvement in health and social care, *Critical Social Policy*, 27 (1): 5–23.

Cox, K. L., Gorely, T. J., Puddey, I. B., Burke, V., and Beilin, L. J. (2003) Exercise behaviour change in 40 to 65-year-old women: the SWEAT study (sedentary women exercise adherence trial), *British Journal of Health Psychology*, 8: 477–95.

CPS (Crown Prosecution Service) (2013) *Guidelines on Prosecuting Cases of Child Sexual Abuse*, www.cps.gov.uk/legal/a_to_c/child_sexual_abuse/.

Crisp, A. H., Gelder, M. G., Rix, S., Meltzer, H. I., and Rowlands, O. J. (2000) Stigmatisation of people with mental illnesses, *British Journal of Psychiatry*, 177(1): 4–7.

Cross, S., Hubbard, A., and Munro, E. (2010) *Reclaiming Social Work*. London: London School of Economics/Human Reliability Associates.

Cui, M., Durtschi, J. A., Donnellan, M. B., Lorenz, F. O., and Conger, R. D. (2010) Intergenerational transmission of relationship aggression: a prospective longitudinal study, *Journal of Family Psychology*, 24(6): 688–97.

Cumming, E., and Henry, W. E. (1961) *Growing Old: The Process of Disengagement*. New York: Basic Books.

Cummings, E. M., and Davies, P. T. (2010) *Marital Conflict and Children: An Emotional Security Perspective*. London: Guilford Press.

Curtis, L. A., Moriarty, J., and Netten, A. (2010) The expected working life of a social worker, *British Journal of Social Work*, 40(5): 1628–43.

Davati, A., Pirasteh, A., Yahyaei, M., and Shakouri, A. (2013) Skin protective behavior amongst girl students; based on health belief model, *Acta Medica Iranica*, 51: 626–32.

De Matt, S., Dekker, J., Schoevers, R., and De Jonghe, F. (2006) Relative efficacy of psychotherapy and pharmacotherapy in the treatment of depression: a meta-analysis, *Psychotherapy Research*, 16(5): 562–72.

Dearden, C., and Becker, S. (2000) *Growing Up Caring: Vulnerability and Transition to Adulthood – Young Carers' Experiences*. Leicester: Youth Work Press.

Department for Education (2016) *Adoption: A Vision for Change*, www.gov.uk/government/publications/adoption-a-vision-for-change.

Department of Health (1998) *Modernising Social Services*, Cm 4169, http://webarchive.nationalarchives.gov.uk/20140131031506/http://www.archive.official-documents.co.uk/document/cm41/4169/4169.htm.

Department of Health (2000) *Framework for the Assessment of Children in Need and their Families*. London: HMSO.

Department of Health (2006) *Our Health, Our Care, Our Say: A New Direction for Community Services*, Cm 6737, www.gov.uk/government/uploads/system/uploads/attachment_data/file/272238/6737.pdf.

Department of Health (2012a) *Prime Minister's Challenge on Dementia: Delivering Major Improvements in Dementia Care and Research by 2015*, www.gov.uk/government/uploads/system/uploads/attachment_data/file/215101/dh_133176.pdf.

Department of Health (2012b) *Transforming Care: A National Response to Winterbourne View Hospital*, www.gov.uk/government/uploads/system/uploads/attachment_data/file/213215/final-report.pdf.

Department of Health (2014) *Care and Support Statutory Guidance: Issued under the Care Act 2014*, www.gov.uk/government/uploads/system/uploads/attachment_data/file/315993/Care-Act-Guidance.pdf.

Department of Health and Home Office (2015) *2010 to 2015 Government Policy: Drug Misuse and Dependency*, www.gov.uk/government/publications/2010-to-2015-government-policy-drug-misuse-and-dependency.

Dickinson, H., and Glasby, J. (2010) Why partnership working doesn't work, *Public Management Review*, 12(6): 811–28.

DiClemente, C. C., Prochaska, J. O., Fairhurst, S. K., and Velicer, W. F. (1991) The process of smoking cessation: an analysis of precontemplation, contemplation, and preparation stages of change, *Journal of Consulting and Clinical Psychology*, 59: 295–304.

Downs, M., and Bowers, B. (eds) (2014) *Excellence in Dementia Care: Research into Practice*. 2nd edn, Maidenhead: Open University Press.

Duckworth, E. (1964) Piaget rediscovered, *Journal of Research in Science Teaching*, 2(3): 172–5.

Dunning, J. (2008) Personalisation, www.communitycare.co.uk/2008/08/07/personalisation/.

Edwards, N., and Rothbard, N. P. (2000) Mechanisms linking work and family: clarifying the relationship between work and family constructs, *Academy of Management Review*, 25(1): 178–99.

Edwards, S., and Turnell, A. (1999) *Signs of Safety: A Solution and Safety Oriented Approach to Child Protection Casework*. New York: W. W. Norton.

Emslie, C., Hunt, K., and Macintyre, S. (2004) Gender, work–home conflict, and morbidity amongst white-collar bank employees in the United Kingdom, *International Journal of Behavioral Medicine*, 11(3): 127–34.

Engel, G. L. (1977) The need for a new medical model: a challenge for biomedicine, *Science*, 196: 129–36.

Erikson, E. H. (1956) The concept of ego identity, *Journal of the American Psychoanalytic Association*, 4: 56–121.

Erikson, E. H. (1959) *Identity and the Life Cycle: Selected Papers*. New York: International Universities Press.

Evans, C. B., and Burton, D. L. (2013) Five types of child maltreatment and subsequent delinquency: physical neglect as the most significant predictor, *Journal of Child & Adolescent Trauma*, 6(4): 231–45.

Evans, S. E., Davies, C., and DiLillo, D. (2008) Exposure to domestic violence: a meta-analysis of child and adolescent outcomes, *Aggression and Violent Behavior*, 13(2): 131–40.

Evans, T. (2010) *Professional Discretion in Welfare Services: Beyond Street-Level Bureaucracy*. London: Ashgate.

Evans, T., and Harris, J. (2004) Street-level bureaucracy, social work and the (exaggerated) death of discretion, *British Journal of Social Work*, 34(6): 871–95.

Fairburn, C. G., and Cooper, Z. (1993) The eating disorder examination, in C. G. Fairburn, and G. T. Wilson (eds), *Binge Eating: Nature, Assessment, and Treatment*. New York: Guilford Press, pp. 317–60.

Fairburn, C. G., Shafran, R., and Cooper, Z. (1999) A cognitive behavioural theory of anorexia nervosa, *Behaviour Research and Therapy*, 37: 1–13.

Farrell, P., Woods, K., Lewis, S., Rooney, S., Squires, G., and O'Connor, M. (2006) *A Review of the Functions and Contribution of Educational Psychologists in England and Wales in Light of 'Every Child Matters: Change for Children'*. Nottingham: DfES.

Farrington, D. P. (1993) Childhood origins of teenage antisocial behaviour and adult social dysfunction, *Journal of the Royal Society of Medicine*, 86(1): 13–17.

Farrington, D. P. (2005) Childhood origins of antisocial behaviour, *Clinical Psychology & Psychotherapy*, 12(3): 177–90.

Farrington, D. P., and Ttofi, M. M. (2011) Bullying as a predictor of offending, violence and later life outcomes, *Criminal Behaviour and Mental Health*, 21(2): 90–8.

Farrington, D. P., Coid, J. W., and Murray, J. (2009) Family factors in the intergenerational transmission of offending, *Criminal Behaviour and Mental Health*, 19(2): 109–24.

Farrington, D. P., Ttofi, M. M., and Coid, J. W. (2009) Development of adolescence-limited, late-onset, and persistent offenders from age 8 to age 48, *Aggressive Behavior*, 35(2): 150–63.

Featherstone, B., Morris, K., and White, S. (2014) *Re-Imagining Child Protection: Towards Humane Social Work with Families*. Bristol: Policy Press.

Feeney, B. C., and Collins, N. L. (2015) A new look at social support: a theoretical perspective on thriving through relationships, *Personality and Social Psychology Review*, 19(2): 113–47.

Fenge, L. A. (2010) Striving towards inclusive research: an example of participatory action research with older lesbians and gay men, *British Journal of Social Work*, 40(3): 878–94.

Ferguson, I. (2008) *Reclaiming Social Work*. London: Sage.

Festinger, L. (1957) *A Theory of Cognitive Dissonance*. Stanford, CA: Stanford University Press.

Finkelhor, D., and Browne, A. (1985) The traumatic impact of child sexual abuse: a conceptualization, *American Journal of Orthopsychiatry*, 55(4): 530–41.

Firmin, C. (2013) Something old or something new: do pre-existing conceptualisations of abuse enable a sufficient response to abuse in young people's relationships and peer-groups?, in M. Melrose and J. Pearce (eds), *Critical Perspectives on Child Sexual Exploitation and Related Trafficking*. Basingstoke: Palgrave Macmillan, pp. 38–51.

Flavell, J. H. (1971) Stage-related properties of cognitive development, *Cognitive Psychology*, 2(4): 421–53.

Forrester, D., and Harwin, J. (2006) Parental substance misuse and child care social work: findings from the first stage of a study of 100 families, *Child & Family Social Work*, 11(4): 325–35.

Forrester, D., and Harwin, J. (2008) Parental substance misuse and child welfare: outcomes for children two years after referral, *British Journal of Social Work*, 38: 1518–35.

Forrester, D., Holland, S., Williams, A., and Copello, A. (2016) Helping families where parents misuse drugs or alcohol? A mixed methods comparative evaluation of an intensive family preservation service, *Child & Family Social Work*, 21(1): 65–75.

Fossey, J. (2012) Psychological treatments for people with dementia who have behavioural symptoms, *Journal of Quality Research in*

Dementia, no. 1, www.alzheimers.org.uk/site/scripts/documents_info. php?documentID=77&pageNumber=6.

Fostering Network (2015) Statistics on children in care, www.thefosteringnetwork.org.uk/advice-information/all-about-fostering/fostering-statistics.

Fraley, R. C. (2002) Attachment stability from infancy to adulthood: meta-analysis and dynamic modeling of developmental mechanisms, *Personality and Social Psychology Review*, 6(2): 123–51.

Francis, R. (2013) *Independent Inquiry into Care provided by Mid Staffordshire NHS Foundation Trust, January 2005 - March 2009*, Vol. 1. London: The Stationery Office.

Fraser, C., McIntyre, A., and Manby, M. (2009) Exploring the impact of parental drug/alcohol problems on children and parents in a Midlands county in 2005/06, *British Journal of Social Work*, 39(5): 846–66.

Frazier, P. A. (1993) A comparative study of male and female rape victims seen at a hospital-based rape crisis program, *Journal of Interpersonal Violence*, 8(1): 64–76.

Freud, S. ([1923] 2001) The ego and the id, in *The Complete Psychological Works of Sigmund Freud*. London: Vintage Books, Vol. 19, pp. 3–66.

Friedman, H. S., and Booth-Kewley, S. (1987) Personality, type A behavior, and coronary heart disease: the role of emotional expression, *Journal of Personality and Social Psychology*, 53(4): 783–92.

Frisell, T., Lichtenstein, P., and Långström, N. (2011) Violent crime runs in families: a total population study of 12.5 million individuals, *Psychological Medicine*, 41(1): 97–105.

Geller, A., Cooper, C. E., Garfinkel, I., Schwartz-Soicher, O., and Mincy, R. B. (2012) Beyond absenteeism: father incarceration and child development, *Demography*, 49(1): 49–76.

Gibbard, I., and Hanley, T. (2008) A five-year evaluation of the effectiveness of person-centred counselling in routine clinical practice in primary care, *Counselling and Psychotherapy Research*, 8(4): 215–22.

Glasby, J., and Beresford, P. (2006) Who knows best? Evidence-based practice and the service user contribution, *Critical Social Policy*, 26: 268–84.

Goffman, E. (1961) *Asylums: Essays on the Social Situation of Mental Patients and Other Inmates*. New York: Anchor Books.

Goforth, A. N., Pham, A. V., and Carlson, J. S. (2011) Diathesis-stress model, in S. Goldstein and J. A. Naglieri (eds), *Encyclopedia of Child Behavior and Development*. New York: Springer, pp. 502–3.

Goldbas, A. (2014) Childhood obesity: can it really be child neglect?, *International Journal of Childbirth Education*, 29(2): 27–40.

Golding, K. S. (2008) *Nurturing Attachments: Supporting Children who are Fostered or Adopted*. London: Jessica Kingsley.

Goleman, D. (1995) *Emotional Intelligence: Why It Can Matter More Than IQ*. New York: Bantam.

Gould, R. A., Otto, M. W., and Pollack, M. H. (1995) A meta-analysis of treatment outcome for panic disorder, *Clinical Psychology Review*, 15: 819–944.

Grant, L., and Kinman, E. (2014) 'Bouncing back?' Personal representations of resilience of student and experienced social workers, *Practice*, 25(5): 349–66.

Gray, D., and Watt, P. (2013) *'Giving Victims a Voice': Joint Report into Sexual Allegations Made against Jimmy Savile*, www.nspcc.org.uk/globalassets/documents/research-reports/yewtree-report-giving-victims-voice-jimmy-savile.pdf.

Gray, M. (2010) Moral sources and emergent ethical theories in social work, *British Journal of Social Work*, 40(6): 1794–811.

Gray, M., and Gibbons, J. (2007) There are no answers, only choices: teaching ethical decision making in social work, *Australian Social Work*, 60(2): 222–38.

Griffiths, J., and Luker, K. (1994) Intraprofessional teamwork in district nursing: in whose interests? *Journal of Advanced Nursing*, 20(6): 1038–45.

Griffiths, S., and Steen, S. (2013) Improving access to psychological therapies (IAPT) programme: setting key performance indicators in a more robust context: a new perspective, *Journal of Psychological Therapies in Primary Care*, 2: 133–41.

Gross, R. (2005) *Psychology: The Science of Mind and Behaviour.* 5th edn, London: Hodder & Stoughton.

Grzywacz, J. G., and Marks, N. F. (2000) Reconceptualizing the work–family interface: an ecological perspective on the correlates of positive and negative spillover between work and family, *Journal of Occupational Health Psychology*, 5(1): 111–26.

Gunnar, M., and Quevedo, K. (2007) The neurobiology of stress and development, *Annual Review of Psychology*, 58: 145–73.

Hagger-Johnson, G., Roberts, B., Boniface, D., Sabia, S., Batty, G. D., Elbaz, A., Singh-Manoux, A., and Deary, I. J. (2012) Neuroticism and cardiovascular disease mortality: socioeconomic status modifies the risk in women (UK health and lifestyle survey), *Psychosomatic Medicine*, 74(6): 596–603.

Hamdan-Mansour, A. M., Puskar, K., and Bandak, A. G. (2009) Effectiveness of cognitive-behavioural therapy on depressive symptomatology, stress and coping strategies among Jordanian university students, *Issues in Mental Health Nursing*, 30(3): 188–96.

Haringey LSCB (Local Safeguarding Children Board) (2009) *Serious Case Review: Baby Peter*, www.haringeylscb.org/sites/haringeylscb/files/executive_summary_peter_final.pdf.

Harris, J. (1998) Scientific management, bureau-professionalism, new managerialism: the labour process of state social work, *British Journal of Social Work*, 28(6): 839–62.

Harris, J. (2003) *The Social Work Business.* London: Routledge.

Harris, J. (2009) Customer-citizenship in modernised social work, in J. Harris and V. White (eds), *Modernising Social Work: Critical Considerations*. Bristol: Policy Press, pp. 67–87.

Harris, J., and Unwin, P. (2009) Performance management in modernised social work, in J. Harris and V. White (eds), *Modernising Social Work: Critical Considerations*. Bristol: Policy Press, pp. 9–30.

Harris, J., and White, V. (eds) (2009) *Modernising Social Work: Critical Considerations*. Bristol: Policy Press.

Harrison, K., and Ruch, G. (2007) Social work and the use of self on becoming and being a social worker, in M. Lymberg and K. Postle (eds), *Social Work: A Companion to Learning*. London: Sage, pp. 40–9.

Hart, D. (2006) *Tell Them Not to Forget about Us: A Guide to Practice with Looked After Children in Custody*. London: National Children's Bureau, www.ncb.org.uk/media/441684/tell_them_not_to_forget_about_us_web.pdf.

Hazan, C., and Shaver, P. (1987) Romantic love conceptualized as an attachment process, *Journal of Personality and Social Psychology*, 52(3): 511–24.

Hazan, C., and Shaver, P. R. (1994) Attachment as an organizational framework for research on close relationships, *Psychological Inquiry*, 5(1): 1–22.

HCPC (Health & Care Professions Council) (2012) *Standards of Proficiency: Social Workers in England*, www.hcpc-uk.org/assets/documents/10003B08Standardsofproficiency-SocialworkersinEngland.pdf.

Health and Social Care Information Centre (2015) Mental health, www.hscic.gov.uk/mentalhealth.

Healy, K. (2001) Participatory action research and social work: a critical appraisal, *International Social Work*, 44(1): 93–105.

Heffernan, K. (2006) Social work, new public management and the language of 'service user', *British Journal of Social Work*, 36(1): 139–47.

Helgeson, V. S., Reynolds, K. A., and Tomich, P. L. (2006) A meta-analytic review of benefit finding and growth, *Journal of Consulting and Clinical Psychology*, 74(5): 797–816.

Hellerstedt, W. L., and Jeffery, R. W. (1997) The association of job strain and health behaviours in men and women, *International Journal of Epidemiology*, 26(3): 575–83.

Heng, S. (2015) Is relying on social policy benefits over a long time an easy life?, in C. Sealey (2015) *Social Policy Simplified: Connecting Theory and Concepts with People's Lives*. London: Palgrave Macmillan.

Herefordshire SCB (Safeguarding Children Board) (2009) *Serious Case Review relating to Baby HA*, http://hscb.herefordshire.gov.uk/media/1042/executive_summary_scr_ha_.pdf.

Hill, L. (2015) 'Don't make us talk!' Listening to and learning from children and young people living with parental alcohol problems, *Children & Society*, 29: 344–54.

Hoare, Z., and Hoe, J. (2013) Understanding quantitative research: part 2, *Nursing Standard*, 27(18): 48–55.

Hodge, S. (2005) Participation, discourse and power: a case study in service user involvement, *Critical Social Policy*, 25(2): 164–79.

Hoe, J., and Hoare, Z. (2012) Understanding quantitative research: part 1, *Nursing Standard*, 27(15): 52–7.

Hollinghurst, S., Carroll, F. E., Abel, A., et al. (2014) Cost-effectiveness of cognitive-behavioural therapy as an adjunct to pharmacotherapy for treatment-resistant depression in primary care: economic evaluation of the CoBalT Trial, *British Journal of Psychiatry*, 204(1): 69–76.

Holloway, S., Black, P., Hoffman, K., and Pierce, D. (2009) *Some Considerations of the Import of the 2008 EPAS for Curriculum Design*, www.cswe.org/File.aspx?id=31578.

Holt, S., Buckley, H., and Whelan, S. (2008) The impact of exposure to domestic violence on children and young people: a review of the literature, *Child Abuse and Neglect*, 32(8): 797–810.

Horner, N. (2012) *What is Social Work?* Exeter: SAGE/Learning Matters.

Hornsey, M. J. (2008) Social identity theory and self-categorization theory: a historical review, *Social and Personality Psychology Compass*, 2(1): 204–22.

House, R. J., and Mitchell, T. R. (1974) Path–goal theory of leadership, *Journal of Contemporary Business*, 3: 81–97.

Howe, D. (2008) *The Emotionally Intelligent Social Worker*. Basingstoke: Palgrave Macmillan.

Hoyle, D. (2007) *Quality Management Essentials*. Oxford: Butterworth-Heinemann.

Hugman, R. (2003) Professional values and ethics in social work: reconsidering postmodernism?, *British Journal of Social Work*, 33(8): 1025–41.

International Federation of Social Workers (2014) Global definition of social work, http://ifsw.org/policies/definition-of-social-work/.

Ixer, G. (1999) There's no such thing as reflection, *British Journal of Social Work*, 2(4): 513–27.

James, A., and Prout, A. (eds) (1997) *Constructing and Reconstructing Childhood: Contemporary Issues in the Sociological Study of Childhood.* Hove: Psychology Press.

Janis, I. L. (1973) Groupthink and group dynamics: a social psychological analysis of defective policy decisions, *Policy Studies Journal*, 2(1): 19–25.

Jast, J. (2011) *Obsessive Compulsive Disorder: The Essential Guide.* Peterborough: Need2know.

Jay, A. (2014) *Independent Inquiry into Child Sexual Exploitation in Rotherham, 1997-2013*, www.rotherham.gov.uk/downloads/file/1407/independent_inquiry_cse_in_rotherham.

Johns, C. (2013) *Becoming a Reflective Practitioner*. Chichester: Wiley-Blackwell.

Jones, C. (2001) Voices from the front line: state social workers and New Labour, *British Journal of Social Work*, 31(4): 547–62.

Jones, K. L., and Smith, D. W. (1973) Recognition of the fetal alcohol syndrome in early infancy, *The Lancet*, 302: 999–1001.

Jones, R. (2014) *The Story of Baby P: Setting the Record Straight*. Bristol: Policy Press.

Karasek, R. A. (1979) Job demands, job decision latitude, and mental strain: implications for job redesign, *Administrative Science Quarterly*, 24(2): 285–308.

Kaslow, F. W., and Massey, R. F. (eds) (2004) *Comprehensive Handbook of Psychotherapy*, Vol. 3: *Interpersonal/Humanistic/Existential*. Chichester: John Wiley.

Kaufman, E., Yoshioka, M. R., and Center for Substance Abuse Treatment (2005) Impact of substance abuse on families, in *Substance Abuse Treatment and Family Therapy*. Rockville, MD: US Department of Health and Human Services, ch. 2.

Kendler, K. S., Lönn, S. L., Maes, H. H., Sundquist, J., and Sundquist, K. (2015) The etiologic role of genetic and environmental factors in criminal behavior as determined from full- and half-sibling pairs: an evaluation of the validity of the twin method, *Psychological Medicine*, 45: 1873–80.

Kendler, K. S., Lönn, S. L., Morris, N. A., Sundquist, J., Långström, N., and Sundquist, K. (2014) A Swedish national adoption study of criminality, *Psychological Medicine*, 44: 1913–25.

Khantzian, E. (2003) The self-medication hypothesis: the dually diagnosed patient, *Primary Psychiatry*, 1 September, http://primarypsychiatry.com/the-self-medication-hypothesis-revisited-the-dually-diagnosed-patient/.

Kiecolt-Glaser, J. K., Marucha, P. T., Malarkey, W. B., Mercado, A. M., and Glaser, R. (1995) Slowing of wound healing by psychological stress, *The Lancet*, 346: 1194–6.

Knight, K. M., Sperlinger, D. J., and Maltby, M. (2010) Exploring the personal and professional impact of reflective practice groups: a survey of 18 cohorts from a UK clinical psychology training course, *Clinical Psychology and Psychotherapy*, 17(5): 427–37.

Knott, C., and Scragg, T. (2013) *Reflective Practice in Social Work*. London: Sage.

Kroll, B. (2004) Living with an elephant: growing up with parental substance misuse, *Child & Family Social Work*, 9(2): 129–40.

Kroll, B. (2007) A family affair? Kinship care and parental substance misuse: some dilemmas explored, *Child & Family Social Work*, 12(1): 84–93.

Laing, R. (1971) *The Politics of the Family and Other Essays*. London: Routledge.

Laming, H. (2003) *The Victoria Climbié Inquiry: Report*, Cm 5730. London: The

Stationery Office, www.gov.uk/government/uploads/system/uploads/attachment_data/file/273183/5730.pdf.

Laming, H. (2009) *The Protection of Children in England: A Progress Report*. London: The Stationery Office.

Lansford, J. E., Chang, L., Dodge, K. A., et al. (2005) Physical discipline and children's adjustment: cultural normativeness as a moderator, *Child Development*, 76: 1234–46.

Lansford, J. E., Deater-Deckard, K., Dodge, K. A., Bates, J. E., and Pettit, G. S. (2004) Ethnic differences in the link between physical discipline and later adolescent externalizing behaviors, *Journal of Child Psychology and Psychiatry*, 45(4): 801–12.

Larsson, P., Brooks, O., and Loewenthal, D. (2012) Counselling psychology and diagnostic categories: a critical literature review, *Counselling Psychology Review*, 27(3): 55–64.

Latane, B., Williams, K., and Harkins, S. (1979) Many hands make light the work: the causes and consequences of social loafing, *Journal of Personality and Social Psychology*, 37: 822–32.

Lazarus, R. S., and Folkman, S. (1984) *Stress, Appraisal, and Coping*. New York: Springer.

Lent, R. W., Brown, S. D., and Hackett, G. (1994) Toward a unifying social cognitive theory of career and academic interest, choice, and performance, *Journal of Vocational Behavior*, 45: 79–121.

Lewis, S., Bates, S., and Murray, J. (2008) *Children of Prisoners: Maintaining Family Ties*. London: Social Care Institute for Excellence.

Li, C. Y., and Sung, F. C. (1999) A review of the healthy worker effect in occupational epidemiology, *Occupational Medicine*, 49: 225–9.

Lietz, C. A., and Zayas, L. E. (2010) Evaluating qualitative research for social work practitioners, *Advances in Social Work*, 11(2): 188–202.

Lipsky, M. (1980) *Street-Level Bureaucracy: Dilemmas of the Individual in Public Services*. New York: Russell Sage Foundation.

Lock, R. (2013) *Serious Case Review re Daniel Pelka: Born 15th July 2007, Died 3rd March 2012 [Full Overview Report]*. Coventry: Coventry Safeguarding Children Board.

McCrory, E. J., De Brito, S. A., Sebastian, C. L., Mechelli, A., Bird, G., Kelly, P. A., and Viding, E. (2011) Heightened neural reactivity to threat in child victims of family violence, *Current Biology*, 21(23): R947–8.

McGregor, K. (2013) Third of UK's social workers not currently receiving supervision, *Community Care*, 18 June, www.communitycare.co.uk/2013/06/18/third-of-uks-social-workers-not-currently-receiving-supervision/ .

Marcus, B. H., and Simkin, L. R. (1994) The transtheoretical model: applications to exercise behaviour, *Medicine and Science in Sports and Exercise*, 26: 1400–4.

Marks, D. F., Murray, M., Evans, B. E., Willig, C., Woodall, C., and Sykes, C. M. (2006) *Health Psychology: Theory, Research and Practice*. 2nd edn, London: Sage.

Marmot, M. G., Davey Smith, G., Stansfeld, S., Patel, C., Head, J., North, F., and White, I. (1991) Health inequalities among British civil servants: the Whitehall II study, *The Lancet*, 337: 1387–93.

Marsh, P., and Fisher, M., in collaboration with Mathers, N., and Fish, S. (2005) *Developing the Evidence Base for Social Work and Social Care Practice*. London: Social Care Institute for Excellence, www.scie.org.uk/publications/reports/report10.pdf.

Maslow, A. H. (1968) *Toward a Psychology of Being*. 2nd edn, New York: Van Nostrand.

Mason, R., (2013) David Cameron orchestrates applause for social workers at Tory conference, *The Guardian*, 2 October, www.theguardian.com/society/2013/oct/02/david-cameron-social-work-conservative-conference.

Matarazzo, J. D. (1982) Behavioral health's challenge to academic, scientific, and professional psychology, *American Psychologist*, 37(1): 1–14.

Mental Health Foundation (2009) *Talking Therapies Explained*. London: Mental Health Foundation.

Mezey, G. C. (1997) Treatment of rape victims, *Advances in Psychiatric Treatment*, 3: 197–203.

Millward, L., Haslam, A., and Postmes, T. (2007) Putting employees in their place: the impact of hot desking on organisational and team identification, *Organisation Science*, 18(4): 547–59.

Mind (2013) *We Still Need to Talk: A Report on Access to Talking Therapies*, www.mind.org.uk/media/494424/we-still-need-to-talk_report.pdf.

Mind (2015a) Mind's response to today's front pages on the Germanwings plane crash, www.mind.org.uk/news-campaigns/news/minds-response-to-todays-front-pages-on-the-germanwings-plane-crash/#.VgBpHvlVhBc.

Mind (2015b) Mental health facts and statistics, www.mind.org.uk/information-support/types-of-mental-health-problems/statistics-and-facts-about-mental-health/how-common-are-mental-health-problems/.

Misca, G. (2009) Perspectives on the life course: childhood and adolescence, in R. Adams, L. Dominelli and M. Payne (eds), *Social Work: Themes, Issues and Critical Debates*. Basingstoke: Palgrave Macmillan, pp. 116–28.

Misca, G. (2014a) The 'quiet migration': challenges for families with children adopted internationally, in A. Abela and J. Walker (eds), *Contemporary Issues in Family Studies: Global Perspectives on Partnerships, Parenting and Support in a Changing World*. Chichester: Wiley-Blackwell, pp. 288–301.

Misca, G. (2014b) The 'quiet migration': is intercountry adoption a successful intervention in the lives of vulnerable children?, *Family Court Review*, 52: 60–8.

Misca, G., and Neamţu, N. (2016) Contemporary challenges in social work practice in multicultural societies, *Revista de Asistenţă Socială*, 15(1): 7–9.

Misca, G., and Smith, J. (2014) Mothers, fathers, families and child development, in A. Abela and J. Walker (eds), *Contemporary Issues in Family Studies: Global Perspectives on Partnerships, Parenting and Support in a Changing World*. Chichester: Wiley-Blackwell, pp. 151–65.

Moffatt, K., George, U., Lee, B., and McGrath, S. (2005) Community practice researchers as reflective learners, *British Journal of Social Work*, 35(1): 89–104.

Molyneux, J., and Irvine, J. (2004) Service user and carer involvement in social work training: a long and winding road?, *Social Work Education*, 23(3): 293–308.

Montanaro, E. A., and Bryan, A. D. (2014) Comparing theory-based condom interventions: health belief model versus theory of planned behavior, *Health Psychology*, 33(10): 1251–60.

Morgan, J., Leeson, C., Dillon, R. C., Wirgman, A. L., and Needham, M. (2014) 'A hidden group of children': support in schools for children who experience parental imprisonment, *Children & Society*, 28(4): 269–79.

Morris, N. (2009) 'Shocking' sickness rates in social work, *The Independent*, 16 September, www.independent.co.uk/news/uk/home-news/shocking-sickness-rates-in-social-work-1787970.html.

Morrison, T. (2000) Working together to safeguard children: challenges and changes for inter-agency co-ordination in child protection, *Journal of Interprofessional Care*, 14(4): 363–73.

Morrison, T. (2007) Emotional intelligence, emotion and social work: context, characteristics, complications and contribution, *British Journal of Social Work*, 37(2): 245–63.

Moskowitz, J. T., Folkman, S., Collette, L., and Vittinghoff, E. (1996) Coping and mood during AIDS-related caregiving and bereavement, *Annals of Behavioral Medicine*, 18(1): 49–57.

Moylan, C. A., Herrenkohl, T. I., Sousa, C.,Tajima, E. A., Herrenkohl, R. C., and Russo, M. J. (2010) The effects of child abuse and exposure to domestic violence on adolescent internalizing and externalizing behavior problems, *Journal of Family Violence*, 25(1): 53–63.

Mullender, A., Kelly, L., Hague, G., Malos, E., and Iman, U. (2002) *Children's Perspectives on Domestic Violence*. London: Routledge.

Munro, E. (2008) *Effective Child Protection*. 2nd edn, London: Sage.

Munro, E. (2011) *The Munro Review of Child Protection: Final Report: A Child-Centred System*. Cm 8062. London: Department for Education.

Munro, E., and Musholt, K. (2014) Neuroscience and the risks of maltreatment, *Children and Youth Services Review*, 47(1): 18–26.

Murray, J., and Farrington, D. P. (2005) Parental imprisonment: effects on boys' antisocial behaviour and delinquency through the life-course, *Journal of Child Psychology and Psychiatry*, 46: 1269–78.

Murray, J., and Farrington, D. P. (2006) Evidence-based programs for children of prisoners, *Criminology & Public Policy*, 5(4): 721–35.

Murray, J., and Farrington, D. P. (2008) Parental imprisonment: long-lasting effects on boys' internalizing problems through the life course, *Development and Psychopathology*, 20(1): 273–90.

Murray, J., Farrington, D. P., and Sekol, I. (2012) Children's antisocial behavior, mental health, drug use, and educational performance after parental incarceration: a systematic review and meta-analysis, *Psychological Bulletin*, 138(2): 175–210.

Myers, D., Spencer, S., and Jordon, J. (2009) *Social Psychology*. 4th edn, New York: McGraw-Hill.

National Institute of Child Health and Human Development (2006) *The NICHD Study of Early Child Care and Youth Development*, www.nichd.nih.gov/publications/pubs/documents/seccyd_06.pdf.

National Working Group Network on Tackling Child Sexual Exploitation (2015) How is child sexual exploitation defined?, www.nwgnetwork.org/who-we-are/what-is-child-sexual-exploitation.

Nelson, C. A. (1999) How important are the first 3 years of life?, *Applied Developmental Science*, 3(4): 235–8.

NHS Choices (2013) Cognitive behavioural therapy (CBT), www.nhs.uk/conditions/cognitive-behavioural-therapy/Pages/Introduction.aspx.

NHS Choices (2016a) Talking therapies explained – stress, anxiety and depression, www.nhs.uk/Conditions/stress-anxiety-depression/Pages/Types-of-therapy.aspx#mindfulness.

NHS Choices (2016b) 'Transformational managers' may be bad for workplace health, www.nhs.uk/news/2016/04April/Pages/Transformational-managers-may-be-bad-for-workplace-health.aspx.

Norcross, J. C. (2011) *Psychotherapy Relationships that Work: Evidence-Based Responsiveness*. New York: Oxford University Press.

Norman, P., Bennett, P., and Lewis, H. (1998) Understanding binge drinking among young people: an application of the theory of planned behaviour, *Health Education Research*, 13(2): 163–9.

Norman, R. E., Byambaa, M., De, R., Butchart, A., Scott, J., and Vos, T. (2012) The long-term health consequences of child physical abuse, emotional abuse, and neglect: a systematic review and meta-analysis, *PLoS Medicine*, 9(11): 1–31.

Norris, W. R., and Vecchio, R. P. (1992) Situational leadership theory, *Group and Organisation Management*, 17(3): 331–42.

North Tyneside SCB (Safeguarding Children Board) (2010) *Serious Case Review re: Child F*, http://hundredfamilies.org/wp/wp-content/uploads/2013/12/MAPASEKA_SHAPUNG_Jan-10_SCR.pdf.

Ociskova, M., Prasko, J., Cerna, M., Jelenova, D., Kamaradova, D., Latalova, K., and Sedlackova, Z. (2013) Obsessive compulsive disorder and stigmatization, *Activitas Nervosa Superior Rediviva*, 55(1–2): 19–26.

O'Connor, D. B., Jones, F., Conner, M., McMillan, B., and Ferguson, E. (2008) Effects of daily hassles and eating style on eating behaviour, *Health Psychology*, 27: 520–31.

Ofsted (2013) *Missing Children*, www.gov.uk/government/publications/missing-children.

Olafson, E. (2011) Child sexual abuse: demography, impact, and interventions, *Journal of Child & Adolescent Trauma*, 4(1): 8–21.

Øverlien, C. (2009) Children exposed to domestic violence: conclusions from the literature and challenges ahead, *Journal of Social Work*, 10(1): 80–97.

Parker, G., Savitch N., Abbott, E., and Ludwin, K. (2015) The personal is political: women's experiences of dementia, http://php.york.ac.uk/inst/spru/research/summs/wed.php.

Pavlov, I. P. (2010) Conditioned reflexes: an investigation of the physiological activity of the cerebral cortex, *Annals of Neurosciences*, 17(3): 136–41.

Payne, M. (2014) *Modern Social Work Theory*. 4th edn, London: Palgrave Macmillan.

Peck, E., Gulliver, P., and Towel, D. (2002) Information, consultation or control: user involvement in mental health services in England at the turn of the century, *Journal of Mental Health*, 11(4): 441–51.

Peterson, C., Seligman, M. E., and Vaillant, G. E. (1988) Pessimistic explanatory style is a risk factor for physical illness: a thirty-five-year longitudinal study, *Journal of Personality and Social Psychology*, 55(1): 23–7.

Piaget, J. (1964). Part I: Cognitive development in children: Piaget development and learning. *Journal of Research in Science Teaching*, 2(3): 176–86.

Pino, N. W., and Meier, R. F. (1999) Gender differences in rape reporting, *Sex Roles*, 40: 979–90.

Prentice-Dunn, S., and Rogers, R. W. (1986) Protection motivation theory and preventive health: beyond the health belief model, *Health Education Research*, 1(3): 153–61.

Prilleltensky, I. (2001) Value-based praxis in community psychology: moving toward social justice and social action, *American Journal of Community Psychology*, 29(5): 747–78.

Prison Reform Trust (2015) Keeping children in care out of trouble: an independent review, Public briefing, www.prisonreformtrust.org.uk/ProjectsResearch/CareReview.

Prochaska, J. O., and DiClemente, C. C. (1983) Stages and processes of self-change of smoking: toward an integrative model of change, *Journal of Consulting and Clinical Psychology*, 5: 390–5.

QAA (Quality Assurance Agency) (2008) *Social Work [Subject Benchmark*

Statement], www.qaa.ac.uk/en/Publications/Documents/Subject-bench mark-statement-Social-work.pdf.

QAA (Quality Assurance Agency) (2010) *Psychology [Subject Benchmark Statement]*, www.qaa.ac.uk/en/Publications/Documents/Subject-bench mark-statement-Psychology.pdf.

Quintana, S. M., Aboud, F. E., Chao, R. K., Contreras-Grau, J., Cross, W. E., Hudley, C., Hughes, D., Liben, L. S., Nelson-Le Gall, S., and Vietze, D. L. (2006) Race, ethnicity, and culture in child development: contemporary research and future directions, *Child Development*, 77: 1129–41.

Radford, J. (2010) *Serious Case Review under Chapter VIII 'Working Together to Safeguard Children': In Respect of the Death of a Child: Case Number 14.* Birmingham: Birmingham Safeguarding Children Board.

Rapaport, J. (2009) The life & times of forensic social work, *Professional Social Work*, September, pp. 26–7.

Rappaport, J. (1987) Terms of empowerment/exemplars of prevention: toward a theory for community psychology, *American Journal of Community Psychology*, 15(2): 121–48.

RCGP (Royal College of General Practitioners) (2015) *Improving Access to Psychological Therapies*, http://elearning.rcgp.org.uk/course/info.php?id=29.

Reader, T., Gillespie, A., and Mannell, J. (2014) Patient neglect in 21st century health-care institutions: a community health psychology perspective, *Journal of Health Psychology*, 19(1): 137–48.

Research in Practice (2014) Adoption and fostering, http://fosteringanda doption.rip.org.uk/.

Richards, D., Timulak, L., and Hevey, D. (2013) A comparison of two online cognitive-behavioural interventions for symptoms of depression in a student population: the role of therapist responsiveness, *Counselling and Psychotherapy Research: Linking Research with Practice*, 13(3): 184–93.

Robboy, J., and Anderson, K. G. (2011) Intergenerational child abuse and coping, *Journal of Interpersonal Violence*, 26: 3526–41.

Roberts, D., Bernard, M., Misca, G.., and Head, E. (2008) SCIE research briefing 24: Experiences of children and young people caring for a parent with a mental health problem, www.scie.org.uk/publications/briefings/brief ing24/.

Rogers, C. R., Stevens, B., Gendlin, E. T., Shlien, J. M., and van Dusen, W. (1967) *Person to Person: The Problem of Being Human: A New Trend in Psychology*. Lafayette, CA: Real People Press.

Rogers, R. W. (1975) A protection motivation theory of fear appeals and attitude change1, *Journal of Psychology*, 91(1): 93–114.

Rosenthal, D. A., Gurney, R. M., and Moore, S. M. (1981) From trust to intimacy: a new inventory for examining Erikson's stages of psychosocial development, *Journal of Youth and Adolescence*, 10(6): 525–37.

Ross, L., Lepper, M., and Ward, A. (2010) History of social psychology: insights, challenges, and contributions to theory and application, in S. T. Fiske, D. T. Gilbert and G. Lindzey (eds), *Handbook of Social Psychology*. 5th edn, Hoboken, NJ: Wiley, Vol. 1, pp. 3–50.

Rothbart, M. K., Ahadi, S. A., and Evans, D. E. (2000) Temperament and personality: origins and outcomes, *Journal of Personality and Social Psychology*, 78(1): 122–35.

Rousseau, D. M. (1995) *Psychological Contracts in Organizations: Understanding Written and Unwritten Agreements*. London: Sage.

Ruch, G. (2005) Relationship-based practice and reflective practice: holistic approaches to contemporary child care social work, *Child and Family Social Work*, 10(2): 111–23.

Ruch, G. (2007) Reflective practice in contemporary child-care social work: the role of containment, *British Journal of Social Work*, 37(4): 659–80.

Rutter, D. (2009) *Practice Enquiry Guidelines: A Framework for SCIE Commissioners and Providers*. London: Social Care Institute for Excellence, www.scie.org.uk/publications/researchresources/rr04.pdf.

Rutter, M. (1970) Normal psychosexual development, *Journal of Child Psychology and Psychiatry*, 11(4): 259–83.

Rutter, M. (1999) Resilience concepts and findings: implications for family therapy, *Journal of Family Therapy*, 21: 119–44.

Rutter, M. (2006) *Genes and Behaviour: Nature–Nurture Interplay Explained*. Oxford: Blackwell.

Saleebey, D. (1996) The strengths perspective in social work practice: extensions and cautions, *Social Work*, 41(3): 296–305.

Sanborne, E. (2002) A value framework for community psychology, www.uml.edu/docs/What%20Are%20Community%20Psychologists%20Revised_tcm18-61922.pdf.

Schaffer, H. R. (2000) The early experience assumption: past, present, and future, *International Journal of Behavioral Development*, 24(1): 5–14.

Schiola, S. A. (2010) *Making Group Work Easy: The Art of Successful Facilitation*. Lanham, MD: Rowman & Littlefield.

Schofield, G., Ward, E., Biggart, L., Scaife, V., Dodsworth, J., and Larsson, B. (2015) Looked after children and offending: an exploration of risk, resilience and the role of social cognition, *Children and Youth Services Review*, 51: 125–33.

Schofield, G., Ward, E., Biggart, L., Scaife, V., Dodsworth, J., Larsson, B., Haynes, A., and Stone, S. (2012) *Looked After Children and Offending: Reducing Risk and Promoting Resilience*. Norwich: University of East Anglia.

Schön, D. A. (1983) *The Reflective Practitioner: How Professionals Think in Action*. New York: Basic Books.

Schroeder, R. D., and Mowen, T. J. (2014) Parenting style transitions and delinquency, *Youth & Society*, 46(2): 228–54.

Schuman, H. (1995) Attitudes, beliefs, and behavior, in K. Cook, G. Fine and J. House (eds), *Sociological Perspectives on Social Psychology*. Boston: Allyn & Bacon, pp. 68–89.

Scott, M. (2011) Reflections on 'the Big Society', *Community Development Journal*, 46(1): 132–7.

Scott, S., Doolan, M., Beckett, C., Harry, S., Cartwright, S., and the HCA team (2010) *How is Parenting Style Related to Child Antisocial Behaviour? Preliminary Findings from the Helping Children Achieve Study*, Research Report DFE-RR185a. London: Department for Education, www.gov.uk/government/uploads/system/uploads/attachment_data/file/197732/DFE-RR185a.pdf.

Sealey, C. (2015) *Social Policy Simplified: Connecting Theory and Concepts with People's Lives*. London: Palgrave Macmillan.

Seebohm Committee (1968) *Report of the Committee on Local Authority and Allied Personal Social Services*, Cmnd. 3703. London: HMSO.

Seligman, M. E. P. (1972) Learned helplessness, *Annual Review of Medicine*, 23(1): 407–12.

Sharratt, K. (2014) Children's experiences of contact with imprisoned parents: a comparison between four European countries, *European Journal of Criminology*, 11(6): 760–75.

Shaw, J. A. (2003) Children exposed to war/terrorism, *Clinical Child and Family Psychology Review*, 6: 237–46.

Shedler, J. (2010) The efficacy of psychodynamic psychotherapy, *American Psychologist*, 65: 98–109.

Sher, K., Walitzer, K., Wood, P., and Brent, E. (1991) Characteristics of children of alcoholics: putative risk factors, substance use and abuse, and psychopathology, *Journal of Abnormal Psychology*, 100(4): 427–48.

Siegrist, J. (1996) Adverse health effects of high-effort/low-reward conditions, *Journal of Occupational Health Psychology*, 1(1): 27–41.

Sirri, L., Fava, G. A., Guidi, J., Porcelli, P., Rafanelli, C., Bellomo, A., Grandi, S., Grassi, L., Pasquini, P., Picardi, A., Quartesan, R., Rigatelli, M., and Sonino, N. (2012) Type A behaviour: a reappraisal of its characteristics in cardiovascular disease, *International Journal of Clinical Practice*, 66: 854–61.

Skinner, B. F. (1948) 'Superstition' in the pigeon, *Journal of Experimental Psychology*, 38: 168–72.

Skinner, B. F. (1971) *Beyond Freedom and Dignity*. New York: Knopf.

Slavin, R. (1997) *Educational Psychology: Theory and Practice*. 10th edn, Boston: Pearson.

Sloper, P. (2004) Facilitators and barriers for co-ordinated multi-agency services, *Care, Health and Development*, 30: 571–80.

Sousa, C., Herrenkohl, T. I., Moylan, C. A., Tajima, E. A., Klika, J. B., Herrenkohl, R. C., and Russo, M. J. (2011) Longitudinal study on the effects of child abuse and children's exposure to domestic violence, parent–child attachments, and antisocial behavior in adolescence, *Journal of Interpersonal Violence*, 26(1): 111–36.

Stephens, C. (2014) Beyond the barricades: social movements as participatory practice in health promotion, *Journal of Health Psychology*, 19(1): 170–5.

Stewart, L. A., Flight, J., and Slavin-Stewart C. (2013) Applying effective correction principles (PNR) to partner abuse interventions, *Partner Abuse*, 4(4): 494–534.

Stiles, W. B., Barkham, M., Mellor-Clark, J., and Connell, J. (2008) Effectiveness of cognitive-behavioural, person-centred, and psychodynamic therapies in UK primary-care routine practice: replication in a larger sample, *Psychological Medicine*, 38(5): 677–88.

Stirling J. (2007) Beyond Munchausen syndrome by proxy: identification and treatment of child abuse in a medical setting, *Pediatrics*, 119: 1026–30.

Stoltenberg, C. D., Pace, T. M., Kashubeck-West, S., Biever, J. L., Patterson, T., and Welch, I. D. (2000) Training models in counseling psychology scientist-practitioner versus practitioner-scholar, *Counseling Psychologist*, 28(5): 622–40.

Suarez, E., and Gadalla, T. M. (2010) Stop blaming the victim: a meta-analysis on rape myths, *Journal of Interpersonal Violence*, 25: 2010–35.

Sulloway, F. J. (1991) Reassessing Freud's case histories: the social construction of psychoanalysis, *Isis: A Journal of the History of Science*, 82(2): 245–75.

Summerfield, P. (2011) *Executive Summary in Respect of Child H*. North Tyneside Safeguarding Children Board, www.northtyneside.gov.uk/pls/portal/NTC_PSCM.PSCM_Web.download?p_ID=526224.

SWRB (Social Work Reform Board) (2010) *Building a Safe and Confident Future: One Year On*, www.gov.uk/government/uploads/system/uploads/attachment_data/file/180787/DFE-00602-2010-1.pdf.

Tajfel, H. (1982) Social psychology of intergroup relations, *Annual Review of Psychology*, 33: 1–39.

Taylor, F. (2006) *The Principles of Scientific Management*. New York: Cosimo.

Thoits, P. A. (2011) Mechanisms linking social ties and support to physical and mental health, *Journal of Health and Social Behavior*, 52(2): 145–61.

Time to Change (2014) *Let's End Mental Health Discrimination*, www.time-to-change.org.uk/mental-health-and-stigma.

Tollefson, D. R., Webb, K., Shumway, D., Block, S. H., and Nakamura Y. (2009) A mind–body approach to domestic violence perpetrator treatment: program overview and preliminary outcomes, *Journal of Aggression, Maltreatment and Trauma*, 18: 17–45.

Torbay SCB (Safeguarding Children Board) (2010) *Serious Case Review C18*, http://hundredfamilies.org/wp/wp-content/uploads/2013/12/KATY_NORRIS_SCR_APR_10.pdf.

Townsend, P. (1962) *The Last Refuge: A Survey of Residential Institutions and Homes for the Aged in England and Wales*. London: Routledge & Kegan Paul.

Tsutsumi, A., Kayaba, K., Theorell, T., and Siegrist, J. (2001) Association between job stress and depression among Japanese employees threatened by job loss in a comparison between two complementary job-stress models, *Scandinavian Journal of Work, Environment & Health*, 27(2): 1 46–53.

Ttofi, M. M., Farrington, D. P., and Lösel, F. (2012) School bullying as a predictor of violence later in life: a systematic review and meta-analysis of prospective longitudinal studies, *Aggression and Violent Behaviour*, 17: 405–18.

Tuckman, B. (1965) Developmental sequence in small groups, *Psychological Bulletin*, 63: 384–99; repr. in *Group Facilitation: A Research and Applications Journal*, no. 3, spring 2001, http://openvce.net/sites/default/files/Tuckman1965DevelopmentalSequence.pdf.

Tuckman, B., and Jensen, M. (1977) Stages of small group development revisited, *Group and Organizational Studies*, 2: 419–27.

Uchino, B. N., Cacioppo, J. T., and Kiecolt-Glaser, J. K. (1996) The relationship between social support and physiological processes: a review with emphasis on underlying mechanisms and implications for health, *Psychological Bulletin*, 119(3): 488–531.

Ungar, M. (2008) Resilience across cultures, *British Journal of Social Work*, 38(2): 218–35.

Unwin, P. (2009) Modernisation and the role of agency social work, in J. Harris and V. White (eds), *Modernising Social Work: Critical Considerations*. Bristol: Policy Press, pp. 51–66.

Unwin, P., and Hogg, R. (2012) *Effective Social Work with Children and Families: A Skills Handbook*. London: Sage.

Unwin, P., and Misca, G. (2013) The changing face of adoption in England: opportunities and dilemmas, *Revista de Asistenţă Socială*, 12(2): 1–9.

Van der Doef, M., and Maes, S. (1998) The job demand-control(-support) model and physical health outcomes: a review of the strain and buffer hypotheses, *Psychology and Health*, 13(5): 909–36.

Van Vegchel, N., De Jonge, J., Meijer, T., and Hamers, J. P. (2001) Different effort constructs and effort–reward imbalance: effects on employee well-being in ancillary health care workers, *Journal of Advanced Nursing*, 34(1): 128–36.

Vaughan, S. C., Marshall, R. D., Mackinnon, R. A., Vaughan, R., Mellman, L., and Roose, S. P. (2000) Can we do psychoanalytic outcome research? A feasibility study, *International Journal of Psychoanalysis*, 81: 513–27.

Viner, R. M., Roche, E., Maguire, S. A., and Nicholls, D. E. (2010) Childhood protection and obesity: framework for practice, *British Medical Journal*, 341.

Von Dawans, B., Fischbacher, U., Kirschbaum, C., Fehr, E., and Heinrichs, M. (2012) The social dimension of stress reactivity: acute stress increases prosocial behavior in humans, *Psychological Science*, 23(6): 651–60.

Vygotsky, L. (1978) Interaction between learning and development, *Readings on the Development of Children*, 23(3): 34–41.

Walker, C. (2009) The Improving Access to Psychological Therapies programme, globalisation and the credit crunch: is this how we put politics into depression?, *Journal of Critical Psychology, Counselling and Psychotherapy*, 9(2): 66–74.

Ward, E., King, M., Lloyd, M., Bower, P., Sibbald, B., Farrelly, S., Gabbay, M., and Addington-Hall, J. (2000) Randomised controlled trial of non-directive counselling, cognitive-behaviour therapy, and usual general practitioner care for patients with depression, I: Clinical effectiveness, *British Medical Journal*, 321: 1383–8.

Watson, J. B. (1913) Psychology as the behaviorist views it, *Psychological Review*, 20: 158–78.

Watson, J. B., and Rayner, R. (1920) Conditioned emotional reactions, *Journal of Experimental Psychology*, 3(1): 1–14.

Webb, C., and Carpenter, J. (2012) What can be done to promote the retention of social workers? A systematic review of interventions, *British Journal of Social Work*, 42(7): 1235–55.

Webster, R. (1995) *Why Freud Was Wrong*. New York: Basic Books.

Weijer, S., Bijleveld, C., and Blokland, A. (2014) The intergenerational transmission of violent offending, *Journal of Family Violence*, 29(2): 109–18.

Weinfield, N. S., Sroufe, L. A., and Egeland, B. (2000) Attachment from infancy to early adulthood in a high-risk sample: continuity, discontinuity, and their correlates, *Child Development*, 71: 695–702.

Weinfield, N. S., Whaley, G. J., and Egeland, B. (2004) Continuity, discontinuity, and coherence in attachment from infancy to late adolescence: sequelae of organization and disorganization, *Attachment & Human Development*, 6(1): 73–97.

Westergaard, J. (2009) *Effective Group Work with Young People*. Maidenhead: Open University Press.

Westmarland, N., and Kelly, E. (2013) Why extending measurements of 'success' in domestic violence perpetrator programmes matters for social work, *British Journal of Social Work*, 43: 1092–110.

White, W. L. (1998) *Slaying the Dragon: The History of Addiction Treatment and Recovery in America*. Bloomington, IL: Chestnut Health Systems/ Lighthouse Institute.

Whooley, M. A., and Wong, J. (2011) Hostility and cardiovascular disease, *Journal of the American College of Cardiology*, 58: 1229–30.

Williams, C. H. J. (2015) Improving Access to Psychological Therapies (IAPT) and treatment outcomes: epistemological assumptions and controversies, *Journal of Psychiatric and Mental Health Nursing*, 22(5): 344–51.

Williams, D. R., and Mohammed, S. A. (2009) Discrimination and racial disparities in health: evidence and needed research, *Journal of Behavioral Medicine*, 32(1): 20–47.

Williams, G. M. G., Bredow, M., Barton, J., Pryce, R., and Shield, J. P. H. (2014) Can foster care ever be justified for weight management?, *Archives of Disease in Childhood*, 99(3): 297–9.

Williams, K. D., and Karau, S. J. (1991) Social loafing and social compensation: the effects of expectations of co-worker performance, *Journal of Personality and Social Psychology*, 61(4): 570–81.

Williams, Z. (2014) Is misused neuroscience defining early years and child protection policy?, *The Guardian*, 26 April, www.theguardian.com/ education/2014/apr/26/misused-neuroscience-defining-child-protection-policy.

Wilson, K., Ruch, G., Lymbery, M., and Cooper A. (2011) *Social Work: An Introduction to Contemporary Practice*. 2nd edn, Harlow: Pearson Education.

Zanca, R., and Misca, G. (2016) Filling the gaps? Romanian social workers' 'migration' into the UK, *Revista de Asistenţă Socială*, 15(1): 41–7.

Zubin, J., and Spring, B. (1977) Vulnerability: a new view of schizophrenia, *Journal of Abnormal Psychology*, 86: 103–26.

Index

action research 85, 92
addiction 11, 19, 60, 94, 109, 111–14, 115
  impact on children 112
  impact on health 60, 111
adoption 14, 27, 35, 45, 47, 75, 128–9
  'forced adoption' 35
  studies 13, 144, 164
Adorno, T. 76
agency social workers 123, 131, 135, 139
Allport, G. 16, 71, 86, 87
anorexia nervosa 60
anti-oppressive practice 16, 71, 73
  ageism 16, 72, 80
  disablism 16, 72, 83, 170
  racism 16, 53, 72
  sexism 16, 72, 80
anxiety-based problems 57
assessed and supported first year of
  practice (ASYE) 125
assessment 14, 38, 95, 96, 101, 108, 112,
  121, 122, 128, 130, 144, 157, 171
  holistic 43, 66
  risk 19, 23, 49–50, 55, 66–7
attachment theory 12, 14, 24, 33–6
  adult attachment 35–7
  see also Bowlby
attitudes 16, 19, 34, 41, 46, 75–8, 94, 98,
  105, 114, 127, 144, 155–8
  formation 75–8
  towards crime 155–8; *see also* victims of
  crime
authoritative practice 25
autonomic nervous system (ANS) 106

Bandura, A. 147
Baumrind, D. 151, 152, 163
Beck, A. 63, 69
behavioural and relationship difficulties
  28
behaviourism 11, 147
Belbin, M. 86–7, 91
Berelowitz, S. 41, 156, 165

Bifulco, A. 36
Big Society 16, 80, 176
bio-psychosocial model of health 96, 170
bipolar disorder 32, 58
Blades, R. 149–50
Booth-Kewley, S. 97, 116
Bowlby, J. 9, 14–15, 33–6, 47
  see also attachment theory
Brightwell family (case study) 20–1, 25,
  36–8, 47, 68, 72, 78–9, 90, 96, 100, 101,
  103, 115, 136, 162–3, 167–70
British Association of Social Workers
  (BASW) 1, 5, 10, 16, 21, 23, 48, 52, 71,
  74, 77, 92, 94, 105, 119, 123, 125–6,
  141, 153, 167, 171
  Code of Ethics 74
British Psychological Society (BPS) 2, 21,
  49, 51
bulimia nervosa 60

Cairns, K. 14
Care and Support Statutory Guidance 78
care plan 75, 129, 150
care proceedings 113
Care Quality Commission 53, 69, 82
Carpenter, J. 120
challenging other professionals 20, 97
child abuse 5, 77, 124, 148, 158, 164, 165
  child protection plans 99
  child sexual exploitation (CSE) 41,
  155–8
  see also victims of crime
Children Act 1989 32, 43, 60, 99
  Emergency Protection Order 60, 129
  Section 20 43, 60
  significant harm 32–3, 46, 59–60, 99
children and young people
  as 'blank slates' 29
  as mini-adults 27
  voices of 150
Chisholm, K. 29
Chomsky, N. 13

Christensen, H. 63, 65
Cleaver, H. 60, 66
Climbié, Victoria 76, 114
cognitive-behavioural therapy (CBT) 4,
    11, 61, 63–5, 109–10
    effectiveness 63–5, 67, 80, 109–10
cognitive development 17, 24, 29, 35, 169
cognitive dissonance 19, 75, 91
cognitive psychology 13
'collaborative empiricism' 63
College of Social Work 124–6, 132, 141,
    167
commitment 8, 12, 15, 35–6, 71–3, 139
compliance 5, 7, 82, 121, 131, 160
congruence 12, 51
Connelly, Peter 15, 136
continuity vs. discontinuity 27
core conditions 12, 51, 89
counselling 48–52
    therapeutic alliance 62
criminal behaviour 143
    intergenerational transmission of
        criminal behaviour 145–6
    and looked-after children 144–7, 149–50
    and parenting styles 151–3
    psychosocial theories of 144
    risk and protective factors in the
        development of 148
criminal justice system 144, 149, 150, 159
critical vs. sensitive periods of
    development 28–9
culture
    and development 31–3
    and factors in health psychology 114–15
    and parenting styles 152
Cummings, E. 14, 67
cyber-bullying 84
cybertherapy 65
    Big White Wall 65

dementia 21, 79, 95, 104–6
    common psychiatric and behavioural
        symptoms 104
Department of Health 12, 16, 78, 83, 92,
    97, 104, 121, 166
depression 7, 11, 26, 50, 55, 58–9, 63, 65,
    68, 69, 105, 137–8, 139, 151
    in adolescence 107
    bipolar disorder 58
    seasonal affective disorder (SAD) 58
    unipolar depression 58
Diagnostic and Statistical Manual (DSM)
    54, 56, 64
diathesis-stress model 107
DiClemente, C. 103

digital communities 84
disengagement theory 14
domestic violence 8, 23, 25, 60, 72, 78, 109,
    112, 145–6, 156, 159, 164
    impact on children 112, 117, 118
    repeat and multiple victimization
        158
    see also victims of crime
drug and alcohol abuse 67
    impact on children 60, 112–15
dry stone wall model of development 31
Duckworth, E. 30, 47

early life experiences 45–6
eating disorders 60–1
ego 10
emotional intelligence 52, 68, 131
empathy 6, 12, 20, 25, 31, 51, 64, 88, 110,
    140
Engel, G. 96
ethology 33
Evans, T. 109, 117
evidence-informed research 8
extroversion 99

'fabricated or induced illness' 59
Ferguson, I. 1, 5, 122
'fight or flight' 106, 109
foetal alcohol spectrum disorder 112
Forrester, D. 113, 117
Fossey, J.
foster care 14, 31, 33, 34–5, 43, 88, 117,
    127–8, 137
    kinship care 129
Framework for the Assessment of Children
    in Need and their Families 66
Francis, R. 16, 76, 81, 92, 122, 133, 141,
    166
    Freud, S. 10–11, 39, 41, 47, 49, 62

Goffman, E. 16, 53, 81, 83
groups 86–8
    dynamics of 86
    'groupthink' 137–8
    'social loafing' 88, 137

Haringey LSCB 4
Harris, J. 1, 3, 15, 21, 52, 121, 122, 132
health behaviours 97, 99
health belief model (HBM) 100, 170
    'healthy worker effect' 120
    heart disease 97, 139
    and hostility 97–8, 116
homosexuality 54, 56
humanist-existentialist tradition 64

immigration 77
Improving Access to Psychological
    Therapies (IAPT) 55
inclusivity 16, 80
International Federation of Social Workers
    74
introversion 99

Jay, A. 83–4, 114, 133, 156–7
Jones, C. 15, 136

Laming, H. 4, 5, 76, 83, 114, 121, 150
leadership 125–6, 132
    in social work 132
    theories of 142
learned helplessness 11, 139
life-course perspective 42, 127
'Little Albert' 37
Locke, J. 26
loneliness 111
    see also old age
low morale 15, 26, 139

managerialism 121, 132, 139, 166–9
mandatory reporting 124
Maslow, A. 12–13
Matarazzo, J. 95
medical model 136, 169
medication 61, 64
mental illness 49–50, 53–6, 61
    and parenting 66–7
Mid Staffordshire General Hospital 16, 76,
    81–2, 92, 122, 133, 141, 166, 170, 182
Misca, G. 6, 13, 27, 28, 29, 34, 35, 45, 46, 47
mobile and flexible working 123, 130
Modernising Social Services (1998) 121
mood disorders 58, 107
multi-agency working 133, 141
multi-disciplinary working 88, 134, 135,
    136, 171
Munro, E. 3, 5, 13, 15, 45, 120, 122, 130,
    131, 134, 167
Musholt, K. 13, 45

National Institute of Child Health and
    Human Development 27
nature vs. nurture 25–7
neuroscience 13
normative development 14, 23

obesity 2, 20, 60, 97
    and child neglect 99–100, 117
offenders
    anti-social behaviour orders (ASBOs)
        160

offending behaviours 146, 149, 150
    programmes for male domestic violence
        offenders 159–60
    young offenders 160
old age 14, 23, 43, 111
    see also loneliness
operant conditioning 11, 37
optimism 97

parenting styles 151–2, 171
    see also criminal behaviour
Pavlov, I. 37
Payne, M. 53, 134
Pelka, Daniel 99, 114
performance management 1, 5, 81–2, 120,
    129–32, 167–8
personalization 4, 52, 57, 72, 85, 111, 121,
    170
persuasion 76
Piaget, J. 24, 29–31, 47
post-traumatic stress disorder 57, 154
    see also victims of crime
prejudice 54, 73, 75, 76, 77, 85, 91
Professional Capabilities Framework
    (PCF) 1, 2, 10, 21, 23, 48, 71, 125, 167
protection motivation theory 101, 102, 116
psychosis 59
psychosocial development 44

Rapaport, J. 144
Rayner, R.
reflective practitioner 51, 123
relationship-based practice 19, 68, 69,
    131–2
research, critical evaluation 8–9, 22
residential care 4, 41, 149
resilience 5, 13, 19, 45, 47, 120, 141, 147,
    163, 164
    see also child abuse
Rogers, C. 12, 69, 85
Ruch, G. 51, 69, 120, 132

safeguarding 5, 9, 12, 69, 114, 127–8, 134,
    137
    local children's safeguarding board 156
    missing children 156
    see also child sexual abuse
schizophrenia 59
scientist-practitioner model 51, 68
serious case reviews (SCRs) 4, 66, 69, 88,
    99, 112, 141, 166
service users 5, 48, 52, 86, 92, 94, 119, 120,
    131, 135, 140
sexual abuse 3, 58, 82, 114, 147, 154, 155,
    158, 159, 164–5

shared decision-making 97
shared knowledge base 95
Shoesmith, Sharon 15
significant harm 32–3,46, 59, 99
Signs of Safety 12
situational knowledge 73
Skinner, B. 11, 37
Social Care Institute for Excellence (SCIE) 8, 67, 124
social cognitions 19, 149, 164
social justice 8, 16, 71, 73–4, 80, 93, 126, 167, 170
social learning theory 147
social norms 14, 53, 81
social support 45, 60, 95, 99, 110–11, 117
socio-cultural theory of development 31
stages of cognitive development 30
    see also Piaget
stages of psychosexual development 40
stereotypes 73, 75–6, 153, 157
strengths-based approaches 12
stress 106–9
stress management techniques 110–11
substance abuse 112–14
Sulloway, F. 11, 40, 47

supervision 51, 52, 120, 121, 126, 129–30, 141, 148–9

talking therapies 53, 61, 63, 69
teamwork 87, 88, 120, 141, 166
temperament 26
'toxic trio' 60, 112
transference 62
transtheoretical model of change 103
Type A behaviour 97–8

unconditional positive regard 12
Unwin, P. 1, 3, 15, 31, 35, 52, 123, 142

victims of crime 153, 155
    families and children of prisoners 161–2
    Giving Victims a Voice (2013) 154
Vygotsky, L. 31–3
    zone of proximal development (ZPD) 31–3

Watson, J. 11, 37
Winterbourne View 16, 81–3, 92
work–life balance 120, 121, 123, 138, 139–40, 141

young carers 67, 113